From Dust to Ashes

Also by Peter C. Jupp

MORTALITY (quarterly journal; *co-editor with Glennys Howarth*)

CONTEMPORARY ISSUES IN THE SOCIOLOGY OF DEATH, DYING AND DISPOSAL (*co-editor with Glennys Howarth*)

THE CHANGING FACE OF DEATH: Historical Accounts of Death and Disposal (*co-editor with Glennys Howarth*)

INTERPRETING DEATH: Christian Theology and Pastoral Practice (*co-editor with Tony Rogers*)

DEATH IN ENGLAND: An Illustrated History (*co-editor with Clare Gittings*)

GOLDERS GREEN CREMATORIUM 1902–2002: A London Centenary in Context (*co-editor with Hilary J. Grainger*)

POSTMODERNITY, SOCIOLOGY AND RELIGION (*co-editor with Kieran Flanagan*)

VIRTUE ETHICS AND SOCIOLOGY: Issues of Modernity and Religion (*co-editor with Kieran Flanagan*)

Forthcoming

A SOCIOLOGY OF SPIRITUALITY (*co-editor with Kieran Flanagan*)

From Dust to Ashes

Cremation and the British Way of Death

Peter C. Jupp

University of Bristol
and
United Reformed Church Minister

First published 2006 by
PALGRAVE MACMILLAN
Houndmills, Basingstoke, Hampshire RG21 6XS and
175 Fifth Avenue, New York, N.Y. 10010
Companies and representatives throughout the world

PALGRAVE MACMILLAN is the global academic imprint of the Palgrave
Macmillan division of St. Martin's Press, LLC and of Palgrave Macmillan Ltd.
Macmillan® is a registered trademark in the United States, United Kingdom
and other countries. Palgrave is a registered trademark in the European
Union and other countries.

ISBN-13: 978–0–333–69298–1 hardback
ISBN-10: 0–333–69298–5 hardback

This book is printed on paper suitable for recycling and made from fully
managed and sustained forest sources.

A catalogue record for this book is available from the British Library.

Library of Congress Cataloging-in-Publication Data
Jupp, Peter C.
    From dust to ashes : cremation and the British way of
death / Peter C. Jupp.
        p.   cm.
    Includes bibliographical references and index.
    ISBN 0–333–69298–5
    1. Cremation—Great Britain—History.   2. Funeral rites and
ceremonies—Great Britain—History.   I. Title.
    GT3331.G7J87 2005
    393′.2′0941—dc22   2005051551

10   9   8   7   6   5   4   3   2   1
15   14   13   12   11   10   09   08   07   06

Transferred to digital printing in 2007.

This book is dedicated to my wife Elisabeth and our sons Edmund and Miles and to the memory of my father Ernest Victor Jupp (1904–1995) and my mother Jessie Frances Jupp (1899–1968).

Contents

List of Abbreviations

ABBA	Association of British Burial Authorities
AGM	Annual General Meeting
BUA	British Undertakers Association
CBA	Confederation of Burial Authorities
CWS	Cooperative Wholesale Society
FBCA	Federation of British Cremation Authorities
FSC	Funeral Standards Council
HC	House of Commons
HL	House of Lords
IBCA	Institute of Burial and Cremation Administration
ICCM	Institute of Cemetery and Crematorium Management
ICF	International Cremation Federation
LCC	London County Council
LCC	London Cremation Company
LH	Lower House (of the Convocation of Canterbury)
NACCS	National Association of Cemetery and Crematorium Superintendents
NAFD	National Association of Funeral Directors
PP	Parliamentary Papers
QQ	Questions
SAIF	Society of Allied and Independent Funeral Directors
SCI	Service Corporation International
UK	United Kingdom
UH	Upper House (of the Convocation of Canterbury)

Preface

This book is the first account of a fundamental change in death customs in British society: the replacement of burial by cremation. Britain was the first modern European country to popularise cremation and thus it has a unique place in the sociology of death. Cremation was first promoted in 1874 and enshrined in the Cremation Act 1902. By 1939, 4% of funerals in the UK involved cremation, 50% by 1968, climbing to 71% by 2000.

The reasons for the emergence of cremation as the dominant form of disposal of the dead in British society are part of a complex story of overcrowded churchyards and cemeteries, changing social and theological attitudes to death, and the secularisation of the custody of the dead body from ecclesial authority to civic. Cremation, placing funerals in an economic, hygienic and rational frame, overlaps with this process. The present acceptance of cremation as the dominant form of disposal covers a long time period but this book focuses on the period 1820–2000. This study, despite its sub-title, does not focus on Scotland where there are considerable differences in the history of the churches since the reformation and in the development of burial law, nor on Northern Ireland (whose first crematorium opened in 1961). Many vested interest groups are involved in this radical shift from burial to cremation, from dust to ashes.

Academic studies, both of burial and of cremation, are in their infancy. Death scholars today have benefited from the taboo upon discussions about death in the twentieth century, just as much as we have sought to combat it. This story of cremation has had to be constructed from journals, archives, conference reports, government reports and from interviews. In 1976, Kenneth Prevette wrote a thirty-page history to mark the centenary of the Cremation Society of Great Britain (Prevette, 1974). He was the then Secretary of the Society founded in 1874 to promote cremation. Studies of the disposal of the dead are like a jigsaw puzzle where both the lid with the overall picture and several major pieces are missing. There is, as yet, no history of the Cremation Society, nor comparable accounts of the Society's two sister societies: the Institute of Cemetery and Crematorium Management (ICCM), formerly the National Association of Cemetery and Crematorium Superintendents (NACCS) and successively the Institute of Burial and Cremation Administration (IBCA); and the Federation of British Cremation Authorities (FBCA). There is no history of either the

Proprietary Crematoria Association (PCA) or the International Cremation Federation (ICF).

There are very few histories of specific crematoria save Manchester (Makepeace, 1990) and Golders Green (Jupp and Grainger, 2002). In 2005, the first full-length account was published about the first British crematorium at Woking (Parsons, 2005e). Stephen White, a specialist in cremation and ecclesiastical law, has written valuable papers on key events and issues in British cremation history: these stemmed from his first research into the Price trial of 1884. Both Parsons and White have uncovered a considerable amount of material that has greatly helped the earlier sections of this study. At the time of writing, both Douglas Davies' *Encyclopaedia of Cremation* and Hilary J. Grainger's *Death Redesigned: History, Architecture and Landscape* are imminent. There are no English-language full-length accounts of the growth of cremation in mainland Europe. Only in the last three years have there appeared histories of cremation in the United States, by Prothero (2001) and in Australia by Nicol (2003).

Studies of burial practice have fared a little better. James Stevens Curl has been writing about cemeteries and the architecture of disposal for thirty years: his *Death and Architecture* (third edition, Curl, 2002) has, with Colvin's *Architecture and the After-life* (Colvin, 1991), assessed the built environments with which death is marked. Curl's recent *Kensal Green Cemetery* (Curl, 2001) and John Clarke's *London's Necropolis* on Woking (Clarke, 2004) are leaders in this genre. In the last fifteen years, Julie Rugg has developed the work and influence of her Cemetery Research Group at York University, and her annual seminar has brought together a young generation of cemetery scholars. A vital and steady flow of papers has followed her doctoral thesis on the private cemetery movement in Britain during 1820–1850 (Rugg, 1992). Douglas Davies founded a Cremation Research Project at the University of Nottingham, now at the University of Durham. The rise of cemetery Friends' Groups has encouraged studies of a number of individual burial grounds.

There are very few scholars for whom the study of death can be a full-time research interest. The long-standing MA courses in death at the University of Wales Lampeter and, until recently, at the University of Reading, have utilised their interdisciplinary resources. The organisation of university departments has not allowed full-time courses; and only in the last ten years has UK Government research money been favourably directed towards the history and sociology of death practices. Death studies have been a sub-discipline or a side interest for scholars whose major responsibilities have lain – and been reimbursed – elsewhere.

Death studies have been more central for the disciplines of archaeology, anthropology and medicine. The sociology of medicine has made a sustained contribution to death, with scholars like David Clark, David Field and Neil Small. Despite the immense importance of Durkheim and the retention of suicide in a central place in sociological theory, the sociology of death has yet to find its place in the mainstream of British sociology.

Anthropologists have a longer pedigree. Maurice Bloch wrote his critical study, *Placing the dead*, about the double funerary rituals of the Merina in Madagascar (Bloch, 1971). Bloch with Jon Parry published the widely influential collection *Death and the Regeneration of Life* (Bloch and Parry, 1982), and Parry published his studies on *Death in Banaras* (Parry, 1994). Richard Huntington and Peter Metcalf wrote *Celebrations of Death: The Anthropology of Mortuary Ritual* (1979). Behind such studies lie the scholars who in the 1960s translated the highly influential Robert Hertz' *Death and the right hand*, first published in 1907, and Arnold van Gennep's *The rites of passage*, first written in 1909. One wonders how much the anthropology of death might have been advanced further if these translations had longer preceded Geoffrey Gorer's *Death, Grief and Mourning in Contemporary Britain* of 1965.

The anthropologists thus made available a framework for categorisation and analysis of death and disposal practices upon which the sociologists could build. Contemporary leading anthropologists include Jenny Hockey (Hockey, 1990), who is currently leading an ESRC-funded Sheffield programme investigating the phenomenon and significance of the removal of cremated ashes from crematoria (over 50% compared with 15% twenty years ago); also in the Sheffield team is Leonie Kellaher, who has completed with Doris Francis an earlier ESRC-funded project on grave visiting as *The Secret Cemetery* (Francis *et al.*, 2005) which was not published in time to be considered in this study. British sociologists might seem to have discovered death only in the 1990s. But by 1990, Zigmunt Bauman, Douglas Davies, Glennys Howarth, Tony Walter and Michael Young were all researching and writing about death; and important doctoral dissertations by Smale (1985) and Naylor (1989) remain unpublished. Tony Walter (1991a) wondered whether sociologists themselves are among those affected or conditioned by a British taboo on death in the twentieth century. Walter's *Funerals and How to Improve Them* (1990) stimulated interest both from sociologists and from funeral reformers, and at Reading University he found sufficient scholars with a sub-interest in death studies to found his inter-disciplinary MA course. The Open University, founded by Michael Young, pioneered a TV-based distance-learning course on death and dying in 1993.

A number of conferences greatly aided the rapid development of British death studies in the 1990s with published papers. The Social History Society of the UK held a conference in 1987 on 'Death, ritual and bereavement' (Houlbrooke, 1989). The Urban Research Committee of the University of Birmingham held a conference on 'Death in Towns: urban responses to the dying and the dead, 100–1600' (Bassett, 1992). Sociologists based at Leicester University founded the annual day seminar on the sociology of death in 1990 (Clark, 1993; Field *et al.*, 1997; Hockey *et al.*, 2001). In 1993 at Oxford, Glennys Howarth and Peter C. Jupp held the first conference on 'The Social Context of Death, Dying and Disposal'; this proved to be the first of, so far, seven conferences. Howarth and Jupp were approached by the publishers Carfax (now Taylor & Francis) to edit the interdisciplinary (and now quarterly) journal *Mortality*, which was established to offer a channel for publication for the growing numbers of scholars studying death from within a variety of disciplines.

The interdisciplinary network of death scholars and professionals took a further direction when scholars began to collaborate with those responsible for burial and cremation facilities. The annual conferences of the Cremation Society of Great Britain and of the Joint Conference of Burial and Cremation Authorities all invited scholars to give papers. The conference proceedings have provided enormous and essential research materials for the present study. These conferences led to research projects of which the two most well-known were Julie Dunk and Julie Rugg on *The Use of Old Cemetery Land* (1994) and of Douglas Davies, who, with Alastair Shaw, published the IBCA-sponsored research on *The Re-use of Old Graves: A Survey of Public Attitudes* in 1995. These stimulated further publications on social policy, like The London Planning Advisory Committee's *Planning for Burial Space in London* (1997).

This academic and professional collaboration took a further step in 2000 with the enquiry by the House of Commons Select Committee on the Environment, whose chairman Andrew Bennett, MP for Stockport, undertook a review of cemetery provision in 2000–2001 (ETRAC, 2001). Bennett's Select Committee is only the latest in a stream of British Government initiatives investigating death issues. The post-1945 Labour Government provided some financial support in bereavement. Government interest might have been expected to peak with the Suicide Act 1961, the successful campaign for the abolition of capital punishment in 1965, and the abortion legislation of 1966, but successive governments have pursued a series of reports. These included the Brodrick Report into death certification and coroners (Brodrick, 1971) and enquiries into funeral directing services (Hennessey Report, 1980); the Monopolies and Mergers Commission report on Service Corporation International (MMC, 1995) and pre-paid funeral plans (1995 and 1996); death registration (2002); the Shipman enquiry (2003); the Coroners Enquiry (2003); enquiries into the retention of infant remains at Alderhey and Bristol hospitals leading to the Retained Organs Commission; and the sequel to the ETRAC report, the Home Office's Burials and Cemeteries Advisory Group, currently sitting.

Issues of public and social policy were also raised by the funeral reform groups which sprang up in the 1990s. Michael Young founded the National Funerals College project (1992–2001) to promote better funerals. In 1996, it first launched *The Dead Citizens Charter* against the background of John Major's Conservative Government's concern for 'charters' as instruments of social improvement. The IBCA published its own *Charter for the Bereaved* (IBCA, 1996) which has proved influential in raising standards at cemeteries and crematoria. Meanwhile, Nicholas Albery founded the Natural Death Centre. With its major publication *The Natural Death Handbook* (Albery *et al.*, 1993), the Centre has successfully promoted woodland burials and the use of cardboard coffins.

Where are religious and theological studies in all this? They seem to have fallen behind in academic enquiry into a territory where the religions have long behaved as if on their own home ground. From a Christian perspective, despite numbers of pastoral and self-help books often based upon personal experience, there has been a dearth of serious theological input. For forty years after the Church of England's declaration in favour of cremation, there was no serious theological study of cremation and its implications until the work of Douglas Davies. Peter Brown has contributed to patristic studies with *The Cult of the Saints* (1981) and Carol Walker Bynum with *The Resurrection of the Body* (1995). John Hick published a comprehensive *Death and Eternal Life* in 1976 and John Bowker has developed theological studies of modern death in *The Sense of God* (1973) and *The Meanings of Death* (1991). At the University of Wales Lampeter, Paul Badham has written successive studies, including *Christian Beliefs about Life after Death* and *Immortality or Extinction?* Geoffrey Rowell published *Hell and the Victorians* in 1974 and *The Liturgy of Christian Burial* in 1977. As Chair of the Churches' Funerals Group, Rowell continues to encourage the Christian churches to improve funeral ministry, but serious theological output from the Churches is meagre (save, e.g., Carr, 1985; Edwards, 1999; Sheppy, 2004; Lampard,

2006), apart from philosophy and the field of liturgical studies, the latter influenced by van Gennep's models. In view of the vital and traditional connection between the facts of death, practices in disposal and beliefs in the afterlife, this is a frustrating tale.

Five principal arguments are embodied in this study to account for the popularisation of cremation. The first relates to burial as a public health issue. The physician G. A. Walker, accepting the miasmatic hypothesis of the spread of infectious disease from, among other places, burial grounds, proved an effective funeral reformer in the 1840s. Consequently, and following cholera in 1847–1848, burial in towns was prohibited from the 1850s. The public health argument was successfully pressed about mortuaries (1880s) and about cremation (1930s). It has resurfaced in a different form in the concern for environmental protection in the 1990s.

Secondly, from 1874 the early cremationists were concerned to ensure their movement would stay within the law. They also sought to equalise lawful access to burial and cremation, a strategy which, like their concern for economy and public health, enabled them to avoid arguments on religious grounds, but it also involved them in seeking reforms to the system of death registration. As a result, some of them were both advocates for cremation and activists against infanticide, both issues which would benefit from more robust recording of deaths and their causes. In subsequent decades, the concern for registration has been allied with that for death certification, issues in which the Shipman murders exposed in 2000 are only the latest stage.

Thirdly, an economic argument had been growing over the extravagance of funeral expenditure, especially for poor people, popularised by the social criticism of Charles Dickens. The early cremationists pressed the economics of cremation in the 1870s, and in the 1930s Sir Arnold Wilson, the reforming Conservative MP, dissected both the industrial assurance and the funerals industries with themes that were echoed by Prime Minister Attlee as he pursued his Government's post-war Welfare State agenda. The 'Sunday funerals' issue of the 1930s and the development of cremation in the 1950s have both led to the reduction of social class differentials in funerals – the democratic way of death.

Fourthly, there was a land resources argument which claimed that cemeteries took up valuable land. In the 1890s, metropolitan authorities sought to introduce cremation because their available cemetery spaces had become landlocked. After 1918, the rapid suburbanisation of housing exacerbated the problem of cemetery space. The Cremation Society adopted the motto 'Save the land for the living'. In the 1930s this ideal crystallised into the slogan 'Cemeteries or playing fields?' Despite a current cremation rate of 71% (2004) a crisis in cemetery space arose in the 1990s and still awaits practical government action.

A fifth theme is the process of secularisation in Britain. The cremation movement, in seeking to avoid religious arguments, pressed what were in effect secular arguments. The Churches, in seeking to defend the burial tradition, chose not to take cremation seriously and thus failed to make significant contributions to the architecture, location, administration or ownership of crematoria. Seventy years passed before the Church of England positively supported cremation. By that time the assumption that the mode of disposal made no difference to post-mortem destiny or beliefs about the afterlife was probably too well cemented into public consciousness, a process further hardened once the Roman Catholics permitted cremation in 1964. It is now 150 years since the Church controlled, through ownership, England's burial grounds. 'Those conducting Christian funerals at crematoria still largely need to come to terms with the fact that they are visiting actors on a stage they do not own, enacting a traditional drama subject to contemporary restraints' (Jupp, 1997c: 10–11).

Thus the Christian churches largely surrendered the benefits of the ritual and symbolism that burial gave their traditional theology. No one seriously expects theology not to develop – else it atrophies – but there is a cost to the churches' passivity over cremation. I am asked why I, as a cremationist and Chairman of the Cremation Society, seem to regret the marginalising of the Christian churches' influence in death, both pastorally and conceptually. I reply that, as a funeral reformer, I assert that cremation has contributed enormously to remove social class differences in death (still very visible up to 1939) and the burden imposed by traditional funerals on many families. As a Christian – and a minister – I find that the Churches' hesitation to contribute to the practical and theoretical issues of death and the disposal of the dead to be a matter of regret. I hope that a recognition of my own two roles will help explain the ambiguity that some feel they discern. This is a lament over the waste of an opportunity to meet people's needs in death better, not over the irretrievable loss of such an opportunity. Just as the founders of the Cremation Society anticipated that some day a better form of disposal might arrive, so do I look forward to a more effective ministry by this country's faith groups to the range of end-of-life issues, where the evolving practices of our culture, politics, government, law, public health and religion mutually inter-react with our private and social well-being.

Unforeseen by Sir Henry Thompson and the early cremationists in 1874 was that by 1888 local government in the United Kingdom would have been transformed. The growth of cities, with rapid rural migration into the towns, and massive problems of public health, education and utilities, had necessitated a root and branch reform of local government, which was by that stage in the century responsible to growing numbers of citizens because of the extension of the franchise. It was through the machinery and institutions of local government that the Cremation Act 1902 was successfully enacted, as local government's best way of discharging its obligations to provide for the disposal of the dead, a problem it had inherited from the Church of England in 1852. In 1902 a change in the law did not effect the change in practice that both cremationists and local councillors had hoped for.

The traumatic and unforeseen experiences of the First World War had enormous implications for the British public. The ten fronts on which the war was fought provided their own forms of death, injury and terror. The war changed attitudes to death and the afterlife, to beliefs and superstitions, to public and private remembrance, to the corpse and to burial places. Nevertheless, the war situation introduced new attitudes and practices about government, religion, diet and health, gender equality, housing and patterns of family life, all of which would be helped to meet their own ends by the adoption of simpler funeral and mourning practices, which included cremation.

Within sixty-five years of the Cremation Act 1902, the course of three generations, half the funerals in England involved cremation. The purpose of this book is to explain this shift. Contemporary funeral arrangements have been subject to the same sets of processes as most other aspects of life: commercialisation and the intrusion of the profit motive; individualisation and the setting of personal preference before the common good; municipalisation and the enhanced role of public services in personal and family life; secularisation and the dwindling of a supernatural frame of reference to daily life; and consumerisation, the exercise of the element of choice and the ascription of a value to a widening range of goods. Funerals are among the personal and public activities affected by these processes.

Acknowledgements

In writing this study, I acknowledge a large number of debts with great pleasure. This study began as a doctoral thesis in sociology at the London School of Economics, partly funded by the award of a Studentship from the Economic and Scientific Research Council. I thank my patient and inspiring supervisor, Professor Eileen Barker, and earlier teachers including Professor David Martin, Professor Graham Stanton and the late Dr Bryan Wilson. Six friends were particularly helpful during the winter of 2004–2005. Dr Brian Parsons, Dr Julie Rugg and Mr Stephen White have all read sections of this book and offered amendments and advice. Dr Kieran Flanagan read carefully two successive drafts of the whole text. Professor Hilary Grainger kindly shared with me the chapters of her forthcoming *Death Redesigned* on crematorium architecture, and the Revd Professor Douglas Davies gave me sections I needed from his imminent *Encyclopaedia of Cremation*. The result is immeasurably better for their suggestions. Misjudgements and all remaining errors are my own. Two friends have helped me enormously with word processing and proofreading, Miss Edith Coole, formerly of the Methodist Publishing House, and Miss Katharine Riley, formerly of the National Funerals College: their wizardry with word processing has been invaluable.

In the months leading upto publication, I wish to thank Jill Lake, Melanic Blair and Satishna Gokuldas and the team at Macmillan Palgrave. Their patience, encouragement and efficiency have been a continual support.

Mr Roger Arber, Secretary, and the staff of the Cremation Society of Great Britain – Sue Jackson, Gill Payne, Julie Forrest and Val Jones – have been generous over many months in affording access to the Society's archives in Maidstone. The major archival holdings are now at Durham and I thank the staff there for their kindnesses. I wish to acknowledge the help of the staff at the following libraries: the Commonwealth War Graves Commission Records Department, Dr Williams's, the Institute of Historical Research, the Institute of Landscape Architecture, the Lambeth Palace Library, Peterborough Public Library, the Reform Club, the Royal Society of Arts, Stamford Public Library and the Wellcome Institute for the History of Medicine. A quiet and inspiring environment was provided for me by Launde Abbey.

I am grateful to the 58 families who, in Leicester and Fensham, shared with me their experiences of bereavement and funeral arrangement; their trust, frankness and generosity confirmed my conviction that in the study of death and experience of bereavement lie vital clues to understanding human experience and aspiration and to the cost of living. I thank the church congregations of Stamford Corby, and Westgate, Peterborough, for their support.

Of the many friends and colleagues who have, perhaps unknown to them, played a part in conversations behind this book are: Roger Arber, Richard Barradell, Andrew and Gillian Bennett, Clyde Binfield, Michael Bray, Sheila Cameron, Clive Chamberlain, Bob Coates, Lesley Cullen, Tam Dalyell, Grace Davie, Brendan Day, Kate Day, Michael Day, Keith Denison, Julie Dunk, Angela Dunn, Cheryl Eva, David Field, Doris Francis, Robert Fulton, Clare Gittings, the Right Honourable the Earl Grey, Vanessa Harding, John Harris, Andrew Helsby, Michael Henshall, David Hill, Jenny Hockey, Ralph Houlbrooke, Glennys Howarth, Trevor Hunnaball, Ian Hussein, Malcolm Johnson, Gerdien Jonker, Lisa Kazmier, Leonie Kellaher, Brian Kurht, Ulf Lagerström, Carol Lambert, Bill Lamers, John Lampard, Clive Leverton, Keith Leverton, Julian Litten, Jon Luby, Tony Macarthy, the late John McDonald, Sandy MacDonald, Kevin McGinnell, Bernard McHale, Alan Mortimore, Baroness Julia Neuberger, Colin Parkes, Debbie Powton, Theresa Quinn, Paul Rosenblatt the late John M. Ross, Geoffrey Rowell, Alan Sell, Brian Simon, Graham Sloan, John Slow, David Smale, John and Chris Steele, Bruce Stuart, Gill Tallon, Tony Walter, Tony Warburton, Sam Weller, Keith Welters, Ken West, Frank Wilson and the late Michael Young.

I have always wondered why authors thank their family last. It is perhaps a reflection that they have supported the project from before its beginning. To my wife Elisabeth whose love and support have been constant, generous and unfaltering; and to our sons Edmund and Miles who, as children, found crematoria to be regular features of holiday stopping places, I owe more than I can possibly say.

1
Introduction

Death interrupts life, frustrates plans, renders roles, ownerships and responsibilities vacant; it bereaves loved ones and dependent ones, and threatens the identity and continuity of families and societies. By removing a player from the social scene, death forces social readjustment. In the face of death, whether seen as a threat or as a relief, human societies and their constituent units – families or work teams, races or nations – all construct and continually develop ways to contain and regulate its impact. Deaths and funeral arrangements provide the living with a view of their priorities for living and an awareness of the resources and networks they need for survival. Our mortality is a fact of all human life and activity.

The range of funeral tasks includes arrangements to acknowledge the death of those who die; to dispose of their dead bodies; to ensure their identity and memory in the land of the living and to do whatever is humanly possible to ensure their identity and welfare in whatever forms of existence are believed to follow; to comfort those who survive and mourn them; to restore survivors to normal life; to commence survivors' readjustments to the social roles which death has made obligatory; and to help restore the rents that death has torn in the social fabric.

From Durkheim onwards, studies of suicide have reminded us that, whilst suicide seems to be the most individual of acts, its repercussions have strong social significance. Genocide has earned a focus both political and academic in the last hundred years. All deaths preclude the future of individuals; generically, death always poses a threat to the continuation of societies. As different societies develop and modify their coping strategies for surviving the deaths of their members, habitual death-ways develop into traditional customs. Changes in death-ways centre on the disposal of the dead.

The funeral is the public recognition of a death. It emerges as the climactic event at which the roles of the dead and their survivors are publicly marked; and the stricken community publicly (Hertz, 1960: 78) moves on to re-form itself in the physical absence of the dead, not back to normal but on to a reordered normality. If funeral customs change, then there is a strong probability both that the social significance of death has changed and that the nature of society has changed, in that it marks the deaths of individual members in a different way. This book explores the social significance of just such a major change in funeral arrangements.

Death, disposal and social structure are related in a number of ways. The intensity of funeral procedures varies according to the social significance of the one who has died. It also depends upon whether society has developed measures sufficient to reduce the problems caused by individual deaths to the wider society's daily life and livelihood. All societies have developed traditions whereby gender roles are allocated in death-work, women having usually been the major bearers of mourning tasks. Family and kinship systems, fertility practices, food production and wealth regeneration, religious identities and political control systems have all taken their shape partly in response to the pressure of mortality: hence the title of Bloch and Parry's 1982 book *Death and the Regeneration of Life*. The end of a human life provides an opportunity to assess both the worth of an individual life and the social arrangements which enabled that individual to live. Studies of such assessments can tell us what different societies prioritise as of value in human life.

The certainty of death is a focus around which human cultures and organisations have developed. It affects family and personal relationships between parents, partners and children. It involves arrangements for the transfer of property and authority. It necessitates action to ensure the transmission of values. It also permits the possibility of innovation: 'If the individual members of any species were everlasting there would be no evolution' (Young, 1988: 255).

The prospect of death has prompted our national policies on health care and pensions. It has fuelled the insurance, house-purchase and entertainment businesses. It has necessitated investment in survival and security: food supplies, fuel supplies and the environment, policing, armed forces and international defence and diplomacy. The prospect of mortality is the scenery for every movement on the human stage. As Evans wrote in his study of Germany in the nineteenth-century cholera years,

In the epidemic, the workings of state and society, the structures of social inequality, the variety of values and beliefs, the physical contours of everyday life, the formal ideologies and informal ambitions of political organisations, were all thrown into sharp and detailed relief. (Evans, 1990: ix)

The shadows thrown by death affect more than the contemporary and the present. Death crosses time barriers. It involves both memorialisation and expectation; and in that setting, religions have a profound part to play. Because death begs questions about the hereafter, and the fate of individuals and their bodies, to decay or extinction, to resurrection, immortality or reincarnation, the whole issue of the disposal of the dead has deep theological implications. For many, especially in the past, the fate of the dead in relation to the afterlife was a matter of anxiety.

Until the modern era, the Churches played a critical role in how death was understood and interpreted, in the rituals for dying and procedures for funerals, and, by their provision and management of churchyards, in the provision of geographical and symbolic space for the bodies of the dead. The history of cremation reveals how the Church lost its traditional role in the disposal of the dead, a shift which created opportunities for new arrangements for disposal and new beliefs about the afterlife. Without the Churches' loss of their urban churchyards in the legislation of the mid-nineteenth century, cremation in Britain would have had a very different history.

The tradition of burial for Christians and for people living in societies with a Christian tradition and culture is strong. Jesus Christ, the founder of the Christian faith, was buried. This was in line with Jewish practice: Jewish bodies were buried as soon as possible and in burial grounds outside towns. Both speed and convenient location were necessary because the hot climate accelerated the decomposition of dead bodies which were a hazard to health. In related ways, dead bodies were regarded as polluting: a series of rituals reflected fears both of death and of supernatural contagion. Jesus' burial was unusual in that He was buried in a cave: most of His contemporaries were buried in the earth. The burial of the dead was one of the important obligations in Judaism, partly because of traditional respect for the person who had died and partly because the corpse was ritually polluting and needed to be buried before mourners could resume normal duties. Jews also observed traditional patterns of mourning – of three, seven and forty days – which still obtain in Judaism today. Catholic Christianity took over these customs which have persisted, where not forbidden, in Reformed countries.

When Christianity began, practices of burial and cremation existed side by side in the Roman Empire. In pre-Roman Britain both methods were used and cremation in Britain actually increased in the first century AD (Hope, 1999: 50–1). Yet, in the Empire overall, cremation lost place to burial over the first two Christian centuries. It was once assumed that this was because of the influence of Christianity, as portrayed in Bishop Wordsworth's 1874 sermon against cremation (Wordsworth, 1874), but the evidence is contradictory. Nock concluded (1932: 338) that the most likely reason was not theological but a change of fashion and that the customs of the rich had spread down the social scale.

Disposal and belief had become linked in a critical way in the second century BC when belief in the resurrection of the dead arose among the Jews (Cullman, 1958; Nickelsburg, 1972). It was linked with revised concepts of God's reward for martyrs and became a major feature of the piety of the Pharisees (Smart, 1968: 117). This was understood as both a physical and a communal event. It concerned God's judgement at the end of the world and therefore acquired moral implications. Whilst beliefs in a communal resurrection were current in Jesus' day, the resurrection of Jesus was the critical event in the development of Christian beliefs about life after death. For St Paul, the first great Christian apologist, Christ was the 'first-fruits' of a whole harvest of the dead (*1 Corinthians* 15). Many in the early church anticipated resurrection in the near future (Davies, 1972). When these hopes were disappointed, concepts of communal resurrection in a distant future were gradually developed into 'the Four Last Things', death, judgement, Heaven and Hell.

When the first generations of Christians realised (*1 Thessalonians*) that their resurrection after death would not be immediate, the problem arose of what happened to the individual Christian in the interval between death and resurrection. This prompted the co-option of the Greek (and hitherto un-Hebraic) concept of the immortality of the soul (Rowell, 1974: 19–23). A continuing tension between belief in the resurrection of the body and the immortality of the soul began (Bynum, 1995). The New Testament offered five alternatives to ease this tension. It suggested, first, that the Christian dead 'slept' until a general resurrection when 'the trumpet shall sound' (*1 Corinthians* 15:52ff.). Secondly, eternal life with Christ was a present reality for Christians: 'This is eternal life, that they know thee the only true God, and Jesus Christ whom thou hast sent' (*John* 17:3). Thirdly, the Christian dead, and especially Christian martyrs, shared immediately in the life of Heaven (*The Revelation of St John* 7). Fourthly, the dead were visited by Christ in Hell (*ad inferos*) in the interval between Good Friday and Easter

Morning. The fifth alternative (*The Revelation of St John* 20) was two successive post-mortem judgements. The general judgement, following the particular, would take place at the end of time. An individual judgement would happen to every person at the time of death; and this would show individual souls the state of their relationship to God.

Biblical texts also provided the extreme points for the afterlife of the Christian: Heaven as a place of salvation and bliss, Hell as a place of torment and punishment. In the centuries leading up to the elaboration of the doctrine of Purgatory in the twelfth century (Le Goff, 1984) the promise of a purgatorial process seemed to ameliorate the passage of the human soul after death and increase, despite antecedent deprivations, the likelihood of its gaining eventual admission to Heaven. The rejection of Purgatory in Reformed countries had implications for traditions of mourning, memorialisation and funerals which recur in this book.

Another tension was prompted by the point of death, the moment after which the dead person either joined his ancestors ('was buried with his fathers') or was alone before God. Daily life and experience easily understood death as the beginning of a journey for the individual soul, a theme most powerfully shown in John Bunyan's *Pilgrim's Progress*; life beyond death was imagined as a dangerous journey for which the traveller would need not only prayers but provisions and a benevolent guide. In pre-Christian Judaism, guidance was the task of angels. Many features of the world's funeral rites adopt the image of a journey to describe what we do immediately after we have died (Grainger, 1988). The most visible symbol of death as a journey is to be seen in funeral processions. These journeys serve many purposes, but as they transport the dead individual from the world of his home to the communal burial ground they symbolise the translation of the dead soul from the world of the living to the world of the dead.

Dying and death were matters of risk. Societies developed rituals to give people greater confidence about life beyond death, both in protecting the individual in his own death and defending survivors against harm from the dead (Bloch and Parry, 1982). Berger's concept of 'plausibility structures' (Berger, 1969) may be fruitfully deployed to describe two key Christian rituals for facing and interpreting death. The first was the weekly Eucharist where the faith that Christ's death and resurrection offered both pre- and post-mortem salvation to believers was symboli- cally available in the bread and wine. The second was the *viaticum*. In Greek mythology this was the coin left with corpses so that their spirits could pay Charon the ferryman to carry them safely across the river Styx to the Elysian Fields. In Christian tradition the *viaticum* became the word for the Communion given to a dying person just before his death, a custom common by the fourth century (Grabka, 1953).

The modes of disposal of the dead also work as 'plausibility structures'. This is particularly relevant to those Christian funeral rites where the dead are committed to the earth 'in sure and certain hope of the resurrection to eternal life'. In 1851, in the context of the British Parliament's debates about the closing of churchyards and the establishment of publicly owned cemeteries, the Ecclesiological Society wrote:

> We are bound to provide that the remains [of our brethren in Christ]...should remain undisturbed and inviolate till the Great Doom; that in the same place where they lie down to rest, in the same place they shall arise to their sentence. (Ecclesiological Society, 1851: 2)

These words marked the cusp of change in Britain. One of the most critical stages in the history of funerals in Britain came with the burials legislation of the 1850s. In a chain of events to be discussed in Chapter 2, this legislation effected the surrender by the Church of England of its monopoly on the provision of burial space. For one thousand years or more, the Church in England had controlled the rite, site and mode of disposal of the dead. The burial Acts of the mid-nineteenth century established the cemetery in succession to the churchyard. Henceforth burying-places would increasingly be owned and managed by local, secular government. The consequences included an increasingly open market for the disposal of the dead. This in turn opened up to choice and speculation not only new modes of disposal but new interpretations of death and concepts of the afterlife. It is a central assertion of this book that the shift of responsibility for the disposal of the dead was a necessary stage for the consideration of cremation as an alternative to burial. In the Christian tradition disposal and belief had become crucially linked in the process of Christian burial in the context of a Christian churchyard. The first Anglican opponents of cremation were certain that it would unravel belief in the resurrection of the body, with consequences both for the authority of the Church and of the morals of society.

Christianity's attitude to death, disposal and the future life marked it out as a religious force to be reckoned with. The Roman Emperor Julian the Apostate (AD 361–363) cited the Christian treatment of the dead as one of the reasons for the conversion of the Empire (Rowell, 1977: 18). Christianity introduced, as from its Founder and the facts and convictions about His life, death, resurrection and second coming, a set of beliefs which harnessed modes of disposal and modes of belief in the afterlife solidly together. The process of separation of mode of disposal from mode of belief in the nineteenth and twentieth centuries speaks either of the declining influence of institutional Christianity or of a shift of popular attitudes by which individual people increasingly see death and disposal as issues without religious meaning (Davies and Shaw, 1995; Walter, 1996).

There were at least three facets to the link between disposal and belief. First, Christianity provided hope for individuals both in and after this life. Baptism and the Eucharist were both spiritually nourishing rites which not only helped people to cope with the demands of daily living but prepared them for life's end. At their baptism, Christians symbolically died and were raised to life again with Christ. At the Eucharist, Christians obeyed Jesus' command at the Last Supper on the night before His arrest and death; and Christian believers symbolically ingested the benefits of Christ's death. Christian funeral liturgies, focusing upon the corpse, the grave and the burial ground, all helped to make more plausible the conviction both that in Christ the individual received the guarantee of life after death and that at a day of general resurrection in God's distant future all individuals would be raised simultaneously.

Secondly, Christianity offered plausible sets of answers to the questions raised for both individuals and societies by the fact of death. For individuals death is certain and inevitable. No one lasts for ever: that is bad news for those in love, just as it is good news for those who suffer under tyrannies. Mortality and suffering both force two responses on humans. Humans have both to cope and to understand; needs for which all belief-systems develop rituals and interpretations. While the fact of death is certain, the act of death seems random and this characteristic has long been illustrated by metaphors of chance, as with dice or arrows, as has the fact of death by the hourglass or the skull (Ariès, 1985; Prior, 1997). What the Christian interpretation of death offered was the conviction that human society could survive the fact and incidence of death because it had been created and introduced by God as a punishment for sin, ordained and therefore controlled by God (Augustine, 1984; Thomas, 1997). This fitted with the tradition inherited from the Jews (Davies, 1965). Furthermore, in the Christian dispensation, death had been defeated by Jesus Christ once for all (*2 Corinthians* 5:14), in a resurrection that (at least) all Christians would share. Thus human society could have a second existence, a new hope beyond death, and experience a renewed corporate existence in Heaven.

Thirdly, the Christian interpretation of death and the afterlife had moral implications for wider society. After all, in human experience, death came to all, washed or filthy, prince or pauper; death was imaged as a social leveller in a large poetic corpus. Christianity not only accepted the levelling function of death but also drew out its moral implications for society at large. There was often a contradiction in practice which the elite practised and protected. Funeral rites for social outcasts and outlaws could be either perfunctory or punitive. Nevertheless, the social levelling implications of the Christian doctrine of death were a continual and parallel source of human hope. Even a good king like Wenceslaus could not live for ever, and neither could the tyrant, whether Timur the Lame, Vlad the Impaler or Stalin the Red Czar.

There is an inherent paradox in these processes. As we have seen, death rituals were developed over time to contain and ameliorate the effect of death on social systems (Marris, 1968). Because the death of leaders is seen as the most acute threat, and because arrangements and values tested by experience (rationalised as 'stood the test of time') are the ones most put at risk, the obsequies and the memorials of the elite are given far greater prominence. The consequence is that those with low social worth are accorded lesser funeral rites. A social tension persists as to how religious groups discharge both their theological responsibilities to privilege human equality before God and their social responsibilities to privilege secular hierarchies.

These three concepts were all expressed with emphases that over time strengthened the Church's control of funerals. 'Whoever is in Christ is a new creation,' wrote St Paul, as he sought to articulate the implications of the saving death of Christ (*2 Corinthians* 5:16). The offer of Heaven as one of these implications was matched from the New Testament onwards by the alternative of Hell, and from the fifth century onwards by a third possibility, the process of purgation. So the Church's authority at funerals was steadily enhanced, preceded by the once-for-all baptism and the weekly Communion, with the priest at the lych-gate and the grave head, the pardoner with indulgences for sale (Rosenthal, 1972), the *Ars Moriendi* (O'Connor, 1942; Beaty, 1970), the prayers before, at or after death, the cult of the saints and their relics (Brown, 1981; Duffy, 1991), which were all symbols and instruments by which individuals might both receive solace about the event of death and have reassurance of a life beyond where a system of rewards and punishments obtained. At root, however, when a person died, their destiny became the responsibility of God with whom at death the individual was alone.

The burial became the point when the survivors and mourners, grief-stricken or relieved, some struggling with indifference but drawn to the graveside by communal solidarity, quitted the visible physical presence of the corpse; this leave-taking was the physical, mental and spiritual sign that, whatever the destiny of the dead individual, he or she was henceforth alone, awaiting God. Just as this life was conceivable as a preparation for the next, so the burial ground became sacred as a waiting room for the physical and religious event of resurrection. The burial ground spoke not of finality but of pregnancy.

> Not vainly did our fathers call the burying-place God's Acre. It is sown with the seeds of God's harvest; and the day of resurrection is God's reaping-day...It is a strange thing to stand in the breathless stillness of some populous cemetery, and to think what a stirring amid its dust the voice of the last trump will make. (Anon, 1864: 261)

Thus the Church's response to death – in successive ages – increased its influence as a controller and invigilator of human behaviour and as a symbol of the impartial divine judgement to come. The Church's response to death, in theology, ritual and pastoral practice, represented and therefore claimed an authority over human behaviour that transcended all sovereign and secular powers of domination. The Church, in its response to the fact of death and conviction about Christ's resurrection, represented a relativisation of secular power (Martin, 1978b). It was a latent symbol of God's ideal community in a hierarchical society.

The thousand-year-old churchyard burial tradition, established within England by the eighth century, became the focus of the Church's authority and control. Whilst some aspects of death and funerals were at times peripheral to the Church's ministry – the shroud, or the coffin, the tombstone or memorial brass, mourning clothes – other items were central: the churchyard (with issues of ownership, consecrated nature and legal status), the burial service (with issues of theology, liturgy, moral message and interpretation of death), the presiding priest (authorised and fee'd), the complex of pastoral networks which enwebbed the dying process (as last rites, vigil and intercessions); all subject to refinement and development. The tradition of burial survived the Protestant Reformation of the sixteenth century, but in ways that profoundly altered attitudes to the afterlife. The Protestant attitudes, of placing reliance on individuals to seek for the signs of their salvation in their own private forms of address, helped to generate the secularisation of attitudes to funerals which later helped prepare a fertile ground for cremation. The Reformers sought to emphasise the power of God and dilute the Catholic tradition by severing relationships between the living and the dead. By forbidding prayers for the dead, the use of relics, and the system of chantry-houses, the Reformers reduced the effectiveness of funeral rituals and customs. The funeral was not allowed to benefit the dead, it could thus only benefit the living (Rowell, 1977; Duffy, 1991; Houlbrooke, 1998; Marshall, 2002).

The time came when the Protestant Churches' refusal or inability to change, to accommodate or respond to alternatives, exacerbated tensions over disposal. These included the development of private mausolea for the landed or very wealthy, the tradition of unconsecrated burial space for the unbaptised, the failure to provide new burial space in the rapidly urbanising areas, the rise of militant atheism, changes in the doctrines of the afterlife and the effect upon the established clergy's role and payment of the new cemeteries. The failure of the Churches to overcome civil distinctions in burial between the rich and the poor was connected to the Church's establishment. The Church of England's alliance with the state, intensified by the course of the Reformation in England, meant that the Church compromised its Gospel about the social consequences of resurrection with its awareness and acceptance of social hierarchies in this world and parish.

When society increasingly realised that the Church's monopoly of the rites of passage exacerbated social divisions in an upwardly mobile industrialising society; that the practical facilities it provided for burial were insufficient; that the Anglican monopoly of increasingly limited grave-space had public health implications; and that the economic implications of its policies either could not solve the tensions of belief, decency and fairness or excluded the Protestant Nonconformist and Catholic churches now increasingly politically assertive; the State had to impose reforms in practical, political and secular ways. In the mid-nineteenth century, the State intervened to close urban churchyards. Cox has written of the rise of cemeteries that it did not need to happen (Cox, 1998). There had been other alternatives. The Church of England could have surrendered its monopoly earlier or followed precedents set by some Reformed and Catholic countries on mainland Europe to close urban burial grounds and build larger ones outside city boundaries (McManners, 1981a). But why did cremation increasingly emerge as an option in England in the second half of the nineteenth century?

Was it, perhaps, that cremation symbolised the more rapid dissolution of family bonds at a time when, with increasing geographical and social mobility, family structures were already loosening? Was it that cremation fitted the increasingly tenuous link between families and the church, between the individual and the religious professional and between the individual and the community in line with twentieth-century changes in social structure? Cremation was capable of bearing a lower voltage of religious belief and denomination affiliation in the later nineteenth century. The Church of England could have accepted cremation, save that it was neither its inclination nor tradition, nor in its financial interest, to do so. It still presided over the vast majority of English funerals in the nineteenth century. But, above all, cremation sat ill with the traditional doctrine of the resurrection of the body which was the symbolic function of the churchyard where the dead waited as in anticipation of the resurrection to eternal life (Healey, 1967). In the twentieth century the cost, in time and money, of the upkeep of a grave, the purchase of a gravestone, the maintenance of a link to a specific locality, all became too irksome for a population increasingly mobile both geographically and socially.

In complex and correlated ways not as yet fully disentangled, the Church's theological understanding of life after death changed. This included the nature of the afterlife; access to Heaven; rewards and punishments post-mortem; relations between the living and the dead; the shape or form of the body in the next life; and the new and more secular concepts of self-identity, status and social security which made certain Christian promises about life after death seem redundant. Meanwhile, industrial society, with slowly improving access to better diets, medical care and public health, offered avenues towards new and greater forms of health, prosperity and leisure activity. These enabled many people to feel that they had found satisfaction and achievement sufficient for their needs on this side of the grave. Concepts of sin and salvation, good and evil, justice and punishment became matters too complex for a church tradition publicly (at least) to bear. Expectations of greater equalities in this life correlated with the extension of the franchise and the rise of the Labour movement. The declining plausibility of traditional Christian images of life after death was first obvious with the debates about Hell (Rowell, 1974) and was intensified for many, many more people – especially men – with the experiences of the First World War (Wilkinson, 1978; Winter, 1995).

Cremation was not the obvious, natural or necessary successor to churchyard burial. Yet the increasing individualism of the age, changes in longevity and causes of death, together with new opportunities for social mobility in a welfare state, made the substitution of burial by cremation increasingly attractive. They enabled those promoting cremation to make an effective case, both to the public and to those responsible for disposal, to extend facilities for cremation and bring its advantages to a wider public. And because, from 1850, burial grounds were owned and managed by secular authorities, the Church found itself in an increasingly weakening position to play a part. From the 1880s, periodic surveys revealed that church attendance was declining, a process accelerated, though in different ways, by the two World Wars. In a parallel process, the Church's institutional role and authority in British society weakened (McLeod, 1974; Gilbert, 1976; Obelkevich, 1976; Gill, 1993).

Changes in funeral customs, including those of the shift from burial to cremation, need to be seen in this context. The process of secularisation has affected individual attitudes not only to death and disposal but to the social facilities and institutions which help people cope with them. It has contributed to breaking the traditional link between disposal and the afterlife. Christian pessimists might be tempted to comment that secularisation and cremation have mutually encouraged each other, yet there was and is no overwhelming necessity for this deduction. Historically, the English churches chose first to oppose cremation and then, for seventy years, to ignore it. This was not the only course of action open to them.

In the fifth century AD, St Augustine, the dominant theologian in the first millennium, had asserted that forms of disposal had no effect on dead bodies because God's grace and love were sufficient for human survival of death. In the nineteenth century, Lord Shaftesbury echoed Augustine when he denied that cremation would exclude the possibility of resurrection; he is said to have commented, 'Pray, Sir, what would then have happened to the blessed martyrs?' Neither dust nor ashes gave the Almighty problems. What God could create, he could re-create. So, theologically, there should have been no necessary connection between cremation and secularisation.

Given the Christian tradition of burial, what were the cultural and theological grounds for Christian resistance to cremation? First, burial as a mode of disposal followed and symbolised that of Jesus Christ. The hope of a physical life and identity after death was almost inextricably connected with Jesus' resurrection from death (Bynum, 1995) and the successive rites and ceremonies of Christians underlay that connection (Rowell, 1977). The funerals of Christians were conducted in the expectation that they would rise bodily again at some future date that God would choose.

Secondly, by contrast, early anti-Christian agitators, states or individuals, deliberately burned the bodies of Christian martyrs to seek to negate their post-mortem hopes of resurrection. For anti-Christian opponents there was nothing so symbolic of a rejection of the Christian message as that the Christian dead should be burned and their remains scattered.

For Christians, however, the promise of resurrection was dependent upon the action of God. Human inititative was in no way involved. There was no biblical tradition for God's being in any way limited by any funeral liturgy or any particular mode of disposal. This had led Augustine to write:

> earth has not been laid over many Christian bodies, yet no one of their souls has He kept out of Heaven... Hence all these things, that is, anxiety about funeral, or place of burial, or funeral pomp, are rather a solace to the living than a help to the dead. (Augustine, n.d.: 12)

These phrases were to be pressed into service by nineteenth-century cremationists to uncouple the mode of disposal from Christian custom.

Thirdly, the Church had adopted a violent mode of disposal when executing those heretics and witches whom its Courts had condemned. These included burning at the stake followed by scattering of ashes, often into flowing water, and the general denial of traditional religious burial rites. Hanging, drawing and quartering were likewise means of authorised contempt for the body of the criminal and rejection of any optimistic hopes of one's life after death. Such actions symbolised how society viewed the outlaw, as an outcast for whom the normal decencies at death should be denied, and for whom social exclusion might also be effective after death.

Fourthly, at times of death on crusade in non-Christian countries, the bodies of the elite were sometimes burned and the hearts embalmed so that Christian remains were portable and brought home. This division of body parts after death was forbidden by Pope Boniface VII in 1299. More commonly, at times of plague, the claims of public health and survival permitted bodies of the plague dead to be burned. Burning the dead was for emergencies.

In the sixteenth century the rising tensions between the European (Catholic) Church and the rising spirit of nationalism were partly resolved – and turned into long-lasting divisions – by the Protestant Reformation. For Protestant countries there was a significant change in the structure of belief in the afterlife (Purgatory was outlawed); in relations between the living and the dead (intercessions for the dead were forbidden); and in liturgies (some of which, for example the Calvinist Directory in Scotland in 1644, forbade all ritual at the graveside). All the mediaeval rites were simplified. The focus was increasingly upon exhortation to the living. For Protestants, no human, only almighty

God, could benefit those who had died. With intercessions for the dead forbidden, the dead were cut off from any benefit at the hands of family, friends or neighbours. The effect of the Reformation refocused the funeral rituals not on the future of the deceased but upon the fate of the survivors. Yet, in simultaneously curtailing religious ceremony but permitting or encouraging civil honours, it exaggerated the secular status both of the dead and of their survivors. Reformation emphases at death served to accentuate the identity of the bereaved family in terms of its secular status and achievements, thus denying in funeral reality the very levelling aspects of death which were fundamental to its Christian theology. Funeral rites no longer had any positive contribution to the destiny of the dead (Rowell, 1977: 23).

As suggested earlier, the Reformation helped to prepare the ground for cremation. When in the late nineteenth century cremation came to be proposed as an alternative to burial, this new mode of disposal proved a good fit with both a decline in belief in the resurrection of the body and a renewed emphasis on the immortality of the soul. In a society partly moulded by Calvinism and by a Protestant work-ethic where people sought status achieved by hard work rather than by inheritance, cremation fitted the mindset of the atheist or socialist who held that man and human societies alone could bring about social justice, progress or equality. And, if there were no life after death at all, the mode of disposal was irrelevant as long as it was respectful of the person. For those who felt that a veil had been drawn over the afterlife, cremation seemed to embody the notion that the form of disposal should reflect human achievements. In that regard funeral rituals became effectively geared for the comfort of the living, who felt they no longer needed consolatory rituals for what could not be seen or expected of the life to come (Flanagan, 2004). This process has been discerned in contemporary trends in funeral liturgies as a shift of focus from 'prospective' to 'retrospective' fulfilment of identity (Davies, 1995b).

Why were Catholic attitudes to cremation more complex and more hesitant? First, Catholics maintained an institutionalised relationship between the living and the dead. A system of rites and prayers as, for example, the week's, month's and year's mind, intercessions for the dead, and the cult of the saints, all encouraged the living in a continuing and efficacious mutuality with the dead. In societies where the counter-Reformation had triumphed, like France, this lasted until the end of the eighteenth century (McManners, 1972, 1981a; Kselman, 1988).

Secondly, Catholics were able to maintain belief simultaneously in the resurrection of the body and the immortality of the soul because the souls of the dead were believed to spend a time in Purgatory. Whilst Protestants found difficulties in positing a location for the souls of the dead whose bodies lay 'sleeping' in the grave (Burns, 1972; Disley, 1991), Catholics had a clear sense of engagement with the dead in ways that entailed duties for the living, often expressed in rituals with parallels in the Orthodox churches (Ware, 1963; Danforth, 1982; Merridale, 2000). Protestantism served to deny such a dynamic relationship between the living and the dead, which even extended to the understanding of ghost narratives (Bennett, 1987). As Rowell commented of the radical Anglican liturgies of 1552, the priest could commit the body but not commend the soul (Rowell, 1977). For Catholics, however, the corporeal remains were still accorded space in a realm where obligations still mattered, for the judgement to come was not solely a matter of divine responsibility, nor beyond human influence or amelioration.

Thirdly, Catholics maintained ritual and pastoral aids for dying people as, for example, prayers, extreme unction, the role of Jesus' mother Mary ('Pray for us sinners now and at the hour of our death') which all bore the dominant notion that people after death commenced a journey for which a 'send-off' was beneficial. To that end, the need to provide a priest for the dying person was a vital obligation placed on the living. This need to supply sacramental provision did not apply in Protestantism, whose theology had rendered the minister's death-bed role perfunctory (Stannard, 1977; Porter, 1989).

Fourthly, there was an association between orthodox belief in the resurrection of the body and a belief that if a person had lived a particularly saintly life this would be manifest in the incorruptibility of his or her corpse. In England, the outstanding precedent was that of St Cuthbert, Abbot of Lindisfarne, who died in AD 687 (Daniell, 1997). Cuthbert's body refused to decay and was found to be incorrupted at the opening of his coffin in 1534 at the orders of King Henry VIII's commissioners. For a corpse to remain incorrupt, its owner is marked out as a person of very special and incorruptible virtue. For example, in Civil War Spain (1936–1939) certain Republican supporters sought to demonstrate, by the opening of monks' and nuns' graves to reveal their decaying skeletons, that religious people were as sinful as anybody else (Lincoln, 1985).

Fifthly, the Catholic tradition of burial was not seriously challenged until the French Revolution and the political upheavals of the mid-nineteenth century. Pope Pius IX began his reign with some openness, but after 1848 – 'the year of revolutions' – he adopted a successive range of conservative policies to protect the Catholic Church. To counter doctrinal, sectarian and political onslaughts, he sought to make the

Church a closed corporation. He lost political control of the Papal States in 1859 and his temporal powers outside Vatican City in 1870. His opponents fastened upon Catholic practices at death as one of a number of institutions critical for Catholic social formation. These included schools, orphanages and colleges as well as baptism, confirmation, marriage and, especially, funerals. Freemasons played a part: in Italy and the Netherlands they were among the first supporters of cremation (Cappers, 1999). Pius' successor, Leo XIII, interpreted the promotion of cremation as deliberately anti-Catholic and anti-clerical. He banned cremation in 1886. This ban was maintained until, under a changed context in theology, pastoral work and world order, the Second Vatican Council removed the ban in 1964.

The Catholic–Protestant divide is critical for the history of modern cremation in Europe (Jupp, 1993b: 132–78) because of the different roles of the Church in matters of mortality and because of relationships between Church and State. When cremation was first promoted in Britain in the 1870s, the pattern and status of the various Christian Churches and their different attitudes towards burial grounds all prohibited a monotone response. First, whilst Catholicism in European countries, like France, Spain, Italy and Austria, generally maintained a religious monopoly (Martin, 1978a), England and (until 1920) Wales had a theoretically dominant Established Church; the Church of England had had to accommodate the existence of Nonconformist and Roman Catholic Churches since their legal position had been improved by the repeal of certain civil disabilities in 1828 and 1829. After 1820 (see Chapter 2) Nonconformist congregations began to flex their denominational muscles by helping to establish private cemetery companies. Catholics also began to provide their own cemeteries later in the century. Both Quakers and Baptists already had their own burial grounds, being excluded from Anglican churchyards because of their beliefs and practices about baptism. Thus, by the time cremation was proposed in 1874, the Anglican Church was only the leading church, but not the dominant one, and had been forced to accommodate both other forms of Christianity and their authority over rites and sites of disposal. In the British situation no united Church response could be offered to cremation.

During the 1840s both public and Parliament became aware of the shortage of burial spaces. The second cholera epidemic of 1848 stimulated public health legislation, which prompted a series of Acts from 1850. This seemed to solve the urban burial crisis. The legislation established new burial grounds – called cemeteries – which were owned and maintained by local authorities. The laws provided both consecrated and unconsecrated space; cemeteries were thus a secular location open to all denominations. Clergy continued to conduct funerals there, but from now on they participated as visitors, not as landlords. Thus ecclesiastical jurisdiction was severely limited. The Church had no control over what visiting relatives did in cemeteries; nor could it influence what they believed. The cemetery did not function as 'the frame for the Church', in Bishop Healey's phrase (Healey, 1967). This meant opportunities for rival forms of memorialisation and of interpretation of death. The concept of cemeteries as a secular solution to a national problem – the disposal of the dead – is inherent in the comments of the social reformer Bishop Fraser of Manchester in 1879. Consecrating the Anglican section of a new cemetery in Stockport, he said both that the establishment of a cemetery implied the removal of 200 acres of food-producing land for ever, and that this was a long way for the poor of Manchester to carry their dead: utilitarian principles both. Fraser was implying that the secular value of burial land balanced, if not outweighed, its religious value. As the decades passed, the secular value of cemeteries was viewed by their owners, local authorities, in increasingly economic terms. For, after 1918, the costs of cemetery maintenance, especially the upkeep of old graves and gravestones, impelled both church and local government leaders towards cremation.

Monopoly ownership of churchyards by the Church of England had other consequences. First, urban Nonconformist Churches who had owned burial grounds since before 1850 lost them under the new laws. Secondly, the religious census of 1851 stimulated the Free Churches to an unprecedented programme of chapel building. Hardly any of these provided burial grounds. This removed the Free Churches' proprietorial interest in burial grounds. I offer the hypothesis that these facts supply a reason why some Free Churches were able to march in the forefront of theological liberalism. No longer having burial ground responsibilities of their own, they were free to jettison such death-related doctrines as the existence of Hell and the resurrection of the body.

The implications of the succession of church-owned burial grounds by public cemeteries facilitated the emergence of cremation as a viable issue of disposal. This move from the churchyard to the cemetery reflected the growing spirit of secularity of the mid-Victorian period. When the eyes of administrative reformers fell upon forms of the disposal of the dead, Church practices that had survived for centuries were found wanting and, indeed, quite unfit for 'the age of improvement'. The burden of the dead on the living was increasingly attributable less to theological anxieties and more to administrative inefficiency and deprivations. Against this background, theological assumptions about the resurrection of the dead began to change. The movements of reform set in train a climate that had become increasingly favourable to the advocates of cremation. The Church, in its management of the dwelling space for the dead, was shown up to be hazardous as regards public health, unfit as regards administration, and inadequate as regards capacity.

The account of the development of cremation in Britain will reveal how its replacement of burial coincided with a process of modernisation, democratisation and secularisation. In the 150 years since the burial Acts of the 1850s, the Church, as an institution, increasingly lost the adherence and loyalty of the general population; as a doctrinal authority, it accommodated its doctrines about salvation after death to new and alternative popular beliefs; and as the dominant provider of burial space, it surrendered its responsibility as the custodian of the bodies of the dead. The English Churches' surrender of burial grounds is only one facet of the secularisation of British society. Yet the burial provisions of the Established Church of England were a key determinant of the way funeral change took place in England, to the analysis of which we now turn.

2
How the Church Lost Its Monopoly of Burial, 1820–1852

In England after 1800, within the rapidly growing cities, pressures developed on the tiny, over-used and rarely extended Anglican churchyards. The shortage of burial space for the new urban populations led to the abuse of the virtual monopoly of Anglican control of funeral services and burial grounds. The reforms initiated by Parliament in the 1850s established the cemetery as the successor to the churchyard. These developments effected the Churches' loss of influence in death. The enhanced role of the state in providing and maintaining burial space promoted non-Anglican funeral services, legalisation for cremation and the increasing secularisation of the interpretation of death.

The power of the State in circumscribing the Anglican Church's role in death was first exercised at the Reformation. Three facets of the Reformation in England are particularly important for an understanding of burial tradition. The first was the outlawing of relationships between the living and the dead (Thomas, 1973; Kreider 1979). The Reformation closed the chantries and forbade intercessions for the dead: the 1552 Prayer Book removed the commendation of the soul and substituted the committal of the body (Rowell, 1977: 87). The doctrine of Purgatory was abolished (Le Goff, 1984). Gittings discerned in late-mediaeval funerals a precarious balance between 'an increasingly individualistic philosophy and a collective approach to the problem of death' (Gittings, 1984: 39). As long as Purgatory was a legitimate belief within the Christian framework, both the dying person and his survivors could together influence his post-mortem destiny by prayer and by charity. When Protestants declared doctrines and rituals relating to Purgatory invalid, Christian funeral services lost half their effect: they could no longer help the deceased, only the bereaved. 'The ritual ties between the living and the dead were severed' (Gittings, 1984: 40). Because of the new

Protestant doctrine, 'each generation could be indifferent to the spiritual fate of its predecessor' (Thomas, 1973: 721) and invest more in its own generation and successors.

The second facet was the secular accompaniment of the new individuality of the soul: the development of the cult of the individual. The evacuation of religious symbols at death made room for secular ones. The Calvinist Directory of 1644 advocated funeral services with few words and without ceremony, but added '...this shall not extend to deny any civic respects or differences at the burial, suitable to the rank and condition of the deceased' (cited in Rowell, 1977: 83). So, whilst the burial ceremony was reduced to little more than a secular disposal of the body, the funeral was permitted to act as an expression of earthly social status. The rising cult of the individual also encouraged those with sufficient wealth to seek burial within church buildings, a practice largely opposed by the mediaeval Church but increasingly accepted in dense urban areas like London (Harding, 2002). This development had its critics. John Evelyn recalled in his diary that his father-in-law was disgusted by the novel custom of burying everybody within the body of the church and chancel, 'making churches charnel-houses being of ill and irreverent example and prejudicial to the health of the living, besides the continual disturbance of the pavement and seats' (cited in Curl, 1993: 135). Nevertheless, this practice continued and was especially conspicuous where attendance at the parish church could be enforced by law. The Church of England found itself in an ambiguous position, strengthened politically but weakened economically under Queen Elizabeth, with its monopoly weakened when the Stuart dynasty legitimised forms of religious Dissent between 1660 and 1714. The Church's response included an alliance between landed gentry and parochial clergy, an alliance illustrated by the Church's sanctioning of class divisions in funerals and memorials. Once commenced, intermural burials, together with the new memorial fashions imported into England with William III, proved popular (Houlbrooke, 1998; Llewellyn, 2000). Indeed, Westminster Abbey became so full of eighteenth-century leaders and warriors that the heroes of the Napoleonic Wars had to be interred and memorialised in St Paul's Cathedral (Irwin, 1981).

The third facet was the decline of the use of the charnel-house and the development of the permanent and individual grave, whether or not accompanied by the use of less perishable grave-markers. Time could rot wood, but not stone; it might efface individual inscription, but not erase ownership. A growing number of the new merchant-class could not buy a permanent tomb in the church but might obtain a permanently marked one in the churchyard. And the more the middle-classes purchased grave-space in hallowed ground, the less room was there for lesser mortals. Some churchyards were so congested with bodies that the churchyard soil level began to rise up above the streets. The overuse of the London churchyards had been perceived as a problem by the 1580s and the wealthier churches had to buy burial ground outside their parishes (Harding, 1998: 55). Given the shortage of space, social status and burial place were critically linked in the early modern city with space within the church being allocated according to wealth, class, gender and occupation (Harding, 1998: 56; 2002).

Thus by 1800 the pressure on burial space was already an old problem. The circumstances which provoked the burials crisis after the battle of Waterloo (1815) date from the Reformation Settlement and particularly the Restoration, which reconfirmed the Established position of the Church of England. Before the Reformation, the vast majority of graves were not marked individually. According to traditional Christian theology, the resting place of human remains was known all along to God, for whom identification caused no problems (Augustine, 1984). Up to the Reformation and with a stable population,

> most churchyards were capable of assimilating a regular intake of corpses that was balanced by the removal of displaced bones to ossuaries and charnel-houses, themselves a distinctive type of funerary building whose history has yet to be written. (Colvin, 1991: 366)

The use of charnel-houses continued in many countries that remained Catholic. Most charnel-houses in England were cleared in the first Protestant century: in 1549, for example, the contents of the charnel-house at St Paul's were deposited at Bunhill (Bone-hill) Fields. So disposing of charnel-houses was to leave a problem for the future, when rising populations or epidemics might increase pressure on increasingly limited space, no longer made regularly available by re-use.

After the Great Fire of London (1666), John Evelyn and Christopher Wren both counselled that the fire had provided an opportunity to build new large cemeteries outside the city (Adshead, 1923). It is reasonable to assume, with Curl (1993: 136), that a major opponent of such proposals was the Established Church, which sought to safeguard clerical income from burial fees (Gittings, 1984: 138). Other likely opponents would have been the existing owners of such prime development land.

After 1689 Protestant Dissenters made their own contribution to meeting burial needs and their Bunhill Fields in London became the most famous, with the graves of Bunyan and Defoe (Light, 1915). Baptists and Quakers needed their own burial space because their baptismal policies disqualified them from Anglican churchyards (Manning, 1952; Jupp, 1997a; Stock, 1998). Other small-scale alternatives to the Established Church monopoly existed: a few private grounds, usually unconsecrated, and some for foreigners (Holmes, 1896). Anglican clergy conducted all funerals, including those of Dissenters, in their own churchyards. Catholics remained in a state too weak to argue for burial land of their own until the 1801 union with Ireland, when Catholics became one-fourth of the British population overnight; but this did not translate into Catholic burial grounds in England until the 1850s after the first post-Famine Irish immigrations. In the non-Anglican regions of Scotland and Ireland, religious pluralism prevented the dominance of any one of the denominations over cemetery arrangements.

An act of 1711 permitted the building of fifty new parish churches and churchyards in the London suburbs. It forbade inter-mural burial but Christchurch, Spitalfields, probably one of many, ignored the Act very swiftly by establishing vaults beneath (Cox, 1996). As London grew larger, the Church of England was seriously handicapped by its refusal to break up the large parishes into smaller ones. McLeod (1974: 101–6) describes how the parish of Bethnal Green was carved out of the parish of Stepney in 1743: a parish church was built in 1745 and a chapel of ease in 1820. A third church was not built until 1837, by which time the population had reached 70,000. The vast majority of the parish would all have been buried in the same single Anglican churchyard.

Vested interests of both church and chapel inhibited proposals to extend burial sites. The crisis was caused by rapid urbanisation and the sharp rise in population at the end of the eighteenth century. There was a massive influx of population into the towns, where new forms of funeral behaviour were forced on people by new forms of communal living (Landers, 1993). Country people had been accustomed (Gordon, 1984) to the help of their friends, neighbours and the local carpenter at times of bereavement. In the city, the role of carpenter was played by the undertaker (Litten, 1991, 1997; Howarth, 1992) and that of neighbour was played for the wealthier by undertakers providing catering and for the poorer by burial clubs. Usually founded by undertakers, these clubs developed in the second half of the eighteenth century (Gosden, 1961; Gittings, 1984; Thompson, 1988). They grew enormously as a result of the Anatomy Act 1832. This transferred unclaimed corpses from workhouses to the charge of medical schools as cadavers for dissection, thus increasing the importance of giving relatives a public and respectable funeral (Richardson, 1987). The Act was intended to defeat the practice of body-snatching but the issue did much to promote public disquiet about burial as a secure mode of disposal.

The English population level had remained on a plateau through most of the eighteenth century (Houlbrooke, 1999). This served to emphasise the rapidity of growth when it came at the century's end and between 1801 and 1831 the population increased by 16% in each decade. The growth of industrialisation was compounded by the country's being on a war footing until 1815. This massing of the proletariat concentrated extraordinary problems of sickness, death and disposal which only became a cause for concern when the Napoleonic War ended. In 1790 twice as many labourers worked on the land as in towns. By 1840 that situation had been reversed (Morley, 1971: 7). In 1840, the government published the report of a Select Committee on the Health of Towns (*Report*, 1840). The report drew attention to the problems of over-crowding. Liverpool, Glasgow and Manchester had each more than doubled in size. In Liverpool, by 1840, one fifth of the working class, estimated at 30,000 persons, lived in 7800 'inhabited cellars'. In St Martin's-in-the-Fields, whose parish stretched to Drury Lane, some houses contained between 45 and 60 people (Chadwick, 1843, cited in Morley, 1971: 8). Chadwick pointed out that the annual loss of life from filth and bad ventilation was 'greater than the loss from death or wounds in any wars in which the country has been engaged in modern times' (cited in Morley, 1971: 9–10).

Commercial interests had, of course, been active in funeral customs for a very long time (Gittings, 1984; Litten, 1991). A 1678 Act for burying in woollen had been intended to stimulate the wool trade. The use of the parish coffin was increasingly discontinued after the Plague of 1665 which encouraged the use of individual coffins, themselves a status symbol. By 1700, the new undertaking trade had a monopoly on coffins. During the next quarter of a century the coffin furniture trade became well established. Urban funerals were becoming an item of conspicuous consumption. It is important to note that elements of the so-called Victorian way of death pre-dated Queen Victoria's accession by several decades.

Gittings relates the commercialisation of death to the twin developments of individualism and of the undertaking business. The undertakers in the later eighteenth century had responded to growing middle- and working-class consciousness by catering for funeral attire, whereas the trade had previously only catered for funeral hospitality. Undertakers responded to expanding class-consciousness with entrepreneurial skill.

When they succeeded in draining money and significance away from the funeral meal in favour of their own business, the consequence was that

> a supportive, communal activity – the funeral meal – was being eroded by a competitive, isolating and individualistic element, the display of ... material commodities ... The profession of undertaking could not have come into being if the premise on which it rested, that death was a fit candidate for commercialisation, had not been acceptable to its potential customers. (Gittings, 1984: 98–9)

The undertaking trade had emerged in the 1680s providing, in a period of increasing stability and prosperity, styles of funeral based on College of Heralds lines (Litten, 1991, 1997). Fairly swiftly, undertakers were given control of upper- and middle-class funerals providing specialist services to classes of people for whom status was important. This represents a shift of institutional power and control in funeral rites. Thus by the nineteenth century, undertaking was a well-established trade offering such a range of services that there was a growing concern that the trade exploited its customers, a theme popularised in the novels of Charles Dickens.

The clergy were also weakened. The place of clergymen at upper-class deathbeds was partly taken by doctors, who began to undertake the medical management of death (Porter, 1989: 87–90; Jalland, 1996). The family's role also increased. Expanding social consciousness both of the self and of the nuclear family (Stone, 1979) led to the death having increased importance for the family above that of the community. The dying person was losing control of his own death (Ariès, 1981; Porter 1989: 89). Death began to assume a greater family and less of a religious importance, which was also caused by theological change including the moderation of Calvinist belief (Almond, 1994). Upon the decline of Calvinism and its doctrines of election, there followed the nineteenth-century hope of reunion, after death, with one's family (McDannell and Lang, 2001). This was fuelled by nineteenth-century evangelicalism, which moulded attitudes to death for much of that century (Jalland, 1996, 1999).

Within Protestant England, there was no doubt of the clergyman's role at the actual funeral. The churchyard was a consecrated ground, God's Acre, where the outlaw could still claim sanctuary. Within it, the Church exercised custody over the bodies of the dead until God's action on the Day of Resurrection (Anon., 1864). The clergyman met the corpse at the lych-gate, to conduct it onto consecrated ground, there to be buried 'in sure and certain hope of the resurrection'. The range of funeral hymns sung by mourners up to 1850 demonstrate traditional and folk beliefs in the resurrection of the body (Gammon, 1988). This belief began to be challenged by secularists after 1850 (Barrow, 1986) and lost much credibility during the First World War (Wilkinson, 1978).

Funeral fees had begun to play an increasing part in providing the clergyman's stipend. This was partly a result of the limits on parish fund-raising imposed by the English Reformation (Duffy, 2001b). Towards 1600, the Church had begun to count the cost of the Reformation, with the loss of fees formerly paid for prayers offered for dead souls, and the loss of property at the Reformation. For a simple funeral, fees were paid to the minister, clerk and sexton of the parish. The Congregationalist Henry Barrow complained around 1590: 'Neither rich nor poor, neither young nor old, can get burial without money in the Church of England: no penny, no *Pater Noster* there' (cited in Gittings, 1984: 142). A century later, John Evelyn was complaining about the Marriage Duties Act 1694, whereby four shillings were to be paid as a burial tax. On 14 July 1695, John Evelyn wrote: 'A very imprudent tax, especially this reading of the names, so that most went out of the church' (cited in Gittings, 1984: 143).

It seems to have been understood that the fees paid to the clergyman were for burial in his freehold ground. Whilst it is easy to understand that church incomes were in need of supplement, it is also easy to visualise how chargeable extras could increase, when an established, but no longer so prosperous, Church had a monopoly upon burial. In London city churches, a sliding scale operated (Harding, 2002). By 1800, clergy incomes in many London parishes (87 in the urban area) were derived in great measure from burial fees. This fact might have remained unnoticed for much longer had not public attention been drawn to burial practices and the state of burial grounds. There were four reasons behind the growing calls for funeral reforms: the activities of the body-snatchers c.1780–1832 (Richardson, 1987); the cholera crisis of 1831 and its emergency burial regulations (Morris, 1976); the advent of the private cemeteries in the 1820s (Rugg, 1992, 1999); and the public health debate connecting fever with 'miasmas' from burial grounds stimulated by Walker (Walker, 1839) and Chadwick (Chadwick, 1843). Notoriety became attached not only to Anglican burial practices but also to those of Nonconformists, as exemplified by London's Enon Baptist Chapel (Jupp, 1997a) and to non-denominational grounds like London's Spa Fields (Walker, 1846). Calls for burial reform began to emerge.

Doctor George Alfred Walker lived in London's Drury Lane, and knew well the situation of the poor who lived in the crowded courts and streets off the Strand and in the area now known as Kingsway. He began a campaign against the appalling burial conditions which were a threat to the health and life of the poor. His book *Gatherings from Graveyards* (Walker, 1839) was widely reviewed. Convinced that miasmas from burial grounds affected the health, particularly of the poor, he called for the closure of urban churchyards, nearly all owned by the Established Church, and their replacement by cemeteries outside the built-up area, under some form of private or public management. These measures were naturally interpreted by clergy as a threat to the authority and income of the Church. The Church seemed to have had no serious thoughts of a major campaign to extend its holdings of burial land, though Birmingham and Oxford were among Anglican exceptions (Rugg, personal communication). It did not seem to have understood the challenge as a threat to its doctrines. It was at the time concerned with issues like the provision of new churches. Blomfield, Bishop of London (1826–1852), is celebrated in Church history as a reforming bishop, but his record on the reform of burial practices is not as satisfactory (*Report from the Select Committee*, 1842, QQ.2947–8). The clergy were a frequent target of Walker's criticisms, for the conditions they allowed at funerals were inconsistent with the Gospel they preached over the coffin, whilst the burial grounds over which they presided as clergy or as chairmen of Vestries were a disgrace to a civilised nation. Walker said:

> I am sorry to find the apathy of my reverend brethren, from the bishop to the curate, so universally prevalent. It must arise either from apathy or from interest. Among the many thousands in our Churchmen of observation, leisure and education, we look in vain for a single champion in so righteous a cause. (Walker, 1847: 21)

Clergy burial fee interests had been defended by William McKinnon, MP, when he conducted his Select Committee on burials in 1842. He was attacked vigorously by John Campbell, the minister of London's Whitfields and Moorfields Tabernacles and the editor of *The Patriot*. He claimed that McKinnon, in defending the Church of England, was endangering the chapels of Dissenters (Campbell, in *The Patriot*, 11 October 1842; Rugg, 1999).

In the 1850 Parliamentary debates on the Metropolitan Interments Bill, Lord Ashley defended clergy burial fees, saying that in many instances clergy received little or no emolument beyond what was derived from churchyard fees 'while in others fifty per cent of the clergyman's income was derived from that source' (HC, 7 June 1850, paras 926–7). For Ashley, if Parliament were to forbid burial within the city, clergy would need financial compensation. The MP for Marylebone, Sir Benjamin Hall, suggested that, under the Bill, the corpse would now be buried in an extra-parochial cemetery; a compensation fee of 6s 2d would be paid for burial to the present and all future incumbents of the parish in which the deceased had last lived (HC, 7 June 1850, para. 917). The actual burial would be conducted by a paid chaplain attached to the new cemetery.

In some cases before 1850, said Sir George Grey, the clerk and church-warden of the metropolitan parish had also received fees (HC, 7 June 1850, para. 918). In St Giles in the Fields, a parish made notorious by the revelations of Chadwick's Supplementary Enquiry in 1843, there was a parish official who practised nearly all the trades involved in a funeral. The rector, Dr J. E. Tyler, employed as his sexton a former soldier who had become a parson. As sexton, he then added to his services both undertaking and stonemasonry. By such means St Giles had become a parish able to charge a lower burial fee: it thus undercut adjoining parishes and attracted their trade. The parish's own statistics for the years 1846–1849 reveal: deaths and funerals in 1846, 896 and 2323; in 1847, 1298 and 2877; in 1848, 1111 and 3578; in the first six months of 1849, 573 and 3440. Whilst the 1849 figure probably indicates increased mortality during the cholera epidemic, there was, nevertheless, no doubt that practices like those in St Giles underlined the inability both of the Church and of parish government to reform themselves: (for Tyler testimony to the Select Committee of 1842 see QQ.1413–1509).

This Parliamentary critique was only part of the story for there were reformers within the Church. The Cambridge Camden Society, founded in 1839, was a High Church pressure group within the Church of England whose reforming purposes included better funerals for the urban poor. They wanted to make funeral services more sacramental by including the Holy Communion. They wanted to reduce expense, break class distinction, revive burial guilds whose duties would include watching over the corpse, and have one grave per person except for married couples. They had witnessed inadequacies in the Church's funeral ministry and were indignant. One report described the 'miserable farce of a modern consecration of a churchyard' where the bishop had conse-crated the churchyard from the altar: 'He might as well have been in his study!' The Ecclesiological Society provided the theological underpinning for their campaign:

Sanitary considerations are the first and greatest ... there are other considerations also ... to them that believe in the resurrection of the dead. They, for the Christian burial of whose remains we are providing, were our BRETHREN in Christ whilst they lived; and now that they have entered on another and higher life, they are our brethren in Christ still. We are bound to provide that their remains, so far as in us lies, should rest undisturbed and inviolate till the great Doom; that in the same place where they lie down to rest, in the same place they shall arise to their sentence. Their bodies which were temples of the HOLY GHOST must be treated as His temple still. (Ecclesiological Society, 1851: 2)

The Ecclesiologists were too late, overwhelmed by the reforming zeal of the age which placed sanitation and public health, the identity of the middle class, and the new local Burial Boards before the considerations of a Church. Had the London clergy and parishes found different and effective ways to accommodate the capital's dead, in ways which honoured their equality in Christ rather than their rank in society, in ways which treated the churchyard as a frame to the church and as effective for the preaching of the Gospel as the pulpit, the challenge for the churchyards and the Church's monopoly might never have been magnified to a crisis point. The cries of the Ecclesiologists were an anachronism. Furthermore, the response to Walker was a nation-wide phenomenon.

The earliest effective proposals for burial reform came from the private sector. After the end of the Napoleonic War (1815) many British tourists admired the Père Lachaise cemetery in Paris, laid out in 1804 (Brown, 1973), and it may well have influenced American reformers (French, 1975; Curl, 1993: 269ff.) A number of scholars have earlier pointed to Paris' Père Lachaise cemetery, as a model for British cemetery reform (Brooks, 1989; Jupp, 1990; Curl, 1993). Certainly, the Parisian model had stimulated British ideas for a national cemetery and in the 1820s Carden proposed Primrose Hill above London's Regents Park as the site of a central cemetery for which Thomas Willson designed a vast pyramid to take five million bodies. Yet Carden's first proposal, the '(British Père Lachaise) General Burial Association of 1825', failed to attract any attention. Rugg asserted that burial enthusiasm for the French cemetery became general only after the mid-1830s, by which time the establishment of private cemeteries in Britain was well under way (Rugg, 1997: 108).

Carden was more successful in 1830 when he organised the General Cemetery Company in London which, in 1831, purchased fifty-four acres at Kensal Green (Curl, 2001). The outbreak of cholera later that year helped to speed Parliamentary action. The Act of Incorporation 'for establishing a General Cemetery', passed in July 1832, acted to neutralise the opposition of the Established Church by ensuring that clergy did not suffer from loss of funeral fees. A precedent was set on clergy fees which were not only to be paid to clergy who conducted the graveside ceremony, but also to the incumbents of those parishes from which the corpses had originated (Meller, 1999: 118). At Kensal Green, new fees for the clergy – ranging from 1s 6d (7.5p) to 5s 0d (25p) – bought off clerical opposition but these fee levels were soon insufficient. When Brompton Cemetery was proposed, the clergy 'wished to protect themselves against the loss of burial fees following their experience at Kensal Green' (Curl 1993: 240).

Kensal Green was the first of eight joint-stock cemeteries to be established in London between 1832 and 1842. Financially, Kensal Green's success was immediate. Not only had shares doubled by 1839, but its social cachet received royal approval when two of the children of George III, Princess Sophia and the Duke of Sussex, were buried there. Kensal Green became one of the sights of London. A precedent for the future was its administrative bureaucracy: Kensal Green burials were mapped and recorded, with a plan kept at a cemetery lodge. This measure was not only a reflection of the recognition of individual ownership and the permanence of the individual grave, it was also a mark of social distinction from the pauper grave. Pauper graves were unmarked and could contain up to thirty bodies. Lack of disturbance was not guaranteed. The immediate appeal of Kensal Green set the standard for the respectability and acceptability of the cemetery movement, whose bubble did not burst for twenty years.

Yet London was late in the field. The first joint-stock cemetery company in the UK was established in 1819 to open Rusholme Road Cemetery, Manchester. Rusholme Road was the first of 113 private cemetery companies which were established between 1820 and 1853. By no means were all of these successful, but the successful ones shared common denominators. Of the thirteen companies successfully founding cemeteries before 1835, ten were closely affiliated with Nonconformist churches, and all ten attracted sufficient capital to lay out a cemetery (Rugg, 1997: 109). Rugg has established that private charity companies, pioneered largely by Nonconformist Christians were *the* model for cemetery reform in the post-1815 period. The Congregationalist George Hadfield wrote that 'it had long been wanted and resorted to by many; but to us it was a particular advantage to get our own ministers enabled to preside at our funerals' (Hadfield, cited in Rugg, 1999: 309). Rugg outlines three reasons for Nonconformist involvement in cemetery reform. First, the Nonconformist Churches had greatly increased their numbers and often their wealth in the early decades of the Industrial Revolution. Secondly, Nonconformists wanted to be free of Anglican control. Not until 1880 could Nonconformists be buried in parish churchyards without Anglican rites led by Anglican clergy. Thirdly, cemetery companies provided Nonconformists with a political weapon with which to campaign against their other civil disabilities, like the mandatory payment of Church rates and the registration of marriages. For Rugg, cemetery companies established by Nonconformist denominations in the UK predominated in the period from 1820 to 1834 and twenty were in operation by 1853 (Rugg, 1999).

Trouble was imminent for London's Brompton Cemetery which symbolised all that could go wrong with private cemeteries. Architects and directors quarrelled. Delayed building work gave clients pause. Maintenance was expensive, salaries were reduced. Designs were simplified, short cuts taken. Its financial problems stemmed from initial outlay on buildings, catacombs and drainage, in a space too small. The income was insufficient to repay capital, let alone shareholders. Built on the edge of town, it was being encircled by new suburbs. Brompton proved that joint-stock cemeteries were unable to prevent the evils of inter-mural burial because they were beyond the purse of the poor majority. The Cemetery Clauses Act was passed in 1847 to facilitate the growth of new commercial cemeteries but with the return of cholera in 1848, the Government was forced to rethink its burials solution. From the decisions taken in the years 1850 to 1852 would be dated the British system of making the disposal of the dead, whatever their survivors' means, a responsibility of local government.

The Cemetery Clauses Act 1847 was one of several similar measures passed by Lord John Russell, essentially as exercises in administrative housekeeping, designed to speed up and tidy up the cumbersome business of obtaining a Private Act of Parliament for works of a public nature, whether carried out by public authorities or private enterprise (Brooks, 1989: 41). It allowed cemetery companies compulsorily to purchase land; cemeteries had to provide consecrated and unconsecrated land, each of which might have its own chapel; it allowed the payment of compensation to any incumbent from whom a body came for loss of his burial fee; burial plots could be sold either for a period or in perpetuity; registers of all burials were to be kept; and no burials were to be beneath the chapels. One significant clause was that cemeteries should be at least two hundred yards from a dwelling house; this 'radius clause', as it came to be known, would cause considerable problems in the twentieth century when a successor for cemeteries was sought. The whole Act, however, was essentially conservative. It did nothing to address the burial crisis for the working classes; there was no provision for inspection and no regulations about the depth of burial. Sanitary precautions were minimal. It did little to meet the objections of Nonconformists and it did nothing to facilitate the building of cemeteries either by local authorities or as a national scheme.

The initiative for burial reform came from two individual campaigners, George Alfred Walker and Edwin Chadwick. Reflecting on the reforms of Dr Walker, the *Provincial Medical Journal* of June 1843 observed that 'in contemplating the advancement of any public good, rarely does it happen that labours such as these originate with, or are maintained by, a single individual' (cited in Walker, 1843 edn: 1). Walker's campaign against inter-mural interment was conducted, over a space of nine years, with substantial medical and public support. *Gatherings from Graveyards* was followed by pamphlets, letters and lectures. These were nationally reviewed and stimulated calls for country-wide reform, for many London problems were paralleled in provincial cities. By the end of the decade, Walker's pioneering work had been taken over by the Government. Yet Walker is not to be credited only for publicising contemporary burial practices and for giving them a medical frame of reference. His work was critical to the development of the cemetery and the demise of the churchyard.

Walker had studied in Paris where the miasmatic hypothesis and 'evidence' relating burial ground emanations and public health was already well established. Before the discovery of microbial pathogens late in the nineteenth century, the prime source of disease was believed to be miasmas, poisonous gases given off by unhealthy environments, like stagnant waters, rotting vegetable and animal matter and by burial grounds (Porter, 1996: 171–2). Walker's campaign was also based on his personal experience of health and sanitation around Drury Lane, London. Between St Clement Dane's and the Savoy there were on or adjacent to the Strand eight burial grounds. Everybody knew of their smell. Walker was concerned to show that the smell was not only capable of causing sudden death, but generally sapped the health and physique of people who lived nearby. Of scores of examples, two must suffice. William Jackson, a gravedigger, died after digging into coffins dating from the cholera years at the Savoy ground and at Russell-Court, Drury Lane (Walker to MacKinnon, PP 1842, 3 May 1884; Walker, 1843: 25: 3). William Chamberlain was preparing a vault in the Green Ground, Portugal Street. He placed one foot on the brickwork, the other on a lead coffin from which gas escaped and overcame him (PP 1842 Q.2341; Walker, 1843: 27: 16).

In the sixteenth century, St Martin-in-the-Fields had established a new burial ground on the west side of Drury Lane. The soil had now become physically incapable of decomposing any more corpses. The smell was intense. The ground level was formerly below the tenements next door: now it was five feet above their lower floor. Where the living slept within a few inches of the dead, wrote Walker, it was not surprising that

> The experience of Insurance Offices and Benefit Societies has long since shown that, *caeteris paribus*, in these localities the mean average duration of life is infinitely lower than in other situations. (Walker, 1843: 18)

Clergy defended themselves with exceptions to his hypothesis. The Bishop of London told the 1842 Select Committee that he had slept in a house next to a churchyard for many years without feeling any ill effects (PP 1842, Vol. X, Q.2948). Walker's usual response was that the better off could afford both better food and homes and thus enjoy a stronger constitution.

As long as the miasmic hypothesis of illness held the floor, there was little to deny Walker's testimony on the grounds of health. What continually vexed him was that, despite the outcry his lectures and pamphlets caused, there was little practical response. Walker was, of course, opposed by several vested interests. He personally directed campaigns against local Anglican clergy and Dissenting ministers, against undertakers and burial ground managers and employers. He gained enemies in each of these ranks, the manager of the Spa Fields Burial Ground taking him to court in 1845, the Minister of Whitfields Chapel attacking him in his newspaper *The Patriot*. Burial abuse proved to be interdenominational. The following churches figure frequently in Walker's writing: St Giles-in-the-Fields, St James, Clerkenwell, and St Mary's, Poplar; to the first two of which poor Irish Catholics were particularly brought for burial (Walker, 1841: 7); the Dissenting chapels of Enon Chapel, of Elim in Fetter Lane and Whitfields in Tottenham Court Road, and the small private ground of Spa Fields.

Nonconformist chapels, as voluntary organisations, needed income even more than the Anglican parish churches. Those chapels which had burial grounds valued the income they provided. The Revd John Campbell of Whitfields Chapel challenged Walker in *The Patriot*:

*

No means whatever were taken by Mr McKinnon, MP, to ascertain the true condition of the dissenting burial grounds and the effect which this bill would have on Dissenting property...We can prove he was fully apprised of the ruinous results of this Bill to many of the most important congregations of the Nonconformist community... This Bill is very largely a question of property; it is still more largely a question of civil and religious liberty. (*The Patriot*, Letter XI, October 1842)

Of course, it was cheaper to be buried in the chapel-yard than in the churchyard, but Walker recognised other, good, motives. Many people preferred to be buried where they had worshipped. Furthermore, only in the chapel-yards or private burial grounds might Nonconformist worshippers be buried by their own ministers and with their own rites. Nevertheless, whilst there was a religious principle behind the Nonconformist interest, it is clear that income was another important factor. Elim and Enon Chapels were among those excoriated by Walker both for unacceptable profits and for immoral practices to make room for yet more dead (Jupp, 1997a). Hence the title of Walker's 1843 pamphlet, *Interment and Disinterment* (Walker, 1843). By the burial Acts 1852 and 1880, Nonconformists later obtained the right to conduct funerals according to their own rites in both urban and rural churchyards (Fletcher, 1974).

Disinterment was a frequent practice. Once the poor of the earth were committed to the ground 'in sure and certain hope of the resurrection to eternal life', there followed the fair statistical probability that disinterment would swiftly follow, long before the day of the General Resurrection (Walker, 1841: 22). Walker told how Thomas Wakley, MP, Coroner for Middlesex, reported that in August 1840 a poor man had died at 'a wretched hovel in Paradise Row', Chelsea, and was buried, said the gravedigger, 'in the usual way' by the parish. A judicial enquiry was instituted, and it was necessary to exhume the body. The gravedigger declared he could not find it. 'Twenty-six bodies in the same plot?' queried the summoning officer, 'Were they rammed in with a rammer?' The reply was that 'the bodies of paupers were packed together as closely as possible, in order to make the most of the space' (PP 1842, Vol. X, Q.878). In the cheapest burial grounds, an unscrupulous manager and his assistants practised all manner of disappearing tricks: disinterment, burning, removal down sewers or into the foundations of new road and bridge-works of bodies and part-bodies. To cut costs, the common graves for the paupers were left open between funerals. Clergymen sometimes buried paupers *en masse* on Sunday afternoons. The Poor

Law Commissioners were told (Walker, 1839: 141) that the cheap burial grounds in Cripplegate were 'left open from one Sunday to another'. The weekend was the only free time for a working man to attend a funeral. It gave the relatives time to collect the money for the funeral bill.

Clergy were aware of the conditions in which they buried their parishioners. The smell at St Luke's Church, in London's Old Street, was so offensive that 'Revd Dr Rice the present curate . . . never volunteered to descend [into the vaults below] but invariably performed the funeral rites whilst standing in the passage, at the top of the entrance to the vaults' (Walker, 1841: 7). But the clergy were caught in a double trap. Their Bishops had far less discipline over them than was popularly believed. The parson's freehold was a bulwark against church reform. Moreover, the burial fees were part of regular income, both for Anglican incumbents and for Nonconformist chapels. Anglicans were also compromised by their position in the local politics of the day. The parishes into which London's local government was divided (sixty-eight north of the river) were independent and jealous of each other. Their burial income was also under threat from the new private cemeteries.

During the Metropolitan Interments Bill debate (HC, 3 June 1850, col. 682) Mr R. B. Osborne, MP, said that credit due to Dr Walker had been given instead to Edwin Chadwick. During the 1840s, Chadwick had argued not for churchyards or joint-stock cemeteries but for public cemeteries. Edwin Chadwick was the disciple and personal friend of the elderly Jeremy Bentham. A lawyer, he became the Chief Commissioner in the enquiry into the administration of the Poor Law. In 1837, a fever epidemic hit east London. Applications for relief increased the poor rates. Chadwick, by then Secretary to the Poor Law Board, sent Dr Southwood Smith to investigate Bethnal Green and Whitechapel. The publication of the report put Chadwick into the vanguard of public health agitation. Tireless, humourless and authoritarian, Chadwick exhibited the paradoxical characteristic of a man devoted to the public good who was incapable of fellow feeling (Brooks, 1989: 37; Finer, 1952). These characteristics and the fact that he was fighting a laissez-faire economic culture would eventually defeat his plans for cemetery reform.

Following the government reports of 1840 and 1842, Chadwick published his *A Supplementary Report on the Results of a Special Enquiry into the Practice of Interments in Towns* (Chadwick, PP 1843, Vol. XII). Chadwick was concerned to whip up public concern as a force for Benthamite changes in burial reform, whereby the government would take a major responsibility. He argued that the current state of administrative information was to be deplored when any views can be entertained of making the small parish and the rude and barbarous service (multiplied, at an enormous expense) of the really unsuperintended common gravedigger and sexton, the prototypes for this important and difficult branch of public administration of the greatest metropolis in the modern world. (Chadwick, 1843: 44)

Chadwick argued for public cemeteries on the basis that 'the common cemetery is not the property of one generation now departed, but is the common property of the city' (Chadwick, 1843: 48). The recommendations of his Report were radical and comprehensive; the existing urban burial grounds should be closed, intra-mural burial forbidden and new cemeteries built beyond the suburbs. For Chadwick, the new cemeteries could not be entrusted either to the joint-stock companies or to the Churches: his solution was national cemeteries, financed by the national government. He proposed the nationalisation of undertaking; the re-use of graves in ten-year cycles, bones being reburied in common graves; the employment of district medical officers of health to promote cemetery use and register the dead; receiving houses (mortuaries) to accommodate the dead between death and funeral; and out-of-town cemeteries which could be approached by canal or by rail. His proposals were astonishingly impractical for such thorough-going research into the problem. They were both inconsistent with the English spirit and impossible within the existing English context. Their fate will be discussed below.

If Walker had placed burial in a medical frame, Chadwick had deposited it in a bureaucratic frame. A third figure gave it a horticultural emphasis which would not only dominate the cemetery movement for forty years, but would do so in a very acceptably English way. John Claudius Loudon had reviewed Walker's *Gatherings* favourably in his *The Gardener's Magazine*. *The Builder* joined *The Gardener's Magazine* in an attack upon churchyards (*The Builder*, Vol. iii, 1845: 588). The architects and landscape-gardeners, already relishing their opportunities in the new joint-stock cemeteries, realised that if monopoly over the majority of burial grounds could be wrested from the Church and put under secular administration, there would be many more contracts for cemetery design, landscaping and monumental memorials. Loudon exercised an enormous influence upon landscape, popular architecture and gardening. His *Encyclopaedia of Cottage, Farm and Villa Architecture* (1833) had a 'tremendous influence on taste' (Curl, 1981: 13) and helped to change the appearance of English houses and landscape from the first half of the nineteenth century. His influence on the cemetery movement would be to make the cemetery a place of beauty, culture and taste. His writings on cemeteries in *The Gardener's Magazine* were published together in 1843 (Loudon, 1843). He designed three cemeteries: a private one at Cambridge, a public one at Southampton, and one for Bath Abbey.

One strong influence upon Loudon's design was the Romantic Movement, two of whose popular channels had been Thomas Gray's poem 'Elegy in a Country Churchyard' and Edward Young's *Night Thoughts* (Young, 1853; McManners, 1981a: 335–8). For Morley, Romanticism 'largely determined the nature and form of Victorian emotion. And death calls for emotion in the most stoic society' (Morley, 1971: 14; Rugg, 1999). Loudon was an early advocate of cremation, 'Every large town will have a funeral pile, constructed on scientific principles, instead of a cemetery' (cited in Curl, 1981: 19). Loudon instinctively knew that the cemetery was the place for reform: he sought to civilise death by making the place of the dead into a garden. There it would express the culture of the age, encourage proper feelings and most moral reflections. Loudon sought to turn the churchyard, which mirrored the future of society as Christianity saw it, into a cemetery which mirrored the culture of the present age. His designs thus evacuated burial grounds of their religious purpose by stressing their practical purpose. He defined this (Loudon, 1843: 1) as

> the disposal of the remains of the dead in such a manner as that their decomposition, and return to the earth from which they sprung, shall not prove injurious to the living; either by affecting their health, or shocking their feelings, opinions, or prejudices,

phrases to be echoed by Sir Henry Thompson in 1874. The discerning of sense in death was henceforth to be determined not by the Divine Creator but by creatures of taste. For Loudon cemeteries should not only reflect culture, they should help form it. He insisted that the resting place of the dead should release things valuable for the living. They should have a civilising influence:

> The improvement of the moral sentiments and general taste of all classes and more especially of the great masses of society. Churchyards and cemeteries are scenes not only calculated to improve the morals and the taste, and by their botanical riches to cultivate the intellect, but they serve as *historical records*. (Loudon, 1843: 13)

Loudon's concern for cemeteries was stimulated by his commission for the design of the grounds at a new commercial cemetery at Cambridge. Freed from ecclesiastical restraint, he was able to develop his ideas for cemetery reformation. Cemeteries should be at a distance from human dwellings, placed in a light and airy place, on a southern-facing, well-drained slope with chalk or gravel soils to enable decomposition. Each grave should contain only one body or one family. Catacombs, vaults and mausolea retarded decomposition and therefore should be discouraged. All grave-plots should be identifiable and recorded and the cemetery walled, with just two gates. This would enable far greater control over the cemetery, its contents and its maintenance. Loudon opposed flowers: they made the cemetery too much like a pleasure garden. He preferred evergreens which were easier for the gardeners to maintain.

If tasteful and moral feelings were to be encouraged, then the cemetery must be made far more appealing. The heavily restricted space in urban churchyards made for frequently overused grave-space, with the earth turned black and grassless, gravestones unkempt and at an angle: the first step to rendering a churchyard a source of amelioration or instruction was to render it attractive. Religion was not the only parent of moral feelings:

> A church and churchyard in the country, or a general cemetery in the neighbourhood of a town, properly designed, laid out, ornamented with tombs, planted with trees, shrubs and herbaceous plants, all named, and the whole properly kept, might become a school of instruction in architecture, sculpture, landscape-gardening, arbori-culture, botany, and in those important parts of general gardening, neatness, order and high keeping. (Loudon, 1843: 12–13)

Loudon's proposals could effectively move the burial ground not only from the Church but from the parish community. They would site cemeteries at a considerable distance from the centre of community life and activity. His intention was to move the dead where they might have all the space they needed for self-expression in mute testimony. Henceforth the cemetery would be the place that specialised in death but was allowed its own witness. Death was distanced from everyday contemplation and increasingly from nightly fears: 'a garden cemetery was the sworn foe to preternatural fear and superstition' (Loudon, 1843: 11). Despite the commission for Bath Abbey, Loudon's proposals were generally on far too great a scale for the Church to implement.

Loudon had three more proposals, each of which meant a break from tradition. First, if the cemetery were to be viewed as a work of art, it should always be kept in the best possible order. This meant that voluntary societies like churches would find it difficult to compete. Secondly, he had a realistic view about the probability of cemeteries being filled to capacity. Cemeteries, once filled, should be closed, and after a decent interval opened as public parks and gardens. He obviously foresaw no financial threat, because, in proposing their reopening, he also advocated that all gravestones and monuments should be retained at public expense. The maintenance of churchyards had always been a church expense. Thirdly, he proposed that the poor, whose lot at funeral time was of the meanest, should be buried outside London. He was the first to propose Woking as a potential site with the use of rail transport to take coffins and funeral parties out from Waterloo Station. This was a break with the old tradition that the dead should be buried in the parish where they lived. In the name of reform, he was rationalising the process. As for paupers, temporary cemeteries might be used, the soil of which might revert when full to agricultural use. Land owners, meanwhile, could be buried on their own ground.

Loudon blamed the Church's traditional east–west orientation for the lack of sun, and the damp and gloom of the northern side of the churchyard, overlooking churches' traditional orientation to symbolise the direction of Jerusalem (Loudon, 1843: 76, 78). Did the Churches realise how the message pronounced by the churchyard was being redrafted in Loudon's designs? The graveyard once spoke of impermanence and decay, as if to underline a Christian message, that only when the body was once subject to corruption might it presume to await a mantle of incorruption; only when once subject to mortality might it inherit the prospect of immortality. Now the graveyard was to signal messages of permanence and security. It was to signal that one's family line, with greater financial security and health, was flourishing with far more assurance than ever. It was to signal that identity with a family had more immediate benefits than identity with the Son of God. Death had once been interpreted by the Church as the occasion for claiming the status of a creature redeemed by God. Security in death was a divine gift. In the Industrial Revolution, as the family re-evaluated what it understood by status and security, it reflected these in its use of death, disposal and memorialisation. Having found more wealth on earth, it could defer expectation of treasure in Heaven. It began to invest in things temporal as well as in things eternal. It demonstrated the rearranged (new) grounds of its confidence. It invested the funeral trappings which formerly symbolised what the bereaved had lost with banners clearly expressive of what the bereaved still owned. No wonder the

Church soon found it more in keeping with the spirit of the age to speak not of resurrection but of immortality. Within twenty years of Loudon's death in 1843, the Protestant Churches began to have increasing qualms about some of the traditional moral consequences of mortality: judgement, Hell and the nature of salvation (Rowell, 1974). It is one contention of this book that the Churches' loss of custody of the dead was linked to their surrender of sanctions over death.

Out of the blue, all these efforts to reform burial were radically changed by the reappearance of cholera (Longmate, 1966; Morris, 1976). On 1 October 1848 the disease broke out almost simultaneously at Newhaven and Edinburgh. Two months later, 180 deaths in a Tooting orphanage awoke London to the danger. The role of cholera in the changing of burial traditions is twofold. At its first advent in 1831, legislation was introduced on hygienic grounds to control the spread of the disease but it disrupted traditional forms of mourning, waking and burial. Its victims

> should be buried as soon as possible, wrapped in cotton or linen cloth saturated with pitch or coal tar, and carried to the grave by the fewest possible number of persons. The funeral service [was] to be performed in the open air. (Morris, 1976: 104–5)

Cholera's return in 1848 found a Government better organised, a medical profession far more competent and less panic than in 1831. The medical men of 1848 were not much closer to understanding the cause of cholera, for the Board of Health was now miasmatist whereas it had previously been contagionist. Yet many more people were prepared to see a link between poor hygiene and vulnerability to infection. The Health of Towns enquiry had raised the middle-class consciousness about a link between poverty and lack of sanitation. The burial reformers (non-existent in 1831) had made their cause a political issue. For them the second advent of cholera turned their proposals into policy. The Churches had been defensive throughout the 1840s. Without alternative plans of their own, they had perforce to accept the changes.

The spread of cholera was a mystery in both 1831 and 1848. It spread invisibly and irregularly. One day a town was clear, the next day it was engulfed. Victims could die within eight to ten hours of exposure and were swiftly buried, but to what had they been exposed, and how? In some towns there was an almost exclusive selection of the lowest and filthiest localities, and a considered preference for persons of drunken or negligent habits. Whilst the connection between poor sanitation and hygiene did not fit every case or locality, it lodged in men's minds. Creighton wrote:

> The disease in its successive visitations so obviously sought out the spots of ground most befouled with excremental and other filth as to bring home to everyone the dangers of the casual disposal of town refuse... The Report of the Health of Towns Commission, 1844, was the great magazine from which sanitary reformers drew their weapons. (Creighton, 1965: 833)

People recalled vividly the regulations imposed on them in 1831. The poor protested, but ineffectually, against the wretched treatment demanded for their dead. For sanitary reasons, the coffins of victims were to be filled with lime and their shrouds dipped in coal tar. The parish clerk of St Stephen's Coleman Lane described the stench and horrid state of the corpse, but for the poor who followed the funeral, quicklime was associated with the execution of criminals. The Board's regulations that funerals should follow within twenty-four hours of deaths disrupted the normal working-class habits and took away their pride.

> A working-class needed time. Relatives often kept bodies in their crowded homes for several days while they sought money for undertakers, mourning clothes and funeral teas. They would wait until Sunday, so that friends and relatives would be free from work and able to attend. (Morris, 1976: 105)

Finally, the Board's regulations sought to forbid the mourners their traditional and most intimate gestures of affection (Richardson, 1987). One purpose of laying out the body in the home was that family and friends could call to pay their last respects to the body. The regulations wanted victims rushed from their homes to the special cholera hospitals and the insensitive practice of some doctors performing the autopsies while still in the victim's home. Both these exacerbated pauper fears of medical authority. A generation later, memories of the bitter experiences would still have been sharp. These included the indescribable scenes in the churchyards, with the ground looking like a ploughed field, queues of mourners miserably waiting their turn, and navvies hired as extra gravediggers cursing or jumping on the coffins (Chadwick, 1971: 327).

In England and Wales 53,000 died. A massive programme of visits by local Boards of Health must have prevented hundreds of deaths. The response to cholera at administrative and medical levels had been vastly changed by 1848. There was a shift in the dominant public mood which reflected great changes in attitudes to health, government, science and religion (Morris, 1976: 200). There was a greater use of statistical records because of the recently systematised registration of births and deaths, introduced in 1837. In terms of consciousness, the public health reports of the 1840s gave public and government opinion a thorough education in science-based, especially miasma-based, attitudes to public health problems (Morris, 1976: 200). The 1848 religious response to cholera was also more muted. In 1831 there had been a national day of fasting, prayer and humiliation in an attempt to avert the judgement of God. Whilst Christian evangelicals rejoiced at such a public trust in the efficacy of prayer, the agnostic radicals and the articulate poor were ready to mock the hypocrisy of the wealthy abstaining from meat to eat fish. In 1848, the churches were far less confident about the connection. There were local celebrations, but no national fast day. Blame was shifting from the sin of disobedience by individuals to the sin of omission by society. The transition is well caught in the declaration of the United Presbyterians of Scotland that:

> there is reason to hope that, under the blessing of God, attention to sanitary regulations issued by the national Board of Health will prove effectual in mitigating greatly if not arresting this awful judgement. (cited in Morris, 1976: 203)

This change may also be observed in the response of Bishop Blomfield of London. In 1832 he had worked to ensure that Providence was mentioned in both Cholera Acts. His sermon at St Paul's in November 1849 indicates that he was accepting that material poverty was a major barrier between the Church and the poor:

> the most acceptable mode of acknowledging the greatness of God in withdrawing the scourge of pestilence...will be by a larger measure of charitable consideration for the physical evils which affect our poorer brethren...want of decent cleanly habitations is one of the chief evils that affect the poor. (cited in Morris, 1976: 204)

The practice of inter-mural burial could not long endure with the calls for reform, the example of the new cemeteries and the awful effects of cholera. When it came to the Parliamentary debates of 1850, the question was no longer whether the Church would lose its monopoly but how the administration of new arrangements would be shared with the competing interest groups.

The legislative response to the cholera was the first Public Health Act, in August 1848. The Act, with Edwin Chadwick behind it, inaugurated the public cemetery movement and laid the foundations for all public health measures up to 1914. It established a General Board of Health as a central authority to supervise public health. It was empowered to create local boards of health outside London, which would be responsible for sewerage, street cleaning, drainage, water supplies, burials, etc. It abolished burial within the walls of churches and chapels. It was not, however, given powers to open new cemeteries nor close burial grounds. Vested interests in the City ensured that London was exempt from the authority of the Board. Public Health in London was to be managed by the Metropolitan Commissioner of Sewers. In October 1848, the Commissioner appointed John Simon as the City's first Medical Officer of Health. In 1849, the cholera returned but Simon had not been inactive. In November 1849, his analysis of the City's sanitation was published in full in *The Times*. It galvanised all the various interests into action.

In February 1850, the General Board of Health put forward a scheme for the reform of burial in London. A Metropolitan Interment Commission would close all the urban burial grounds. It would buy up the existing joint-stock companies, extend Kensal Green and open a Great Eastern Cemetery further down the Thames estuary. It would introduce a rationalised system of funerals, so that even the poorest families could afford a decent funeral. The proposals became law as The Metropolitan Interments Act 1850. By this Act, the General Board of Health had authority for the whole of the city area as the Metropolitan Burial District. It was directed to build new burial grounds, with consecrated parts for Anglicans and unconsecrated parts for the remainder. It was empowered to buy up the existing joint-stock cemeteries. It could recommend to the Privy Council that any religious burial ground could be closed, on the grounds of public health. All parishioners, Anglican or Nonconformist, were allowed burial in whatever new cemetery was provided for them. Incumbents of closed churchyards were to receive compensation of 6s 2d for each body from their parish buried in a local authority cemetery. Nonconformist ministers officiating in the new cemeteries would receive the same amount. There was compensation for parish vestries, clerks, sextons and private cemetery owners. The Board was allowed to establish a funeral service at fixed cost and contract with railway companies for funeral transport. To pay for this, the Board could order increases in the Poor Rate, and order the levying of a Burial Rate. It could not, however, incur any expenditure over £100 without the permission of the Treasury.

The Metropolitan Interment Act 1850 represented a significant state investment in public welfare. It involved nationalisation of private business. It recognised equality between Anglicans and Nonconformists. Yet, item by item, it proved unworkable. Brompton was the only cemetery willing to be nationalised. No one was willing to lend money for the larger cemeteries, for the Public Health Act had given the Board only five years of life. The Board was outside parliamentary control. In short, the £100 limit implied that the Treasury had no intention of letting the 1850 Act work. Lord Shaftesbury, a member of the Board, listed the interests whose combination had wrought its downfall. It included the Treasury 'for the subalterns there hated Chadwick' (Hammond, 1939: 158). In 1854, the powers of the General Board of Health were given to the Local Government Board. Chadwick never held another major administrative post (Finer, 1952).

In 1854, the last and the largest of the private cemetery companies and owned by the London Necropolis Company opened at Brookwood, Woking (Clarke, 2004). Its founders, Sir Richard Broun and Richard Sprye bought 2000 acres of Woking common land from Lord Onslow. The early years of the company were dogged by profligacy and directors' in-fighting, in which Broun and Sprye lost control of their project. Only in 1854 was the London Necropolis Company reorganised and the cemetery opened. Special trains ran between Waterloo and Brookwood until after 1945 (Clarke, 1995). Clarke reckoned that, had the London Necropolis Company managed its business affairs better and faster, it would have attracted funerals from a far larger number of central London parishes who lost their churchyards (1850, 1852) and would have been able, by the 1852 Act, to elect a burial board to treat with companies like the London Necropolis Company (Clarke, 2004: 14). In the event, whilst a number of central London parishes regularly used Woking, only 32% of expected annual business was actually achieved between 1854 and 1874, and the London Necropolis Company was continually beset by financial problems.

The 1850 Act was replaced by one which extended across the nation, the Metropolitan Interments Amendment Act 1852. Under the new terms, old churchyards could be closed by the Privy Council on grounds of public health and the advice of the Secretary of State. The Secretary had to give permission for the creation of any new cemeteries. He was empowered to appoint Burial Boards for the vestry of any metropolitan parish. These Burial Boards could fund new cemeteries from the Poor Rate, and had the responsibility of managing them. If a consecrated portion were provided, there had to be an unconsecrated portion as well. The Metropolitan Commissioner of Sewers retained authority for burials in London. The Act was extended to Scotland in 1855 and in 1856 to Ireland, where provisions, of course, included those for Catholics. In 1857, an Amendment Act consolidated the changes. Town Councils, local Boards of Health and local Improvement Commissioners could all be constituted as Burial Boards. Inspectors could be appointed, and the Privy Council was empowered to ensure the maintenance of public health in all cemeteries, public or private.

The series of burial Acts from 1852 to 1857 provided a response to the burial crises of the 1830s and 1840s that has, given the salience of cremation to reduce drastically the space required for burials, survived until this day. For Brooks, the Acts worked because they were the product of compromise and existing practice (Brooks, 1989: 49). For Rugg, the success of the public cemeteries rested upon the model copied from private companies, local initiative. She concluded that 'in organisational terms all power under the new legislation was vested in the parish, and so the provision of cemeteries still remained a community response to a community problem' (Rugg, 1997: 117). After the 1850s, virtually no more private cemeteries were set up. The Acts created a nationwide system of public cemeteries that were entirely decentralised. Once the Burial Acts applied outside London, vestries throughout the country established Burial Boards. That this happened with remarkable speed is testimony to the widely felt dissatisfaction with the churchyard system, whose disadvantages had been worked up into a reform campaign by Dr George Walker. The successor to the churchyard was the public cemetery, a shift goaded by a public health movement stimulated by the cholera epidemic, and which found its best working model in the private cemetery movement. After the establishment of the London County Council in 1888, the London Government Act 1899 created twenty-eight metropolitan borough councils who took over burial provision responsibilities from Burial Boards.

Thus was the public cemetery system established. It was organised on local units and with administrators remaining accountable to ratepayers. As long as ratepayers and elected members were satisfied that their money was well spent, and as long as resources of burial land were forthcoming, the cemetery system would work well as a successor to the churchyard. As the 2001 Select Committee on Cemeteries reported of the 1850s burial Acts:

[the] government was faced with a burial crisis of such proportions that it began to rush through an unthinking series of legislative enactments that ensured an effective short-term solution to the burial problems of the day, but left Britain with a disastrous short-term legacy. The combined Burial Acts established the principle that burial issues were a matter for local decision, leaving central Government with extremely limited responsibility and powers...The cemetery as a wasting asset had been born. (ETRAC, 2001, p. xi)

Until the 1850s, the Church had exercised responsibility for the bodies of the dead until, according to its creed, the Day of Resurrection. Churchyards had thus functioned as a testimony to the Church's faith that this life was to be lived as a prelude to the next, based on its belief in Jesus' physical resurrection. With the passing of the burial Acts, God's urban acre vanished first from use and, more slowly, from sight; only in the countryside could its traditional role be practically fulfilled. With the burial Acts, therefore, urbanisation aided secularisation. Yet, as urban populations continued to grow, the failings of the burials legislation were progressively exposed. Local authorities, having inherited from the Church responsibility for the dead, realised that they needed to seek more economical ways of discharging this responsibility. It is against this background that interest in cremation grew and local government made efforts to realise legislative recognition. The duties of the custody of dead bodies shifted from the Church to local government. The development of cemeteries set in motion this process of transference from the sacred to the secular which would be further accelerated by cremation for which, unlike burial, the Churches possessed few good precedents. It is curious that that Church seemed oblivious to the implications of this change.

3
Cremation Legalised, 1852–1884

From the Dark Ages until the nineteenth century, human cremation in the West had been by funeral pyre in the open air, associated with the dead gods of the Norsemen and with the burning of heretics and witches. If cremation were to fire the modern Western imagination, then it needed a new mode of burning, free from these associations. Archaeological evidence was, if not then plentiful, sufficient to remind the British of its earlier history: the discovery of cremation urns at Old Walsingham, Norfolk, had prompted the Catholic apologist Sir Thomas Browne to write *Hydriotaphia, or Urn Burial* in 1658 (Browne, 1658). The development of cremation awaited adequate technological facilities.

The isolated precedents of modern cremation were not encouraging. In England, Mrs Honoretta Pratt had requested the burning of her dead body in the Bayswater Road burial ground of London's St George's Church, Hanover Square, in 1769 but she created no immediate precedents (White, 2001a). In 1822, the poet Percy Bysshe Shelley and his friend Edward Williams were drowned off the Italian coast. Italian sanitation laws required their bodies to be burned. Lord Byron, Leigh Hunt and other witnesses were revolted by the sight. In 1844, the City of London considered cremating the bodies of prisoners who died at Bridewell Hospital (Eassie, 1878: 230) but it was judged that the British were not yet ready for this reform. In the early nineteenth century there were very occasional writings, like Jamieson's 1818 paper 'On the origin of Cremation or the Burning of the Dead' and Wylie's 1858 'The Burning and Burial of the Dead'. *The Lancet*, founded in 1851, was for thirty years supportive of the cremation concept. In 1857 it favourably reviewed an anonymous pamphlet entitled 'Burning the Dead, or Non-Sepulture, Religiously, Socially and Generally Considered', commenting that if cremation could be shown to be practical it appeared 'as decent, speedy and effectual a method as could well be conceived' (*The Lancet*, 22 August 1857: 199–200). In 1864, Dr Edmund Parkes recommended cremation for those dying on the battlefield. Parkes, a medical doctor with an interest in hygiene, had met the engineer William Eassie at the Crimean War. Whilst at Smyrna, Eassie had also discussed cremation with the surgeon Thomas Spencer Wells. The sparse literature suggests that no one at the time expected their proposals to be put into practice. How and why was the Cremation Society of England formed?

War has ever been the spur to technology. Bessemer's process for developing steel to withstand higher temperatures was hastened by his work on cannon in the Crimean War. From 1856 he revolutionised steel-making. The German firm of Siemens developed furnaces capable of human incineration in the 1870s. An Italian scientist, Brunetti, demonstrated his work on cremator technology at an international exhibition in Vienna in 1873. Among the English visitors was Sir Henry Thompson.

Thompson was the son of a Baptist shopkeeper in Suffolk. He had risen, as in a characteristic Victorian success story, to be Surgeon to Queen Victoria, by way of a successful bowel operation on King Leopold of the Belgians in 1862 (Cope, 1951). Thompson returned from Vienna an ardent pioneer of cremation. A member successively of the Reform Club and of the Athenaeum, Thompson was neither short of cultured friends nor short of outlets for his ideas. Both Thompson and Eassie published cremation articles in January 1874. In an essay entitled 'The Treatment of the Body after Death', Thompson made a powerful argument for cremation. Thompson wrote:

After Death! The last faint breath had been noted, and another watched for so long, but in vain... and the tranquil sleep of Death reigns where just now were life and movement. Here then begins the eternal rest... Rest! No, not for an instant. Never was there greater activity than at this moment exists in that still corpse. Already a thousand changes have commenced. Forces innumerable have attacked the dead. The rapidity of the vulture, with its keen scent for animal decay, is nothing to that of Nature's ceaseless agents now at full work... (Thompson, 1874: 318–19)

He asked, 'how, given a dead body, to resolve it into carbonic acid, water and ammonia, and the mineral elements, rapidly, safely and not unpleasantly. The answer may be practically supplied in a properly constructed furnace' (Thompson, 1874: 325). Thompson's journey to Vienna was not a conversion on the Damascus Road: his interest in cremation had been evolving for some years. It was the sight of Brunetti's cremating apparatus at Vienna in 1873 that showed him that modern cremation was practically possible and propelled him to action (Cope, 1951: 120). Thompson needed to test the practicality for himself. He arranged for experiments on animals early in 1874 to test, in particular, body weights and cremation times. Bodies of animals weighing 47, 140 and 227 lbs were cremated in a Siemens furnace in 25, 55 and 55 minutes respectively (see Parsons, 2005e: 26).

On 13 January 1874 Thompson invited to his London house at 35 Wimpole Street a number of influential friends (White, 1999) to draw up a declaration:

> We, the undersigned, disapprove the present custom of burying the dead, and we desire to substitute some mode which shall rapidly resolve the body into its component elements, by a process which cannot offend the living, and shall render the remains perfectly innocuous. Until some better method is devised we desire to adopt that usually known as Cremation. (*Cremation Society Council Minutes*, 13 January 1874)

The declaration was proposed by Shirley Brooks and seconded by the Revd H. R. Haweis. The other signatures were those of Frederick Lehmann, Charles F. J. Lord, Ernest Hart, John Cordy Jeafferson, the Revd Charles Voysey and Sir Henry Thompson. The Declaration was also signed later by sympathisers not present at the initial meeting: Rudolf C. Lehmann, John Everett Millais, John Tenniel, Anthony Trollope, Thomas Spencer Wells, E. B. Gayer, Alex Strachan and Rose Mary Crawshay (White, 1999). The January meeting also agreed to request Mr Crowdy, a solicitor, to prepare a case for Counsel as to the laws affecting cremation. The Declaration effectively launched The Cremation Society. The Society became the pressure group whose persistence was for nearly eighty years the largest motivating force behind the replacement of burial by cremation in Britain.

At the next meeting on 19 March 1874, there was no news from Crowdy but it was agreed to advertise in the newspapers for subscriptions to establish a crematorium (*Cremation Society Council Minutes*, 19 March 1874). At the third meeting, the Cremation Society of England was formally constituted and a provisional Council elected (*Cremation Society Council Minutes*, 29 April 1874; White, 1999). Eassie was appointed Honorary Secretary and Frederick Lehmann Honorary Treasurer. Anxious to push ahead with practical action, the fourth meeting itemised the other interest groups from whom practical co-operation might be elicited: 'Cemetery Companies, parochial and municipal authorities or other public bodies' (*Cremation Society Council Minutes*, 14 May 1874). Clearly, Thompson's Council realised that their allies would not, at this stage, include undertakers. By contrast, they needed to enlist the support of the groups owning burial grounds for whom cremation could offer practical and economic advantages. At this stage, it is likely that these first active cremationists, perhaps inspired by the metaphor of urn-burial, assumed that after cremation ashes would be *buried*. The Society (*Cremation Society Council Minutes*, 29 July 1874) also contemplated forming its own company.

In the *Contemporary Review* Thompson had refrained from attacking religious belief, for it was part of his policy to dissociate the physical mode of disposal from its religious interpretations. He wrote about the corpse from the sanitary and medical perspective (Thompson, 1874). His concern both for hygiene and for financial saving was sincere. Nevertheless he miscalculated public attitudes to the corpse and its funeral. The Protestant culture of England knew that funeral expenditure could not benefit the dead, but families in most social classes invested in funerals to declare their identity, their affection and their status (Morley, 1971; Litten, 1991). Nevertheless, Thompson drew immediate opposition from the Church and the funeral trades. Many people were intrigued by his campaign, but few believed he would ever succeed. Thompson's position in society, however, was such that the issue, having been raised, could not and did not go away. His journalist friends kept cremation before the public eye. This parody is typical:

> To burn, or not to burn, that is the question.
> Whether 'tis nobler in the tomb to suffer
> The vile encroachments of prolonged corruption,
> Or to take fire against the soulless body,
> And, by destruction, save it? To burn – cremate –
> Awhile: and in incineration say we end
> The death-rot, and the thousand festering things
> That flesh is heir to . . .
>
> (*St Stephen's Review*, 16 May 1885)

It is, of course, the task of the written word to feed the imagination. In 1884, Judge James Fitzjames Stephen commented that the processes of burial and burning were alike 'so horrible that every healthy imagination would turn away from its details' (Queen's Bench Division, 1884: 255). The fear of premature burial, a subject regularly featured in *The Lancet*, was a late-Victorian fascination (Wilkins, 1990; Bourke, 2005). The body had always been food for worms, but now that thought became poison for the imagination. Leaney suggested that what lay at the bottom of cremationist thought and behind the sanitary and economic motives for its advocacy was 'an intense loathing for the physical remains of the beloved' (Leaney, 1989: 129), but the first cremationists' concerns to obtain 'the purest white ash, contained in urns' suggest they were seeking to beautify human remains. Elias described how the nineteenth-century bourgeoisie, in everything from table manners to speech, progressively 'refined' life by imposing controls upon the expression of the 'grosser' biological aspects of human activity, and upon the linguistic expression of such acts (Elias, 1978; Stone, 1979).

It seems the affront to decency was at the forefront of opposition to the idea of cremation, as instanced by the address of Bishop Fraser of Manchester (1818–1885). Paradoxically, whilst he was personally revolted by the thought of the cremation of his own family members, he realised the social benefits of cremation. Personal sentiment vied with beneficial and rational calculation. He said in October 1879 that he had

> just consecrated a portion of a new cemetery [Stockport, October 1879]... but two thoughts occurred to me as I was consecrating the portion of it assigned to those who desire to be buried according to the rites of the Church of England. In the first place, this is a long distance for the poor to bring their dead; in the second place, here is another hundred acres of land withdrawn from the food-producing areas of the country forever. (Fraser, 1891: 117).

The most widely read attack upon cremation was delivered by Christopher Wordsworth, the Bishop of Lincoln, in a sermon in Westminster Abbey on 5 July 1874 (Wordsworth, 1874) and was printed as a pamphlet. For Bishop Wordsworth, the destiny of Christians after death was inextricably dependent upon the death, burial, resurrection and ascension of Jesus. Jesus, as God and man, had hallowed not only the human body but the human tomb (Wordsworth, 1874: 4). There was a relationship between the Passion story; the Church's doctrines about the Sacraments; the resurrection of the flesh and the continuance of personal identity beyond death; and its traditional pastoral practices at death-beds and funerals. Belief in these doctrines produced a tender regard for the dead and dying, and funeral rituals exercised a holy influence upon the living. Bishop Wordsworth held that cremation had been the general rule in the Roman Empire prior to the introduction of Christianity. Burial of the dead had become obsolete when Christianity was first preached but Christianity had extinguished the funeral pyres which once blazed in all parts of the Roman Empire (ibid.: 7–8). The substitution of modern cremation for burial would be a lapse from Christianity to Heathenism.

Aware of recent burial reform, the Bishop allowed that the burial of the dead ought never to be a cause of injury to the living and that burial in the urban context had been justly prohibited by law. He expressed concern about the cost of funerals, estimated at about £1,000,000 pounds a year in London, but was convinced that the saving of money was not as profitable as the saving of souls. 'Which of the two processes – Burial of the dead, or Burning – is more conducive to the maintenance and promotion of Christian faith?' (ibid.: 10). In Wordsworth's judgement, 'The sound Christian believer' did not feel that his faith was rocked by contemplation of the death of martyrs by fire at the stake. By contrast, for the mass of other Christians, the introduction of cremation, by placing human bodies in public furnaces for their extinction 'the popular belief in the Resurrection of the body would be weakened.' He continued:

And since public morality, and public happiness, depends on the maintenance of this doctrine of the Resurrection, great injury would thus be inflicted upon the living ... The condition of a nation is not only influenced by regard for the burial of the dead, but it may be safely tested by it. If the reverential care of the living for the bodies of their departed friends is impaired, its moral and social, and religious condition will decline also. (ibid.: 12)

The Bishop's protection of the resurrection of the body was attacked by *The Lancet* (11 July 1874: 57) which understood St Paul's distinction between the physical body and the resurrected body to mean that the mode of death and decomposition, whether by obliteration in an explosion or by consumption by sea creatures, could not affect Christian prospects of the resurrection of the body. Bishop Fraser, in words reminiscent of Lord Shaftesbury's, foresaw no problems for Almighty God at the general resurrection morning, whether confronted by human dust or human ashes. Cremation would not limit the Almighty's power to resurrect dead bodies any more than burial:

Could they suppose that it would be more impossible for God to raise up a body at the resurrection, if need be, out of elementary particles which had been liberated by the burning, than it would be to raise-up [*sic*] from dust, and from the bodies which had passed into the structure of worms?' (cited in Robinson 1889: 86 cited in Parsons, 2005e: 40)

The Bishop of Lincoln was shrewd enough to realise that a mode of disposal which claimed to have no theological but only sanitary pretensions was actually a proposal to secularise death and thus reduce the importance of human mortality as a focus of God's sanctions on human behaviour:

> We could not conceive anything more barbarous and unnatural than cremation, and one of the very first fruits of its adoption would be to undermine the faith of mankind in the doctrine of the resurrection of the body, and so bring about a most disastrous social revolution, the end of which it is not easy to foretell. (cited in *The Times*, 6 July 1874)

The *Times* quotation is probably more verbatim than the published text. And what had cremation to do with morality? In the popular mind the burial of the body was a prologue to – and burial in God's Acre was a guarantee of – resurrection of the body whose first call was to await the Judgement. *That* was the Church-threatening connection, not so much between disposal and decency as that between disposal (of the corpse) and discipline (of the Church). If the Church were ever to reconcile itself to cremation, it would first have to effect some other disconnections. It could, for example, shift the scenery for the judgement process from the next world to this, or abandon the process altogether. It could extend the possibilities for redemption beyond the confines of this world or of this life, suggest that Christ had descended into Hell, or that Protestant dead might legitimately be consoled by the prayers of the Church militant. It could discard confidence in traditional belief about the resurrection of the body, or abandon faith in mortality as a sanction for ethics.

In the 1870s, however, it was not the atheist take-over of death that was pressing, it was the Nonconformist Churches' designs upon rural churchyards. Burial disputes were an arena for Victorian Church–Chapel conflict (Manning, 1952; Mackintosh, 1972; Fletcher, 1974; Rugg, 1999). Ever since the 1850s burial Acts, the Nonconformist Churches had sought equality of treatment in the new local authority cemeteries. Their grievances were largely met by the Burial Acts Amendment Act 1857 and the Burial Laws Amendment Act 1880. The latter originated from a law case where two Anglican and Congregationalist clergy had almost come to blows in Akenham churchyard, Suffolk, over the burial of an unbaptised child (Fletcher, 1974). The intensity of the resistance may have acted as a smoke-screen curtaining the issue of cremation. It was against this background that the first crematoria in England were planned.

The Cremation Society was, above all, law-abiding. Its supporters were not only respectable, but cultured and well-to-do. Their campaign for reforms in the disposal of human remains was from the start to be conducted in a respectable, legal and practical manner. Eassie, an engineer as well as Honorary Secretary of the Cremation Society, spoke to a meeting of the British Medical Association in 1874 about his practical proposals (*The Lancet*, 4 July 1874: 21). His ideas were developed in *Cremation of the Dead: Its History and Bearing upon Public Health* (Eassie, 1875). It recommended Siemen's design from the cremation apparatus available.

Hesitant about precipitate action in England, the Society keenly followed developments on mainland Europe. In the summer of 1874, the first formal cremation of a British person caught public attention. The first wife of the politician Sir Charles Dilke died in childbirth aged 26. Her body was embalmed and taken to Dresden for cremation. Among the witnesses were Eassie and the Dilkes' son Ashton who reported that the cremation lasted one and a quarter hours and the ashes weighed three and a quarter pounds (letter in *Cremation Society minute book*, from Ashton W. Dilke, 13 October 1874). The Dilke cremation was a *cause célèbre* both in Germany and in Britain (White, 2002; Parsons, 2005e).

Meanwhile, the Society was awaiting its legal advice. Shirley Brooks had consulted Crowdy, who in turn consulted Dr T. H. Tristram, Chancellor of the Diocese of London, and F. M. White, QC, Recorder of Canterbury. According to a printed report, pasted into the Minutes for 12 March 1879, Lord Selborne also gave a written, but unofficial, favourable opinion. Crowdy's response was cautious but favourable: 'such as to warrant the Council in concluding that the performance of the process was perfectly legal, provided that it involved no consequences which could be construed by any one as a nuisance'. This was pasted into the Minutes at 10 February 1876. White has commented that at the time [1876], the legality of cremation in the UK was uncertain. There was no statutory rule specifically prohibiting it, nor any statutory rule requiring dead bodies to be buried. 'Cremation's legality depended on the vague ambit of a motley collection of common law misdemeanours and on the debatable weight to be attached to judicial remarks about a person's "right to Christian burial" and other people's correlative duty to arrange one' (White, 2002: 173).

Alongside these legal enquiries, the Cremation Society was seeking a suitable site and selecting a cremator. By 15 February 1875 it had secured a piece of ground 'for accomplishment of cremation by the best method, and for the erection of a building for religious services' to be performed prior to the incinerating process (*Cremation Society Council Minutes*, 11 February 1875). The cost was estimated at £3500, of which £830 was pledged at the Council meeting. It was agreed to place advertisements seeking further subscriptions.

The Society had been in contact with the directors of the Great Northern Cemetery at New Southgate, founded in 1861 (Meller, 1994: 135). The cemetery had the additional advantage of being close to a disused railway line from King's Cross Station. A crematorium at New Southgate would enable a direct parallel with the arrangements for cemeteries: a chapel for religious services immediately prior to the cremation, followed by either the removal of ashes by the family or the deceased's executor or burial in consecrated ground, two-thirds of the site having been consecrated by the Bishop of Rochester in 1861. This plan indicates the Society's cautious approach to Christian burial traditions. Thompson was so enthusiastic that at the Council meeting on 30 June 1875 he declared that if the Society would buy one acre of land at the Great Northern Cemetery he would himself pay for both a Siemens furnace and a reception room for bodies. He had been in contact with a leading London undertaker, whom Parsons is convinced was William Garstin (Parsons, 2005d) and they agreed upon a remuneration system whereby the undertaker would charge the bereaved family a moderate fee and both the Great Northern Company and Sir Henry (for the next five years) would receive £1 per body cremated. The Council agreed on the price of £500 for the acre and to accept Thompson's offer of the furnace. Unfortunately, an obstacle arose.

'As the land had been consecrated, it appeared desirable to apply to the Bishop of the Diocese, in relation to any jurisdiction he might have in the matter' (*Cremation Society Council Minutes*, 30 June 1875). For reasons unknown, it was not the Council but the cemetery proprietor who wrote to the Bishop, on 16 August, for his agreement to set aside a portion of the Cemetery for cremation. At that time the diocesan boundaries of the Church of England had not yet been redrawn to adjust to the rapid suburbanisation of London (Parsons, personal communication). In 1875 the Rochester Diocese included three North London Archdeaconries, including St Albans within which New Southgate

Cemetery lay. The Bishop's reply stopped the project in its tracks. His short letter (of which the original cannot now be traced) ran: 'Gentlemen, I beg to acknowledge your letter of the 16th inst., asking my consent as Bishop to the setting apart a portion of the Great Northern Cemetery, in my diocese, for the purpose of cremation. I cannot consent – moreover, I have not the power to consent – to the introduction of such a mode of disposing of the bodies of the dead' (copy in *Cremation Society Council Minutes*).

This response was a great disappointment to the Society. There was no Council meeting until the following February. With the response of the Bishop of Lincoln and now that of the Bishop of Rochester, the energies of the Society seemed as if they might dissipate and no further immediate steps to seek a site for a crematorium were planned. As the Minutes stated (*Cremation Society Council Minutes*, 10 February 1876) a report was prepared for circulation to subscribers, offering to return building fund subscriptions:

> It seemed so desirable to inaugurate the system in connection with an existing Cemetery, in order to offer on the same spot the option of either process, that the original idea of making an independent establishment for cremation is deferred for the present.

While the Council insisted that it was undeterred, the time being 'not far distant when cremation would be realised', its meetings then became sporadic.

If the Bishop had agreed, the history of cremation in Britain might have been very different. First, the doctrine of the resurrection of the body might have been more rigorously re-examined and believers come to accept the advice both of St Augustine (1984: 21–2) and, more recently, of Lord Shaftesbury that neither dust nor ashes posed any obstacle to Almighty God on the day of resurrection: 'What, in such a case, would have become of the blessed martyrs?' Secondly, the first crematoria, if welcomed by the Church, would have tempered the earliest secular designs with religious ones (Grainger, 2000b, 2005). Thirdly, the burial of ashes, which the first cremationists actually favoured, would have set a precedent; for their burial in consecrated ground would thus have avoided the alternatives of columbaria, of scattering, or of ashes taken home. If the first purpose-built crematorium had been not only situated on consecrated ground but adjacent to a chapel, the geographical context for liturgies sanctifying this new mode of disposal would have been more of a piece and not a truncation

(Lampard, 1993; Trasler, 1998), with crematoria following a precedent of being located in local cemeteries. As it was, after 1875 the general opposition of the Church, both Anglican and (from 1886) Roman Catholic, assured for the cremation lobby an association with atheism and Free Thought which lasted for well over forty years.

The mood of disappointment was not confined to Britain. As Eassie reported to the 14 December 1876 meeting, the first wave of the movement in favour of cremation seemed to have spent itself. The many societies which had at first sprung up in several countries had apparently flagged in their action, or disappeared altogether, checked by some sentimental reaction. Meanwhile, cremating equipment was being developed not only by Siemens in Dresden but by Polli and Brunetti in Italy, where there was a vigorous anti-clerical campaign and twenty-six cremation societies had been established. Eassie outlined the progress of cremation on the continent in his 1878 lecture (Eassie, 1878). At International Medical Congresses in Florence (1869) and Rome (1871) motions were passed in favour of legalising cremation. Brunetti's wood-burning furnace model was used for three human cremations in 1869 and 1870 and was the one displayed at the 1873 Vienna Exhibition. In 1872 Polli and Clericetti built a gas-fired furnace, but this proved expensive, a revised version being used in 1876 in Milan for the cremation of Chevalier Alberto Keller, a public event witnessed by clergy and local officials. Keller had given 50,000 lira towards a 'crematory temple' in the Cimitero Monumentale; he had died in 1874 but his cremation had to await the practical development of a furnace. In 1877 seven cremations using gas fuel were carried out in a Terruzi-Batti cremator. Meanwhile, Gorini was developing a reverberatory cremator, using wood. Six cremations were carried out in 1877 in the crematory he had built in Lodi Cemetery. At the same time, Frederick Siemens had been working at Dresden on a regenerative furnace. Capable of very high temperatures and using the superfluous heat from escaping gases, this design could use coal, wood, charcoal or peat. The Siemens furnace had been used in Dresden for the Dilke cremation. This was the cremation witnessed by Eassie in his search for a suitable model for the project at New Southgate, although he then decided on the gas design of Frederick's brother William who was based in London (Parsons, 2005e: 57).[1]

Developments at Gotha began in 1876 when the Duchy of Gotha had legalised cremation. This galvanised the German cremation societies. A meeting of German and other national societies was called for in June 1876 at Dresden. Eassie called the congress the second wave of the movement. The subsequent Council meeting on 14 December 1876 agreed that an epitome of the Cremation Society of London's [*sic*] history be printed together with Eassie's enthusiastic account of the Dresden meeting. A public meeting at Dresden drew 700, 'comprising members of the most fashionable and influential circles at Dresden, many of them ladies'. Switzerland's Professor Kinkel surveyed the international scene. There were cremation societies in Germany, Italy, Austria, Switzerland, France, Belgium, England and the United States, that is supporters were in both Catholic and Protestant countries. Religious support would be essential if the hygienic arguments for change were to be widely accepted. If cremation could be shown to be not inconsistent with religious belief, and if people were offered choices in the mode of disposal which were equally legal, cremation would prove far more attractive. Kinkel emphasised that legislation was the proper and most direct course of action; the current preference for burial, however inarticulately expressed, rested upon religious and sentimental grounds (*Cremation Society Council Minutes*, 14 December 1876).

It is clear that the early cremation movement tried to align itself to Christian traditions but was unsuccessful in winning the Churches' support. Thus, in hindsight, it is significant that Kinkel, like other early cremationists, proposed that cremation should be followed by the interment of ashes, in his phrase 'burial by cremation'. Had the interment of ashes been accepted from the outset, there would never have been a need for columbaria. The symbols of cremation would have been far more traditional and akin to burial: earth-bound not air-blown, fixed not portable, localised not dispersed, religiously orthodox not free spirit. When the Churches' reaction to cremation also included the rejection of buried ashes as a mode of disposal, the result was a double rejection by the Church of the opportunity to take cremation into its system. This hardened the association of cremation with a rejection of Christianity which many of the European cremationists already proposed. Holmes, who favoured both earth-to-earth burial and cremation, wrote of cremation:

if the practice is to become at all general it must be advocated by a different set of people. It has, to a certain extent, happened hitherto that those who have been cremated have been more or less associated... with the advanced school – those that consider themselves 'enlightened', Radicals, or Socialists, or persons of little or no professed religious views... I venture to think that cremation will not be taken up very largely until a few such men as the Archbishop of York, the Chief Rabbi, the Rev. Prebendary Ward Peploe, and Father Stanton pronounce in its favour. (Holmes, 1896: 270–1)

Certain church leaders argued for cremation, like Bishop Fraser. Yet his was a lone voice in the 1870s. The majority of Christians knew that Hell and post-mortem judgement were under intelligent attack, and at local level Church and Chapel were locked in battles for status over education and politics, as well as evangelism and the rites of passage. The 1880s proved to be the Churches' high water mark: although there were more Church members in a 1902 survey, their proportion as a percentage of the UK population had begun its decline (Currie *et al.*, 1977). These were not times for ecclesiastical radicalism over funeral ministry.

The Council, with fresh determination, set out to find alternative sites and chose Woking (*Cremation Society Council Minutes*, 30 May 1878). Council members had clearly been busy as individuals, despite no formal meeting for eighteen months. At the May meeting a report was given on an exhibition of models of crematoria at Leamington and London; Gorini's first furnace at Milan had been inspected; and the Council was pledging funds to purchase land at Woking, Sir Henry Thompson again leading the way with £200. Woking was chosen because of the advantages it shared with New Southgate: outside the urban area but within railway reach of London, and with the possibility of additional revenue from burials. There was a financial incentive for the London Necropolis Company and the Society to co-operate. The Society bought one acre from the London Necropolis Company on which to site its cremator. Relations between the two organisations proved difficult, with the London Necropolis lending support to and then finally distancing itself from local objectors (Clarke, 2004; Parsons, 2005e).

The Society simultaneously bid for the site and chose its design of cremator. Eassie went to Milan to witness the cremation of William Crookenden in a Gorini (wood-burning) cremator (White, 2002: 215). For factors which included the need for a gas supply and infrequent cremator use, Eassie recommended the Gorini model. In December Gorini began construction at Woking. Three months later, Society members watched Gorini cremate a horse. The horse weighed 140 lbs, and its ashes 6 lbs. There was neither the slightest odour nor visible escape of smoke, and the ashes were 'perfectly white' (Gorini, 1879: x).

Work on the cremator had aroused the vicar of Woking, the Reverend F. J. Oliphant. On 4 December 1878 he wrote to Richard Cross, the Conservative Home Secretary, protesting that Woking residents viewed the prospect 'with feelings of great abhorrence and are anxious to prevent its accomplishment' (Strutt, 1976: 3). The controversy over the Woking site lasted for three months in the local and national press. Koskinen has interpreted the protests as largely self-interested – Victorian 'nimbyism' – but behind them there was the opposition of the Earl of Onslow, whose family had owned much of the land around Woking since 1752 (Koskinen, 2000). Oliphant's letter to *The Times* of 31 December 1878 claimed that the chosen site for 'the erection of a funeral pyre' was too distant from a railway, in the midst of a growing neighbourhood, and that Woking had sufficient space for burial in the parish church-yards and the London Necropolis Company cemetery. He continued that if cremation were ever to be permitted and that if 'cremation socie-ties are at liberty to purchase land and to erect funeral pyres wherever they please...grave injury would be done to landed proprietors'. On 30 January 1879, a ten-strong party from Woking met with the Home Secretary and presented a signed petition against the crematorium site. Parsons has analysed both the petition and the press accounts of the meeting (Parsons, 2005e: 70–74). Four issues are paramount: the legality of cremation; the siting of crematoria; annoyance to persons or injury to property values; and whether or not the cremation process represents an unacceptable departure from 'the recognised Christian rites and norms'.

Cross wrote to Eassie on 21 February 1879 through Godfrey Lushington, Under-Secretary of State:

> Mr Cross does not propose to enter into the question whether or not the system of cremation is in accordance with the feelings of the Public, or with the respect due by law to dead bodies; it is sufficient for him to point out that it is a system which, in this country, is entirely novel, and that whether or not the law forbids it altogether, the public interest requires that it should not be adopted until many matters of great social import have been duly considered and provided for. (Lushington to Eassie, 21 February 1879, in *Relations*, 1884)

The concern was also forensic: while burial could be followed by exhumation, '...the process of cremation is final; the result of the practice therefore would be, that it would tend, in cases where death has been occasioned by violence or poison, to defeat the ends of justice'. The letter continued that the Home Secretary could not

> acquiesce in the continuance of the undertaking of the Society to carry out the practice of cremation, either at the works now in progress in Woking or elsewhere in this country, until Parliament

has authorised such a practice by either a special or a general Act, and that, if the undertaking is persisted in, it will be his duty either to test its legality in a court of law or to apply to Parliament for an Act to prohibit it until Parliament has had an opportunity of considering the whole subject. (Lushington to Eassie, 21 February 1879, in *Relations*, 1884).

As Parsons points out, a slightly different interpretation of the legality of cremation was in existence (Parsons, 2005e: 76; text at Appendix 2). It was a copy of Counsel's Opinion prepared by John Pearson, QC, and F. A. Bosanquet for the Woking local residents (dated 24 January 1879) and it was probably available to the Vicar's deputation on 30 January 1879. The response was guardedly favourable towards cremation:

We are of opinion that the practice of cremation is not in itself illegal. There are expressions in some reported judgments that serve to imply that burial is the only legal mode of disposing of dead bodies. But such expressions are not directed to the legality or illegality of disposing of dead bodies in any other decent manner, but to the leaving of bodies unburied or treating them indecently. It is a misdemeanour to treat a dead body indecently or in such manner as to cause a physical nuisance. It is impossible to say whether the mode intended to be adopted at Woking will be objectionable on either ground. (Parsons, 2005e: Appendix 2)

However, Counsel advised the residents' group that, in order that they might not by apparent acquiescence lose the right of applying for an injunction later, they should give notice to the owners of the Crematory that 'the practice of cremation intended to be carried on there will be illegal and a nuisance and that they will take legal proceedings to stop it if necessary' (Parsons, 2005e: 76). Counsel advised that actual proceedings should not be commenced at present.

Some days later, after the Vicar's deputation met, Thompson learned that the Home Secretary was considering drafting a bill to make cremation illegal. Thompson wrote to Cross on 17 March 1879 to curtail this possibility. Thompson's deputation met Cross on 20 March. Cross told the deputation not to rely on its own earlier Counsel's opinion, that before the practice of cremation was established by an individual company it would be better for a private individual to bring a Bill to have the matter thrashed out in Parliament. Thompson gave a verbal undertaking, confirmed in a formal letter the same day, that he and his friends intended 'to act in strict conformity with the wish and directions of the Government' in regard to the practice of cremation. On 21 March the Earl of Onslow spoke against cremation in the Lords. The exchanges received considerable press exposure, but *The Lancet* (29 March 1879: 436–7) strengthened its opposition with an emphasis against cremation on forensic grounds and *The Times* (25 March 1879) judged that, whilst it approved of funeral reform, cremation was not the solution. A Cremation Bill, it seemed, would only have a slender chance of passing in either House. The Society published the exchange of letters as *Relations between the Cremation Society of England and Her Majesty's Government* (1884).

Thereafter the cremator stood idle, though the building fund appeal continued. Rebuffed by the Home Office, the Council of the Cremation Society agreed it did 'not consider the present a suitable time to move in the matter, and besides they [the Council] have no finance available' (*Cremation Society Council Minutes*, 6 May 1879). The advantage of the Woking debate was that the pros and cons of cremation had received a wide press both serious and satirical in content. In 1875 the Bishop of Rochester's response had been so short and blunt – and the Society so fledgling – no defence had been attempted to discuss cremation according either to theology or to ecclesiastical law. So far, the Society would not proceed with cremation unless supported by law. As White has written (White, 2002: 171), the Cremation Society of England was always concerned to appear respectable; although it was not clear that cremation was lawful, it was far from certain that it was illegal – indeed, the Society received legal advice that cremation could be conducted lawfully. One consequence of the Society's concern for respectability, however, was that it was unwilling to take the risks involved in testing the law. It wanted legislation expressly permitting cremation or assurances from the Home Office that it would not be prosecuted should it carry out a cremation. Neither was forthcoming.

It was, however, clear that the advance of cremation would require robust legal safeguards; these would involve cremationists for decades in the parallel struggle for better death certification, a double act personified in the work of Dr Charles Cameron, MP (see e.g. Rose, 1986: 82ff.), a Scottish cremationist who succeeded Sir Henry as President of the Cremation Society in 1904. The Society settled down to a long programme of persuasion (the first category of those eligible for honorary membership of the Society was to be 'members of scientific eminence' (*Transactions*, Vol. I, 1880: 7), promoting the value and respectability of cremation for politicians, the law, the funeral and mourning industries, sanitary engineers, officers of health, doctors and clergy. This long-term prospect may have daunted Sir Henry who, at the 6 May 1879 Council, sought to resign but was restrained. He was probably also encouraged the next year when a distinguished funeral reformer was elected as a member of the Cremation Society, Dr George Alfred Walker (*Cremation Society Council minutes*, 10 December 1880).

In its propaganda campaign,[2] two avenues were immediately open to the Cremation Society: professional associations and the parliamentary process, avenues often combined. The Society benefited from its talented leadership. Ernest Hart, a founding signatory to the 1874 Declaration, was the editor of the *British Medical Journal*. He had set an excellent model for campaigning journalism (employing undercover methods) in his 1868 enquiry into abortion and baby-farming (Rose, 1986: 79). William Eassie was a tireless supporter as Secretary of the Society from 1874 until his death in 1888. An engineer, he was particularly interested in cremator design. He regularly deployed the public health arguments, befitting one who, with Hart, had founded the *Sanitary Journal* and was in large part responsible for founding the Sanitary Institute of Great Britain. Thomas Spencer Wells was as indefatigable: he was editor of *The Medical Times and Gazette* and a Surgeon to Her Majesty's Household. He spoke on cremation at the August 1880 meeting of the British Medical Association and gained 120 signatures for a Declaration which extended the Society's January 1874 declaration with the words,

> As this process [cremation] can now be carried out without anything approaching to nuisance, and as it is not illegal, we trust the Government will not oppose the practice when convinced that proper regulations are observed, and that ampler guarantees of death having occurred from natural causes are obtained than are now required for burial.
> (*British Medical Journal*, 21 August 1880, p. 317; Parsons, 2005e: 89)

Dr Charles Cameron had first qualified as a doctor, then turned to journalism, becoming, aged 23, editor of the *North British Daily Mail* in 1864. He was elected Liberal MP for Glasgow in 1874. His support for cremation was based on public health arguments.

In 1880 a Liberal Government had been elected, and a first election pledge had been to enable a partial funeral reform, the Burial Laws Amendment Act 1880 (Fletcher, 1974). This allowed Nonconformist ministers to conduct funerals in Anglican churchyards, without an obligation to use Anglican rites, but also permitted burials without any religious service. On 24 December 1880 the Society wrote to the Liberal Home Secretary, Vernon Harcourt, seeking his permission for the Society to alter its undertaking to his predecessor. The Society had been encouraged by the British Medical Association's 'Memorial to the Home Secretary in favour of cremation' (see *British Medical Journal*, ii, 794, 13 November 1880; 879, 20 November 1880). Would the Government give an assurance not to oppose the use of the Woking crematorium provided no nuisance was caused and that medical guarantees as to the cause of death were more stringent than those required for burial? The Society told Harcourt that it regarded itself as absolved from its promise to Cross and invited Harcourt disingenuously not to regard himself as bound to fulfil Cross' threat to obtain a prohibitory Act (White, 2002: 177). The letter received only a bare acknowledgment.

In the event, the progress of cremation was both threatened and ultimately promoted by three unconnected cremations which could each have thrown almost immovable obstacles in the Society's path.

The implications of the case of Henry Crookenden and his double disposal – burial and cremation – were analysed by Stephen White (2002). Crookenden had died in December 1875 and had been buried in Brompton Cemetery, London, with Roman Catholic rites. Eight months before, he had requested cremation in a codicil to his will, sent to Eliza Williams, his executor. In March 1878, Eliza Williams had the body exhumed from Brompton and shipped to the crematorium at Milan. The Home Office had not given permission for exhumation, and Crookenden's other relatives were cross that they had not been consulted. Eassie had been active in arranging for the body's shipment. Eliza Williams sought to recover the funeral expenses from her executors, who resisted. In the subsequent court case, Mr Justice Kay dismissed Eliza Williams' claim (1881). It is clear from the accounts of the case that Kay believed cremation to be illegal and it was fortunate, as White notes, that his judgment did not disclose the part the Cremation Society had played in Henry Crookenden's cremation (White, 2002: 176–9).

Another celebrated case was that of Captain Thomas Hanham, of Manston House, Sturminster Newton Dorset. In January 1881 he asked the Cremation Society's Council, whether, if he directed his body to be cremated at Woking, his executors would be liable to prosecution? Hanham's mother and wife had each requested cremation. Hanham had kept their bodies in a purpose-built mausoleum at Manston; by 1881 his mother had been dead for four years and his wife for five. The Council meeting on 29 July 1881 decided it had no objection to Woking being used for the

cremations of Captain Hanham's wife and mother but on three conditions: that Hanham pay all the expenses, that Eassie be authorised to
carry out the cremations, and 'provided it be done without causing a
nuisance' (*Cremation Society Council Minutes*, 29 July 1881). The next
Council meeting on 20 December 1881 spoke of the arrangements being
prosecuted with 'all convenient speed', adding 'Dissentient Sir Henry
Thompson'.

This heralded a crisis. Sir Henry Thompson had been absent at the
July meeting. Later on the day of 20 December, Sir Henry wrote a letter
of resignation from the Council (copy in *Cremation Society Council
Minutes* for 20 January 1882). '[H]olding as I do a strong conviction that
it is neither right nor politic on the part of the Society to take such
action until it has been legalised in this country,' Sir Henry submitted
his resignation. This crisis clearly made for a testing Christmas season.
The Revd Hugh Haweis threatened his own resignation, dated 'Xmas,
1881', and, on Boxing Day, Rose Mary Crawshay also resigned. Higford
Burr, who did not resign, was also concerned about the legality issue and
wrote on 5 January 1882 with a straightforward question: '[S]upposing I
were to die now directing my executors to have my body burnt in our
crematory at Woking, would my executors be liable to prosecution?'

An Extraordinary General Meeting was held on 20 January 1882, with
Wells in the Chair. The Society had clearly reached and peered over a
precipice which would have plunged them into lawlessness. Reluctant
to do this, they pulled back. Discussion produced four resolutions. First,
to stay within the law, they withdrew the offer to Hanham to use the
Woking crematory. Secondly, they asked those who had resigned to
return. Thirdly, they sought to move forward by agreeing to press the
Home Secretary with Burr's question about legality. Fourthly, they
responded to public concerns about murder evidence by a (unanimous)
resolution on retaining forensic evidence: 'That no body be burnt in the
Society's Crematorium, except under approved regulations, securing the
preservation of such parts of the body for preventing the destruction of
the evidences of poison – whenever necessary, and that medico-legal
experts be consulted upon this subject.' On 22 January, Sir Henry wrote,
'I will cooperate with my old colleagues if the other resigning members
will do the same.' They did. This series of actions steadied the ship.

Eassie did indeed write to the Home Secretary on 28 January 1882 not
only with Burr's question but about the two Hanham cremations: 'the
Society was extremely unwilling to proceed with any cremation without
the knowledge of the Home Secretary, and under conditions which will
ensure the legality of the proceedings'; and 'could you let us submit to

you for approval regulations in the practice of cremation, intended to prevent the destruction of evidence by poisoning?' Harcourt would not rise to the bait. His office replied on 14 February 1882: 'Sir William Harcourt can give no opinion in matters which belong to the jurisdictions and decisions of Courts of Law...In Sir William Harcourt's opinion the practice of cremation ought not to be sanctioned except under the authority and regulation of an Act of Parliament' (*Relations*, 1884: 57–8). The Cremation Society set about tackling the forensic issue. At the 22 November 1882 meeting, with Sir Henry in the chair, a sub-committee was formed to draft regulations 'so that all possible precautions might be taken against the Cremation of persons who have died otherwise than from natural causes'. Medical men would be needed to convince judges, and Drs Thompson, Wells and Hart were appointed to the sub-committee. Meanwhile, the Council sought an additional route, through Parliament. In August 1883 (*Times*, 27 August 1883) Cameron gave notice that he would seek the opportunity to introduce a Bill to Parliament to legalise cremation (notice of the Bill being pasted with the Society's *Minutes*, 12 December 1883).

Hanham meanwhile had proceeded with his family's wishes. He had built his own crematorium at his home at Manston. On 8 and 9 October 1882 he performed the cremations, with the help of William Robinson, the horticulturist and a Society Council member. There was much talk in the press, but no comment from the Home Office. The Home Office bluff, if bluff it was, had been called (for fuller description of the Hanham cremation, see White, 2002; Parsons, 2005e). In December 1883 Hanham himself died. The local MP presided over a Masonic funeral ceremony followed by cremation. Hanham's cremation drew the attention of the press but no reaction from local people. White notes, 'There appear to have been no moves to prosecute anyone involved in any of these cremations' (White, 2002: 179). The Home Office refused to comment and the Church of England seems, surprisingly, to have been muted. This is possibly because of yet another controversy arising from Nonconformist claims upon Anglican privilege, this time at Oxford University (Johnson, 1987: 210–15). The Church of England was also concentrating on the Disused Burial Grounds Act 1884 which encouraged closed churchyards to be reopened as public gardens (Conway, 1992).

The next month, January 1884, a most unlooked-for and initially a most inauspicious ally of the cremation movement appeared in South Wales. Dr William Price was 83 years old. He had qualified as a doctor in London and established a practice at Nantgarw, six miles north of Cardiff. He was a radical of radicals: one of the leaders of the unsuccessful

Chartist attack upon Newport in 1839 (ap Nicholas, 1940). He opposed orthodox forms of religion, proclaimed himself a druid and wore a fox-skin head-dress. He hoped that his son, by his common-law wife Gwenllian Llewellyn, would restore a new line of Welsh druids. He named the boy Jesu Grist. The boy died, just five months old, on Thursday, 10 January 1884. Price refused to submit a medical certificate of the cause of death. The Coroner gave Price notice on 12 January that unless he sent the certificate an inquest would be held on the following Monday, 14 January. Price deliberately courted sensation by choosing Sunday evening 13 January for what he had planned to do. On the Caerlan fields, on the top of Llantrisant Hill, he placed the body of the child in a cask containing half a barrel of paraffin oil. This he set alight. People coming out of the churches (there were Anglican and Baptist congregations at Llantrisant) hurried to the scene of the flames and smoke. The police were called. The partly burned body was pulled from the barrel. The crowd, in vengeful mood, turned on Price. He was arrested and detained at the police station.

One context of the Price trial was the contemporary national outcry against infanticide (Rose, 1986), an outcry in which a number of the leading cremationists were involved. Price's was not the only case that winter. Dead baby George Stephenson had been burned by his mother and a neighbour on 10 January in Scarborough. The religious conscience of South Wales rushed Price to court over the burning of his dead baby, but the legal ground of his first being brought to court was his failure to obey the Coroner and produce a certificate of cause of death. An inquest was held and the jury decided that the death was due not to foul play but to natural causes. The police asked the coroner for permission to bury the boy, but Price objected. The Stipendiary Magistrate was reluctantly compelled to pass the body back to him, having extracted a verbal undertaking that he would not burn his child. Price took back the body of his son, which he would eventually cremate on 21 March.

Meanwhile, Price had been bailed in the sum of £200 at Pontypridd. On 12 February he was tried before Sir James Fitzjames Stephen at the Cardiff Assizes. Stephen White has long ago made the analysis of the Price trial his own, and this account is dependent upon his (White, 2002: 179–85). Stephen was a brother of Leslie Stephen (the clergyman turned agnostic), a founder of the Bloomsbury Group and a member of the Victorian 'intellectual aristocracy', whose biographer commented that among the things that set this intellectual aristocracy apart from the governing class was 'their interest in obtaining reforms which many in the ruling class resisted' (Annan, 1984: 7). Stephen, the legal star of a family that sought the removal of religious tests and the abolition of the celibate qualification for Oxbridge fellowships, was a prolific contributor to journals on politics, philosophy, history and criminal law. He was defence lawyer for the authors of *Essays and Reviews* (challenged as heresy in 1860), author of much of Charles Voysey's defence at his heresy trial, the drafter of bills for the National Secular Society in their campaign against the blasphemy laws, and, White notes, he clearly liked Price.

Price was tried first on the charge of cremating his son. Stephen rejected prosecuting counsel's submission that this was an offence even if it did not amount to a public nuisance, but on whether it was a public nuisance the jury was unable to agree and was discharged. A different jury was assembled for the second charge that Price was guilty of attempting to dispose of the body with intent to prevent the holding of an inquest on it. After a false start, the jury returned a verdict of not guilty. The next day, 13 February, a third jury was assembled to retry the first charge. The prosecutor announced that he would offer no evidence on the charge and Price was dismissed.

Stephen's technique was to speak first to the Grand Jury, on 12 February. White has adduced three reasons for this procedure: to discourage lengthy – and confusing – submissions before the jury, to pull rank over and thus disarm counsel and, in what Stephen reckoned would be a very important test case, to ensure a written record which would not have been made were Price to have been acquitted by a petty jury (White, 2002: 183–4). White is convinced that Stephen probably arrived in Cardiff with his charge to the jury ready prepared, and that Stephen discussed his mind with his fellow Assize judge, Lord Justice Fry, who agreed both with his conclusion and his reasons. In White's words:

> In his charge to the Grand Jury, Stephen examined both the legal precedents and canonical authorities. He realised that, to substantiate its contention that the only lawful method of dealing with a dead body was burial, the prosecution would rely on the repeated judicial dicta about everyone's common law right to Christian burial. He demonstrated that these had never been uttered in a case where the crucial issue was how a dead body was to be dealt with. Rather they had been delivered when the issues had been, for example, who must deal with it. The use of the term 'burial' in these contexts he explained away as natural when the only conventional method of dealing with a dead body was inhumation. (While, 2002: 184)

With an eye solely on the official law report of Williams versus Williams [Eliza Williams' claim for funeral expenses in the Crookenden cremation], Stephen was able to say that Judge Kay had 'expressed no opinion on the question on which it now becomes my duty to direct you'. Stephen said

> the canonists...were interested only in the question of who was entitled to Christian burial and what Christian burial consisted of, and they were not in the least concerned with what was to be done with the bodies of those who were not entitled to Christian burial. He was therefore able to direct the jury that Price's cremation was not an offence unless it amounted to a public nuisance. (ibid.: 184)

Stephen concluded:

> I am of opinion that a person who burns instead of buries a dead body does not commit a criminal act unless he does it in such a manner as to amount to a public nuisance at common law.... As for the public interest in the matter, burning, on the one hand, effectually prevents the bodies of the dead from poisoning the living. On the other hand, it might no doubt destroy the evidence of crime. These, however, are matters for the legislature and not for me. (Queen's Bench Division, 1884: 254–6)

He dismissed religious scruples:

> There are, no doubt, religious convictions and feelings connected with the subject which everyone would want to treat with respect and tenderness...I do not think, however, that it can be said that every practice which startles and jars upon the religious sentiments of the majority of the population is for that reason a misdemeanour at common law. (ibid.: 255)

This was extraordinarily good news for the Cremation Society and its supporters. Cremation was now, if not legal, not illegal provided no sensible nuisance was caused to the public.

Six weeks later, on 21 March, Price made a second attempt to burn the body of his son, this time using half a ton of coal; the burning was successful (ap Nicholas, 1940). The funeral by fire, by night, in the open air, and – as at the first attempt – on a Sunday, was designed to provoke the prevailing Christian and cultural orthodoxy of South Wales.

Nine years later, in 1893, Price was himself cremated, to his own instructions, within a closed iron coffin burning outdoors for eight hours. Twenty thousand people watched. Two Anglican clergy adapted the Anglican service appointed for 'The Burial of the Dead at Sea', using the Welsh language (ap Nicholas, 1940). The order of service had been approved by the diocesan Bishop. This was indicative of the problems Anglican clergy were now beginning to face over cremation. By law they were required to use only authorised forms of service of which none yet existed for cremation, a mode of disposal that the vast majority of them disliked. The Anglican authorities would soon be faced with the mismatch between the words of the traditional burial service and the liturgical actions required by legal cremation. Whether the Welsh clergy were within the ecclesiastical law to adapt the service is an open question.

Today Price has the status of a Welsh folk hero, and those who tell his story have hijacked for him something of the credit for the introduction of cremation. In fact, he was only the *deus ex machina*. The existing law on burials was unclear about the legality of cremation. Hanham had already proved that the Home Office had fewer teeth for biting than its bark had threatened. Without the Price case, whilst the legalisation of cremation would probably have come at some time in the future, the promotion which the Cremation Society would increasingly have given it would have made cremation more popular much earlier. The legalisation of cremation had been accelerated, with a success that pitchforked both proponents and defenders into a new situation. The Price verdict obviated the need for the Cremation Society's legal campaign and made irrelevant the defence of the Christian churches. The Cremation Society could be much bolder in promoting crematoria. As the next chapter will show, local authorities were now able legally to turn to cremation to solve the urban burial crisis which they had inherited from the Churches thirty years before.

4

The Early Years of Cremation, 1884–1914

Regina v. Price was a great encouragement to the Cremation Society. It was a verdict for which they had not worked and an outcome they had not expected. It solved at a stroke the problems of the legality of cremation to which the Home Office had set so many obstructions. Yet the Price verdict had provided cremationists with a legal victory before they had had a serious chance to persuade the Churches. The ten years since 1874 had been quite insufficient to connect cremation meaningfully to Christian tradition and rituals. So the advocates of cremation had to set about inventing a morality and precepts for this new kind of disposal; instead of offering cremation as a preparation for physical regeneration after death according to the Christian resurrection tradition, cremationists offered a more secular cleanliness and health for the sake of survivors and the living.

To anticipate a slightly later development, uniqueness of the Britishness of cremation was emphasised in 1886 when the Roman Catholic Church placed a ban upon cremation. The Catholic Church forbade Catholics to join societies promoting cremation, or to leave funeral instructions involving cremation. It deprived such Catholics of burial with Christian rites and forbade them the last sacraments. The ban lasted until 1964. The background was as much political as religious. Pope Pius IX (1847–1878) had reorganised and promoted the Papacy as an institution in the modern world, but his stance was resolutely conservative in doctrine and morals. The opposition to cremation was a by-product of the Catholic Church's response to threats from Italian nationalism, as well as from modernist movements within the Church and rising secularisation in the European mind (Chadwick, 1975; Duffy, 2001a). The Papal States which girdled the very centre of the Italian peninsula were a major obstacle to Garibaldi's plans for the unification of Italy. Freemasonry had also attacked the Church's domination of public institutions. The greater the defeats suffered, the more intransigent the Pope became. In 1884, Pope Leo XIII (1878–1903) forbade Catholics to be Freemasons. In 1886 and 1892, he acted against cremation and cremation societies (Vaughan, 1891). As Chapter 1 indicated, the Catholic ban on cremation provided the critical context for the eventual patterns by which cremation was at first resisted and then established in certain Western European societies. In the British context, it meant that, generally, denominational opposition was neutralised because both Anglicans and Nonconformists had to live with the fact that cremation was legal after 1884. Tensions about cremation versus burial were apparent *within* and not *between* Protestant denominations.

Meanwhile, in 1884, British cremationists set about pressing home the advantages they had won in the Price case. Paradoxically, the Cremation Society was diffident about its good fortune in the Price case. The embarrassment was displayed by Dr Cameron twenty years later when he referred to 'a fortunate accident in the shape of what was known as the Welsh Druid case' eliciting the crucial judgment (*Cremation Society Transactions*, 1904: 15). Yet Price and Stephen both deserved credit; and the Society was grateful enough at the time, printing a pamphlet reproducing Stephen's charge to the Grand Jury.

Four facets of the Society's stance are important. First, it was concerned that nobody was to be cremated against his executors' will. Secondly, 'practical' objections were now a judicious target to tackle because, although Anglican and Catholic voices were opposed to cremation, Anglicans had not officially forbidden it. Thirdly, the Society's insistence on medical assessments and certification about the cause of death was designed to meet current public concern about poison. Fourthly, it had to challenge 'sentiment', that is the burial culture with all its rituals, expectations and commercial interests.

The Price verdict accelerated the Society's formulation of its own proposed regulations for cremation. The first Parliamentary questions (Mr Labouchère, 15 March 1884, Dr Cameron, 17 March 1884) elicited no positive encouragement from the Home Secretary. '[A]ware that the chief practical objection which can be urged against...cremation consists in the opportunity which it offers...for removing the traces of poison or other injury which are retained by an undestroyed [i.e., buried] body', the Society laid out three conditions for the use of Woking Crematorium in these words:

    I An application in writing must be made by the friends or executors of the deceased – unless it has been made by the deceased person himself during life – stating that it was the wish of the deceased to be Cremated after death.

II   A certificate must be sent in by one qualified medical man at least, who attended the deceased until time of death, unhesitatingly stating that the cause of death was natural and what that cause was.

III   If no medical man attended during the illness, an autopsy must be made by a medical officer appointed by the Society, or no cremation can take place.

These conditions being complied with, the Council of the Society reserve the right in all cases of refusing permission for the performance of the Cremation, and, in the event of permitting it, will offer every facility for its accomplishment in the best manner. (*Cremation Society Council Minutes*, 26 February 1884)

The use of the Woking crematory was to depend upon 'a strict and systematic enquiry into the causes of death in every case', and Sir Henry not only drew up the questionnaire to be used but examined the reports himself for many years until Dr H. T. Herring succeeded him.

On 30 April, Cameron introduced the Second Reading of his 'Disposal of the Dead (Regulation) Bill' (*HC*, 30 April 1884, cols 959–98). His main purpose was to press for cremation: 'Cremation is quick, clean, cheap, and harmless; burial is slow, disgusting, expensive, and dangerous to the public health.' His Bill proposed that cremation should not be allowed until the death had been registered; that the registration of death, in towns of over 5000 people, was to be preceded by the certification of the cause of death to the Medical Officer of Health; that cremation could not proceed until the death had been registered and could only be carried out in premises licensed by the Home Secretary and in accordance with his regulations.

Cross and Harcourt, past and present Home Secretaries, opposed the measure. Cross commented, 'Nothing but imperative necessity should induce a Parliament to do anything which would shock the feelings of the masses of the people on the subject of the burial of the dead.' The Second Reading was supported by 79 Members, but opposed by 149 Members. The high number of favourable votes gave great satisfaction to the Cremation Society. The Society's Council expressed its gratitude to Cameron, Sir Leon Playfair, MP, and Dr Farquarson, MP, with a request to publish a corrected report of their speeches (*Cremation Society*

Council Minutes, 6 May 1884). Cameron commented (cited in Parsons, 2005e: 109) that the number of votes in favour, although the motion had been lost, made it 'abundantly clear that any attempt [by the Home Office] to solve the problem by means of legislation vetoing the practice would be a work of much greater difficulty than the Home Office had anticipated'. Meanwhile, the Council decided that the Price verdict enabled them to offer the crematory at Woking for public use. An advertisement was issued through suitable newspapers stating the conditions upon which the Crematorium at Woking might be used could be obtained from Eassie (*Cremation Society Council Minutes*, 6 May 1884, 3 December 1884).

Parsons has mastered the materials from which the early history of Woking Crematorium can be reconstructed, and the following account draws in part on his detective work. The Woking cremator had been left unused for five years. A fortnight after the Price verdict Eassie was authorised to prepare the cremator for the cremation of human bodies (*Cremation Society Council Minutes*, 26 February 1884). Two more animal tests followed, the ashes being exhibited to the Commons by Dr Cameron on 30 April 1884. One day's work nearly set back the promotion of cremation. Forty years after their first enquiry in 1844, the Commissioner of Sewers for London travelled to Woking when considering whether to plan a crematorium in the grounds of the City of London Cemetery at Ilford. His party assembled – along with some Society members – to witness the cremation of part of a horse. In what must have looked and smelt like a cookery demonstration gone awry, the wooden parts of the cremator caught fire. The editor of *Sanitary Engineering* was not impressed, 'It is only by an educational process that [the mind of civilised man] is at all reconciled to a mode which cannot be called natural, around which no poetry can cast any halo, and which would kill many fine sympathies and delicate emotions.' (*Sanitary Engineering*, 1 May 1885, cited in Parsons, 2005e: 86). The London visitors made a negative report, and it was only in 1904 that a crematorium was eventually opened at Ilford, the tenth crematorium in the country when it might have been the second. Whatever the reasons for the City of London's protracted decision the burial problems of landlocked London boroughs only continued to swell in the 1890s.

In January 1885 the Society advertised through the press that its Woking crematory was ready. There was no chapel at Woking for, unlike later crematoria, it had not at first been intended that funeral services should take place there. The religious (or secular) ceremony would take place elsewhere either *before* the body was sent to Woking or *after* the ashes had been returned to the executors. The Society expected that the cremation would take place on the same day as the funeral service and that the ashes would be taken away afterwards for burial by the executors. No body would be obliged to be cremated in a coffin, to ensure the purity of the ashes. There was no special place for witnesses to wait. Indeed, the Woking cremator was a somewhat lonely building in a lonely place, as the criticisms of a journal of June 1888 (see pp. 75–6 below) would reveal. These criticisms would lead to rapid action.

Woking's first cremation, the first legal cremation of modern times, took place on 30 March 1885. Mrs Jeanette Pickersgill, the widow of the late H. H. Pickersgill, was 'well known in literary and scientific circles' (*The Times*, 27 March 1885). She joined the Cremation Society on 24 January 1885 and died at her London home on 20 March. She had left instructions for cremation in her will, and she had signed the Society's form of declaration. Medical certificates were signed by J. Langdown and Francis Walmer. An autopsy was completed satisfactorily on her body, which was taken from London by William Garstin's subsidiary, The Funeral Company of Blackfriars. The cremation took one and a quarter hours. The ashes were removed by her executor and, as Parsons discovered (Parsons, 2005d), were eventually placed in a vault in Kensal Green.

The first 'legal' cremation received little attention in the press. This is unfortunate because the two principal accounts, in the *Surrey Advertiser* (28 March 1985) and the Society's *Transactions*, differ in some detail. The *Transactions* starkly states that the one hour cremation 'was attended by two friends of the deceased, who expressed themselves perfectly satisfied with the system employed ... during the time of the cremation no smoke escaped from the chimney-shaft, whilst the ashes were of the purest white and small in volume' (*Cremation Society Council Transactions*, Vol. 2, 1885: 49–50). According to the *Surrey Advertiser*, the inhabitants of Woking were up early, with local children shouting 'a lady for burning'. A number of people came to watch. The body arrived encoffined but was removed, covered with a black cloth and placed on a rack before the cremator door. The coffin was broken up and the wood added to the flames. After an hour the wreaths were added to the fire. Volumes of smoke went up. After an hour and a half, the furnace was opened and 'the principal bone' was taken out using a pair of tongs. The paper commented 'The remarks of the bystanders were not the most appropriate to accompany the disposal of the dead.' For the immediate future of cremation, it was well that the cremation was not widely reported, for clearly the process of the first legal, public cremation lacked a rehearsal in etiquette.

Cremation was so new a process that problems arose at several turns. First, screens needed to be erected to protect the cremator from the weather and cremation ceremonies from people watching from the bank. Secondly, the next year, a record book was opened showing the name of the deceased, names of certifying doctors, length of cremation times, and so on. Thirdly, the first crematory provided for the disposal of the body but without religious ceremony. Within four years, a chapel was built at Woking so that a service could precede the committal. Subsequent crematoria all included a chapel from the outset. Fourthly, the Society intended (after New Southgate) that ashes would be taken away by executors. Indeed, relatives often waited throughout the cremation process to remove the ashes at the end. The Society began to offer urns, of wood or earthenware, for the ashes. Ashes were clearly buried elsewhere, but from 1890 the Vicar of Woking allowed them to be buried in his (consecrated) churchyard. In 1888–1889, the Society provided twenty-seven niches behind the altar at Woking crematory. In 1890 it set aside an unconsecrated burial area for ashes. Cremations at Woking slowly increased.

Progress of cremation in the United Kingdom between 1885 and 1895 with specific reference to Woking

Year	No. of crematoria	No. of deaths	No. of cremations		Percentage
			UK	Woking	
1885	1	597,357	3	3	–
1890	1	641,252	54	54	0.01
1895	3	650,849	209	150	0.03

Source: Mortality Statistics from ONS and General Register Office, Scotland. All other figures from Cremation Society of Great Britain.

There were considerable difficulties in maintaining an adequate service at Woking with so few funerals and so little income. Parsons has analysed a highly critical report of Woking in the eyes of a visiting undertaker who reported in *Undertakers' and Funeral Directors' Journal and Monumental Masons' Review* (22 June 1888: 63–4, cited in Parsons, 2005e: 153). The visitor wrote of a rutted road leading from the gate to the cremator, which stood somewhere forlorn under a damaged canvas shelter. There were no facilities for mourners. The cremator looked dilapidated, and its surroundings were bleak. An open hut nearby contained coal, coke and faggots. There was no information available about rules or fees. The Woking arrangements were a disgrace and, unless something was done, 'the already strong prejudice against cremation will take generations to remove' (ibid.: 63–4). The Society acted with some speed and chose E. F. C. Clarke as their architect. It launched an appeal for the buildings; by far the greatest donor was the Duke of Bedford who contributed £4100 to ancillary buildings which included a chapel area (without music facilities until 1921). In 1911, when the Duke of Bedford provided a family chapel and crematory at the new Golders Green Crematorium, the crematory he had previously commissioned at Woking for his family's sole use was offered for use as a columbarium.

The first religious service took place at Woking in December 1889. The coffin rested upon the catafalque. At the clergyman's words of committal, staff lifted the coffin and carried it through to the cremator room, accompanied by mourners if they wished. Mourners could bring their own clergyman for a service. The Churches probably did not realise how far their traditional authority was being eroded. Here was a novel mode of disposal, dispensing with a church-owned, church-consecrated, visible tract of ground, providing an entirely indoor setting for a funeral where the remains, having travelled for some distance, bore only rarely any relationship to the local parish and its community of the dead. Secularity, individualism and non-localism had entered the British funeral process: Church professionals increasingly now acted unconsciously as sub-agents for family funeral directors and for crematorium owners.

In the early days of cremation, the Cremation Society made an arrangement with the West End of London firm of William Garstin to provide Woking Crematory with funerals (Parsons, 2005d, e), and it is easy to see how, as cremation numbers grew (and despite Cremation Society advertisements), the first cremations were at least as expensive as burials. London undertakers grew jealous of this special relationship, though some south coast firms brought funerals to Woking. Halford Mills, who bought the Reformed Funeral Company in London's West End in 1880, complained both to the Cremation Society (of which he was a member) and to the *Undertakers' and Funeral Directors' Journal and Monumental Masons' Review* about removing the overt preference for Garstin's. The Society gave way in 1891 and the Woking cremation trade was opened to all undertakers. In retrospect, had the complaint raised by men like Mills not been successful, we might well have seen in Britain, as cremation grew, a whole series of commercial relationships between crematorium proprietors and funeral directors, rather on the US pattern which, as Sloane (Sloane, 1991) and other American commentators have shown, gives the funeral directing industry far greater power over bereaved families' choice and powers of judgement. Another factor prevented such combination and ensured the relative independence of the cemetery or crematorium in the UK (Curl, 1993). In the US, there was no overall denominational monopoly by the Churches that, given the size of the continent, had little control over urban burial grounds almost from the beginning; from the early 1800s burial grounds were secularly owned and maintained. By contrast, the vast majority of English and Welsh burial grounds were owned and maintained by the Established Church until the 1850s. At that point local ownership and management of Church burial grounds were passed to local government, for whom, whatever the cost, it has been the tradition, unchallenged until the 1980s, that burial is a locally owned activity, and maintained, even if requiring subsidy, as a public service rather than a profit-making business. The campaign for cremation needs to be understood against this background of change.

Grainger has summarised the hostile circumstances: 'The history of cremation in Britain is a story of struggle against conservatism, custom and prejudice in the attempt to reform the burial system' (Grainger, 2000b: 53). Cremation's principal allies were drawn from medicine and public health. Its advocacy took place amid the regular press coverage on general matters of funeral reform. The legal situation after 1884 stimulated certain local authorities to test whether cremation might offer them an economical solution for their mounting urban burial problems. For the time being, the first generation of crematoria were built and operated by private money and philanthropic enthusiasm.

The Government changed and in June 1885 Cross was reappointed Home Secretary. As the Earl of Dalhousie responded to a complaint about the Woking Crematorium in May 1885, 'Her Majesty's Government did not consider it any part of their duty to encourage or discourage the practice of cremation... the Government had no power to interfere, and until the practice became more common it was not their intention to deal with it' (cited in Parsons, 2005b: 226). The Liberals were as cautious. Cross' minute in response to the second Woking cremation on 21 October 1885 asked whether 'this practice is to become usual and allowable by inches?' (Strutt, 1976: 7). Cross asked the Law Officers whether they considered cremation legal or illegal, whether they could recommend any proceedings either to stop the practice or settle its legality and whether legislation would be necessary if it were to be suppressed. The Officers upheld their predecessors' views of 1879, sanctioned by the authority of Mr Justice Stephen, that cremation was not necessarily illegal, but that if it were, it would be a criminal offence, and the only way to settle the issue would be a criminal prosecution against those concerned in a case. In the Officers' view legislation would be required to suppress cremation. When Cross received this Opinion in January 1886, he wrote, 'It must be brought before my successor.' The next month he was succeeded by Erskine Childers. Childers examined the file on cremation on 22 March: 'My individual opinion is in favour of legislation to regulate cremation but public opinion is not yet ripe for this' (cited in Strutt, 1976: 7–8).

Sir Thomas Spencer Wells, Dr Charles Cameron, MP, and William Eassie were regular speakers at a variety of medical, sanitary and public health conferences. The public and professional lives of these men, intersecting with several networks of social reform and charitable work, enabled the cause of cremation to be asserted. Publications appeared regularly, of which the most influential seem to have been: Wotherspoon's *Cremation, Ancient and Modern: The History and Utility of Fire Burial* (Wotherspoon, 1886); Emrys-Jones' *Disposal of the Dead: present system of burial – earth to earth – objections to and advantages of cremation* (Emrys-Jones, 1888); and Holder's *Cremation versus Burial: An Appeal to Reason Against Prejudice* (Holder, 1891) (this was followed by a motion calling on Hull Corporation to invest money in a crematory); the first edition of Thompson's *Modern Cremation* (Thompson, 1889); and the 1889 new edition of Robinson's 1880 book, *God's Acre Beautiful or the Cemeteries of the Future* (Robinson, 1880), retitled as *Cremation and Urn-Burial* (Robinson, 1889). There are times when these campaigning lectures seem to be the cremationists' main activity. The Council met only sporadically, its *Minutes* complaining on 18 August 1887, 'on more than one occasion, . . . there's been no Quorum'.

There were local attempts to found branches of The Cremation Society of England. First, in April 1886, a branch was formed at Leicester (*Cremation Society Council Minutes*, 20 July 1886) and its meeting in November 1888 carried a motion to raise funds to build a crematorium for the city (*The Lancet*, 10 November 1888: 946, cited in Parsons, 2005e: 227, 230). As a consequence of Emrys-Jones' paper, when the Roman Catholic Bishop of Salford, Dr Vaughan, was in the chair, the Manchester Cremation Society was formed. Dr Vaughan presumably had to reconsider his position following the Papal pronouncement, for by March 1890 he was warning Catholics not to become involved with the Cremation Society (Makepeace, 1990: 8). Local support was sufficiently strong for a Manchester Crematorium Company to be formed in May 1890.

Whilst the first generations of cremationists needed to wage a continuous campaign on many fronts, some opponents also functioned as promoters. Several congresses organised by Churches and other organisations had featured Sir Henry Thompson and Francis Seymour Haden as rival speakers. Haden (1818–1910) was a surgeon who, at the age of 57, changed his career to etching. In funeral history he is famous for promoting earth-to-earth burial. Haden's *Earth to Earth* (Haden, 1875) was first published as letters to *The Times*, on 19 January, 19 May and 16 June 1875. At this point, it is appropriate to emphasise my comment in Chapter 2 that cremation was by no means the next stage in funeral reform. Had not Thompson been first in the field, Haden's ideas might not have received so much attention. Had Thompson not chosen to promote cremation, Haden's might well have been the idea which became acceptable to churchyard and cemetery proprietors. Haden was a great supporter of Brookwood Cemetery on account of its sandy soil conditions, which supported his particular scheme. To some extent he was supported by the Church of England Burial Reform Association, of which little has so far been published. After a series of exchanges in *The Times* in 1891, Haden gave a lecture, 'Cremation as an incentive to crime?' (Haden, 1892). In 1893 he was among those meeting Home Secretary Asquith, a meeting which led to the *Select Committee on Death Certification*.

Despite his forensic concern and his own favourite system, Haden was unable to persuade the Church of England Burial Reform Association to condemn cremation or to persuade influential voices to make it illegal. His passionate advocacy helped to ensure that funeral reform became a regular staple diet in the media and contributed not only to ensuring that forms of legislation were actually passed (Burials Act 1900, Cremation Act 1902) but possibly also to the protective and educational associations established within the funeral industries, the British Undertakers Association (now the National Association of Funeral Directors) in 1905 and the National Association of Cemetery and Crematorium Superintendents in 1913 (successively renamed the Institute of Burial and Cremation Administration and, today, the Institute of Cemetery and Crematorium Management).

Dr Abraham Emrys-Jones was the Secretary of the Manchester and Salford Sanitary Association. His lecture on 'The Disposal of the Dead' in March 1888 led to the formation of the Manchester Cremation Society on 6 July. Had Bishop Fraser still been alive, it might have received greater Anglican encouragement. Whilst the society had no original intention of building its own crematorium, the process mirrored the

way joint-stock cemeteries had been first established. Its proposal to the City Council's Parks and Cemeteries Committee in January 1890 was that it should establish a crematorium in the Council's Southern Cemetery. At this stage, the Home Office's advice was still that local authorities and burial boards would need legislation for cremation, and so the Council felt it could not proceed. In March 1890, the Manchester Society took matters into its own hands.

The ground-swell of support included several wealthy people. Henry Simon was a German-born engineer who settled in Manchester; by the 1870s he concentrated on flour-milling and the manufacture of coke for steelmaking. He was to be involved in many innovative institutions in the new city's life, including the crematorium (Simon, 1997). The middle-class make-up of the Society is evidenced by Makepeace's analysis of 189 subscribers in 1892, with 25% being merchants, 9% doctors and 'gentlewomen' 12% (Makepeace, 1990: 63). This probably indicates the middle-class initiative for simpler, more private funerals and the turning away from duties of visiting and grave maintenance; this is parallel to the middle-class rejection of mourning crêpe, a process threatening the crêpe fortunes of Courtaulds (Coleman, 1969). An analysis of whether or not these subscribers were ever cremated would be revealing of attitudes in these formative years.

In March 1890 the Manchester Society sought subscribers for a capital of £10,000, of which £2000 had already been guaranteed by local donors. On 23 April, the Society agreed to establish a company which would build its own crematorium. Incorporated on 23 May, the Company had the Duke of Westminster as President, the Chancellor of the Manchester Church of England Diocese as Vice-President, Henry Simon as Chairman and Emrys-Jones among the directors. Three-quarters of an acre was purchased from Lord Egerton at Chorlton-cum-Hardy, close enough to the Southern Cemetery to make a future merger possible. The building took two years to complete, but several lessons were learned from Woking, especially the planning and completion of the buildings as a unit. The chapel, built in the Romanesque style, was one of the first in the city to have central heating. The catafalque faced the main entrance. There was a vestry, a rest room and toilets. The cremating equipment was designed and built by Henry Simon's company. A columbarium formed one part of an external colonnade, which also protected mourners from poor weather. Mourners were encouraged to view the coffin being charged into the cremator. Floral decorations were provided, a conservatory being built in 1900. The Manchester Crematorium was opened by the Duke of Westminster on

2 October 1892. To make cremation more attractive for the working classes, both subscriptions and cremation fees were at first kept deliberately low.

On the completion of the project, it was decided to close the Manchester Cremation Society as it was considered that the Company could both manage a crematorium and promote cremation. In 1911, A. E. Piggott, who had served as Company Secretary, reckoned this decision had been a mistake (Makepeace, 1990: 12). At this stage it is difficult to judge whether the education of public opinion might have been better performed independently of the Company; others may have held that the crematorium was cremation's best advertisement. After the opening of Golders Green Crematorium twelve years later, the London Cremation Company and The Cremation Society continued to live separate lives, albeit interlinked by key personalities serving on the committees of each. In the 1920s when the Society had set up the Federation of Cremation Authorities, the appropriateness of the Society being itself a Cremation Authority was questioned; this was solved by the transfer of the Woking Crematorium to the Company.[1] Yet within ten years of Manchester's opening, private initiatives in crematoria-building were supplanted by those of local government, a factor that would become dominant in cremation provision between the 1920s and the 1980s.

The 1880s proved to be a decade of considerable social reform, empowered by the extension of the franchise (Lynd, 1945). This provided the supporters of cremation with an additional and powerful weapon. The Local Government Act 1888 transferred the administrative powers of the Justices of the Peace to Councils elected for each county. This meant that there was now a system of elected local government not only distinct from national government but also able to override the competing interests of Boards, Vestries and Guardians. Health was a major concern of the new Councils:

> Legislation on health and sanitation resulted less from concern for the poor than from the growing realization that – whatever the theory of individualism – epidemics occasioned by bad sewerage and bad housing and by food and clothing produced under insanitary conditions, affected all of society. (Lynd, 1945: 160)

The Local Government Act now enabled cremationists to work through Local Councils and especially through Medical Officers of Health. Cremationists realised that if cremation could be promoted in a specific community on health and sanitary grounds its attractions could increase.

White has analysed the background to the local applications for crematoria in the 1890s. After the Price verdict, no one could doubt the legality of cremation. The issue was whether it was lawful for public authorities to spend rate-payers' money on providing crematoria, in particular whether or not specific local authorities and burial boards were statutory bodies whose powers were limited to those conferred by the statutes which established them. In so far as these Statutes related to the disposal of dead bodies they all referred to 'burial', and the legal view was that when the words 'bury' or 'burial' or 'inter' or 'interment' were used in a statute they did not include cremation. (For a discussion of relevant cases, see White, 2003.)

In 1894, the Home Office changed its mind about cremation; until then it had been discouraging or neutral. Until 1894 local authorities and burial boards were told they needed legislation before they could build a crematorium. White cites the examples of Manchester, Darlington and Yardley (Birmingham). The Manchester Cremation Society at first hoped that the City Council would build a crematorium at its own Southern Cemetery. In March 1890 the City Council's Parks and Cemeteries Committee rejected the Society's request on the grounds that the Committee had the powers neither to perform cremations themselves nor to allow others to provide cremation on their properties (Makepeace, 1990: 9).

In 1890, the Darlington Cremation Society offered to build a crematorium in the cemetery at Darlington and then present it to the Corporation. The Home Office advised the Corporation that it would not be lawful to use ratepayers' money to maintain it. Darlington Cremation Society responded by incorporating itself as a Limited Company, opening its crematorium in 1901. According to White, Yardley Burial Board in Birmingham was given similar advice by the Home Office in 1892 (White, 2003: 18).

In 1887, Tunbridge Wells became the first local authority to seek statutory powers. The Tunbridge Wells Improvement Bill contained a clause which enabled the establishment and maintenance in their cemetery of

> a Crematorium or place where (all requisite consents to the conducting of such a mode of burial having been received and fulfilled) corpses may be burned instead of or prior to being interred. (cited in White, 2003: 15)

Thus Tunbridge Wells sought to ensure that 'burial' should be interpreted as a general word for 'disposal' – as Judge Stephen had decided at Cardiff in 1884 (White, 2002: 171) – and thus include cremation. The clause also ran:

> and in interpreting the Public Health Acts the expressions 'burial' and 'cemetery' shall unless there be anything in the context repugnant to such construction be deemed to include such burning of a corpse in a crematorium and such crematorium respectively. (cited in White, 2003: 15)

Tunbridge Wells' application was rejected on the ground that the establishment and regulation of crematoria should be dealt with by general not local regulation (White, 2003: 15). Whilst Home Secretary Matthews had refused to support Tunbridge Wells, his Permanent Under-Secretary Lushington wrote a note: 'Personally I am in favour of cremation' (cited in Strutt, 1976: 8).

In 1893 the Home Office was reminded of the existing inequality of the laws on burial and cremation. Some of the leading cremationists, like Hart, were also leaders in the campaign against infanticide (Rose, 1986). The last quarter of the nineteenth century saw a massive growth in children's burial insurance. The National Society for the Prevention of Cruelty to Children, founded in 1889, began to tackle the issue of infanticide and insurance after the Prevention of Cruelty to Children Act was passed that year (Rose, 1986: 125). The abuse possible in the current registration procedures was obvious. Until stillbirths were registered by law, there could be no proper picture of infant mortality, licit or illicit. The Scots physician, R. R. Rentoul, reckoned that the incompetence of unqualified midwives was responsible for many stillbirths (Rose, 1986). He collected statistics of known stillbirth burials from a hundred parish burial boards and sent the results to Charles Cameron, MP.

In 1892–1893 a House of Commons Select Committee considered Midwives Registration. In March 1893 Cameron successfully proposed a Select Committee on Death Certification and both he and Dr Farquarson were among its members. Thompson led a deputation to Home Secretary Herbert Asquith (later Prime Minister 1908–1916). He cited the Registrar General's Report for 1890 which indicated that 2% of total deaths (16,000 persons) were buried without any certificate. The inference was clear: if cremationists were willing to undergo stringent conditions to facilitate the detection of crime, should not burial regulations do the same? Thompson outlined his recommendations for a secure system of cremation documentation addressing the forensic concerns about evidence of poisoning, violent death or criminal neglect. He recommended that to deal with cases of death where there was no certificate from a medical practitioner in attendance, there should be set up in each sanitary district a registrar medical practitioner appointed as public medical certifier of the causes of death; and

> that a medical practitioner in attendance should be required, before giving a certificate of death, to inspect personally the body, but if, on the ground of distance or other sufficient reason, he is unable to make this inspection himself he should obtain and attach to the certificate of the cause of death a certificate signed by two persons, neighbours of the deceased, verifying the fact of death. (*Select Committee on Death Certification*, London, 1893, pp. xxvi–xxvii, cited in Parsons, 2005e: 243)

The Select Committee's recommendations included a number of reforms of the British system for the disposal of the dead, including the cessation of the practice of burial in pits or common graves and the registration of stillbirths. It also proposed a Ministry of Health. Nevertheless, none of the Report's recommendations were implemented. Successive governments maintained their reluctance to make stillbirths registrable. Some of the 1893 recommendations were eventually incorporated in the Births and Deaths Registration Act 1926, by which time the demography of English mortality had vastly changed. Sir Henry Thompson revised his recommendations and published them as a pamphlet (Thompson, 1897: 30–4). His proposals were to provide the basis for the Cremation Regulations passed in 1903.

Meanwhile, new opportunities for building crematoria arose because of the pressure on urban burial sites caused by rapid urban population growth (Brooks, 1989; Meller, 1999). As cremation was now a lawful alternative to burial, a number of urban local authorities sought to extend their options for disposal, *The Times* reporting that 150 Local Councils were interested (*The Times*, 22 December 1897). They had discovered the cost of urban cemeteries – especially where the neglect of old memorials by families and prior choices of planting deciduous trees had significantly increased the cost of maintenance. Spare land was increasingly neither cheap nor as locally accessible; if crematoria could be provided in existing cemeteries, and if the public could be persuaded to use them, local authorities would find their responsibilities easier to discharge.

In 1894, an opportunity appeared for a joint project: the Paddington Burial Board invited the Cremation Society to build and manage a crematorium in an area of their Willesden cemetery (White, 2003: 13–14). Had this proposal borne fruit, the first crematorium built in London would have been a joint Society–local authority project which, with all the advantages of a cemetery setting, would have provided a model for (what would be called a century later) 'public-private partnerships' for urban communities throughout the country. In the event, the scheme fell through. Whilst the Paddington Burial Board had taken the initiative and received the consent of the Home Secretary to lease its land to the Society, the Society was dissatisfied with the cost estimates (£5000), the shortness of the lease (21 years) and the size and location of the site (*Cremation Society Council Minutes*, 1 August 1895). The Society withdrew from negotiations, but the affair had whetted its appetite for a crematorium within the London catchment area, for which Golders Green Crematorium would be the eventual outcome in 1902.

In 1894, the attempt by Cardiff Corporation to build a crematorium seemed to demonstrate that the attitude of the Home Office had changed (White, 2003: 15). Either the pressures from within metropolitan and local authorities towards solving their burial responsibilities through cremation were proving too economical to resist, or Lushington had found a kindred spirit in the new Liberal Home Secretary, Asquith. For Asquith, 'there may be great advantages in the establishment and working of crematoria by local authorities rather than by private bodies and this...may be permitted even in a local Bill' given sanitary and forensic provisions (cited by Strutt, 1976: 9). The then third busiest port in Britain, the city had built an isolation hospital at Flat Holm Island for cholera patients, and in 1893 had built there a small crematorium (of wood). The Bill gave permission that the City Corporation 'may in a convenient and proper place in their cemetery set apart for and build provide set up equip and maintain a crematorium proper and sufficient for the cremation of human remains...' Those who died of cholera shall 'without any other sanction than this Act but subject to the regulations made thereunder be cremated in such crematorium of the Corporation as their medical office of health may in each case direct...' (cited by White, 2003: 16). This would have proved a significant precedent arguing from specific public health needs (that is cholera) to a general reform.

The crematorium was never built (White, 2003: 16–17). First, two different committees were responsible for the proposed crematorium – the Port Sanitary Authority and the Burial Board – and communications became haphazard. Secondly, the City discovered that it could not use the crematorium on Flat Holm unless its plans were approved by the Home Office. Thirdly, but most important, was the opposition of Roman Catholic councillors in the City. They felt a crematorium should not be funded through the public rates. A fourth influence was, however, that the Marquess of Bute, the owner of much of the land and shore upon which the City and its prosperous docks were built, was a Roman Catholic. Cardiff did not proceed with its crematorium. Crematoria were later provided nearby at Pontypridd (1922) and at Thornhill (1953).

Nevertheless, two other authorities followed Cardiff's lead with local Acts. Leamington Corporation (1896) and Hull Corporation (1897) acquired powers similar to Cardiff's. Leicester became a third in 1899. The same year, the Corporation of Nottingham proposed a scheme for the dual provision of burial and cremation on the same site. It held a competition for new cemetery chapels and crematoria. The competition winner was declared but, for reasons not yet assessed, the project was abandoned (Grainger, 2005: 71). Had the project been completed, then a new model of cemetery-cum-crematorium would have been inaugurated that would have been greatly helped by the imminent Burial Act 1900 and the Cremation Act 1902. In the event, the Corporation did not provide cremation facilities at Nottingham until 1931.

None of these communities, however, had the burial problems faced by London, the extension and maintenance of whose vast cemeteries were causing increasing problems. London consisted of a number of local boroughs, nearly all of whose inner boroughs, landlocked by the outer boroughs, were unable to expand existing cemetery space. In 1891 the Association of Municipal Corporations asked the Local Government Board to receive a deputation to press for burial authorities to be allowed to build crematoria. The Board replied that since it had jurisdiction only over cemeteries provided by sanitary authorities under the 1879 Public Health Interments Act, the Association should refer to the Home Office (White, 2003: 17). In 1892 the Association sent a deputation to the Home Secretary, Henry Matthews, urging that 'their civil bodies and burial boards should be authorised to expend public money for the provision of crematoria' (cited in Strutt, 1976: 8). Matthews promised to consider their request, but failed to act. Later that year Lushington wrote a minute, 'It is lawful now to cremate but the question is whether the power to provide burial grounds includes the power to provide crematoria; if not, is power to be given to provide crematoria and under what restrictions?' (cited in Strutt, 1976: 8).

In 1893 the Association of Municipal Corporations was informed that legislation was necessary, but that none would be forthcoming from the Government. It determined to proceed on its own and introduced a Bill into the House of Commons in 1895 (White, 2003: n. 19). Clearly the Association would have welcomed the Cremation Society's support but the latter was unwilling, particularly concerned to guard against the old forensic challenge and preferring that the provisions of the Association's Bill should be in accordance with the report of the 1893 Select Committee on Registration. The Bill did not have a Second Reading (HC, 9 May 1895, col. 775). With this setback, the Association of Municipal Corporations withdrew from its attempts to promote crematoria.

The initiative was taken up by the London County Council (LCC). The LCC instructed its Public Control Committee to report on whether local authorities should be empowered to provide crematoria. In 1897 the Committee's positive report recommended the introduction of a Bill which would empower Burial Boards under the Metropolitan Burials Acts to provide crematoria. White suggests that growing local government support for cremation was partly organised by authorities who had been circulating each other for support, including Kings Norton District Council (Birmingham), Islington Vestry and Camberwell Vestry (White, 2003: 18). At the end of 1897 Camberwell asked the LCC to obtain the required power, and this request coincided with the LCC's independent decision to do so. A number of London local authorities then consulted the Local Government Board together. The Board felt the time had come to invite the Home Office to introduce a Bill giving local authorities the appropriate powers. The impetus was not simply capital-based but country-wide: *The Times* reported on 22 December 1897 that 150 Councils were interested in cremation.

In 1899 the LCC drafted a Bill, at the request of twenty Metropolitan Burial Authorities, to enable them to provide facilities for cremation. The Home Secretary, Sir Matthew White Ridley, gave general approval of the clauses, but he maintained that cremation legislation should still be dealt with by a Public General Act applicable to all burial authorities. If such a measure were introduced, he would be prepared to support it. The LCC's Bill was introduced in the Lords by Lord Monkswell. The Bill passed the Lords but was too late for the Commons. Monkswell reintroduced the Bill in March 1901. The April debate in the Commons was controversial: one of the resulting amendments 'prohibited the construction of a crematorium within 200 yards of a dwelling house' without the written consent of the owners and occupiers and within fifty yards of a public highway (Cremation Act 1902, S.5). This precedent was drawn from the Cemeteries Act 1847. The consequence would effectually limit the number of available urban sites for crematoria for fifty years.

In 1902 Lord Monkswell made his third attempt. One Commons amendment indicates a measure of clerical opposition. The Commons agreed that the incumbent of a parish should not be obliged to perform a funeral service before, at or after the cremation of the remains of 'parishioners or persons dying in his parish', within the ground of a burial authority. When a Church of England clergyman refused to take such a service, another might do so in his place, but only with the permission of the Bishop and at the request of the dead person's executor or of the burial authority (S.11). There was less support in both houses for Lord Cecil's proposal that crematoria should not be built on the consecrated portions of public cemeteries, but this restriction was retained in the Act (S.5). The Act received the Royal Assent on 22 July 1902. It drew on the 1884 Bill presented by Dr Charles Cameron and on the text of Sir Henry Thompson's *Modern Cremation*. Similarly, the Cremation Regulations 1903 drew, in addition, on the documentation prepared by the Cremation Society for use at Woking. The groundwork prepared by the Cremation Society Council had borne good fruit.

The Cremation Act 1902, *An Act for the Regulation of Burning Human Remains and to enable Burial Authorities to establish Crematoria*, provided definitions of 'burial authority' and 'crematorium' (S.2). It extended the powers of burial authorities to include the provision and maintenance of crematoria (S.4). Burial authorities could accept gifts of money or land towards crematorium building (S.6) and charge cremation fees (S.9). No cremations were to take place until the Local Government Board had approved its plans and site and until the Burial Authority had certified to the Secretary of State that the crematorium was complete and equipped (S.4). The Secretary of State was to make regulations for the operation of crematoria, including maintenance, inspection and disposal of ashes (S.7). With modifications made in 1926 and 1952, the Cremation Act 1902 stands today. The last by-laws to be approved under Private Act were those for Leicester Crematorium in June 1902; they lapsed when general Regulations came into force.

The low level of formal Church opposition to the 1902 Act is notable. Three reasons may be advanced. First, cremation had been lawful for nearly twenty years. A second reason is likely to be that the Cremation Act was preceded two years earlier by the passing of the Burials Act 1900. This represented, at last, a settlement of the old quarrels between Anglicans and Dissenters. It provided for three contentious issues to be resolved: first, the division of cemeteries into consecrated and unconsecrated ground; secondly, the dual provision of chapels (which from now on would be at the cost of the denominations, not the Councils which had funded them since the Acts of 1850 and 1852); thirdly, the payment of fees to (Anglican) incumbents as compensation for the funeral fees was no longer required where there was no longer a cemetery in the parish. Henceforth, fees paid to parish ministers without cemeteries were phased out (HC, 26 June 1900, cols 1046–7).

Thirdly, the Church of England had adopted an ambiguous position. On the personnel side, allowances were made in the 1902 Act for clergy whose conscience forbade them from officiating at cremation services. Anglican reluctance, if not distaste, towards legal cremation was emphasised by the complications placed on clergy willing to substitute for conscientious incumbents. The Church of England had, on the one hand, stood back from supporting cremation but, on the other, had allowed secular authorities to extend their control over the provision of arrangements for the disposal of the dead. Crematoria, forbidden to be built on the consecrated parts of Burial Board cemeteries – i.e. outside the pale of ecclesiastical law – were to be built on the unconsecrated part. Thus the location of crematoria in the UK would remain on secular territory and be subject to secular law and to local political and financial priorities. Grainger has noted (Grainger, 2005) how the Church's refusal to participate in the first crematoria meant that it had little influence on crematorium architecture and thus on the retention of an Anglican or Christian frame for the ritual. Liturgically, the Church of England did not introduce liturgies for cremation services until the late 1930s, fifty years after the first legal cremation. This all amounted, so far as the Church was concerned, to its further withdrawal from control in the disposal of the dead and thus to a further stage in the secularisation of death (Jupp, 2001).

The Conservative Home Secretary, Akers Douglas, was required to make Regulations for cremation. Now that cremation was not only legal, but to be a public service provision, the arguments about public decency needed no further defence. The committee concentrated on the forensic concern, how to minimise the risk of undetected crime whilst avoiding delay of the funeral. Given the infrequent access of the general public to doctors before the National Health Service, it was not surprising that death certificates were sometimes given by doctors who had neither seen the deceased in the last illness, nor seen the body after death. The committee drafting the Regulations quoted the case of Mary Anne Cotton (1873) who had murdered twenty victims, apparently for insurance money (Smale, 1992: 110). The certificates had recorded various 'natural causes', a stepson being subsequently found to have died of arsenic poisoning. Rose supplies additional cases, all of which would have been familiar to reformers pressing both for cremation and for stricter certification procedures (Rose, 1986: 120–35).

Whilst the danger of undetected crime could not be entirely eliminated, certain proposals were designed to reduce it. The voluntary regulations were reassessed and the following proposals made: (1) A medical referee should be appointed by the cremation authority. He should not be the Medical Officer of Health or the Coroner, but one who would be qualified to hold such office. (2) The second referee should be a doctor, but not the patient's own. This provided a further degree of objectivity, for two separate certificates would now be required. The Regulations were presented to Parliament on 1 April 1903.

Cremation was now legal and orderly. Yet cremation was not thereby popularised overnight. One of the preconditions for its acceptance was the wider provision of facilities for cremation. Cremationists later realised how the effect of these Regulations was to shift a measure of responsibility for the authorisation of cremation more decisively to the medical profession. This may not have seemed important in 1902, when there were only 431 cremations in all. The problems later raised by dual certification and levels of doctors' fees were issues from the 1920s onwards, both for the Society and for its sister organisations.

Meanwhile, a new phase in cremation had begun, with the building in 1902 of the Golders Green Crematorium, the opening of which was, for Grainger, a key point in the development of cremation in England (Grainger, 2005). Golders Green Crematorium set new standards in cremation architecture. The London initiative seems to have been the proposal of Martin Ridley Smith, a City banker, a former High Sheriff of London and a member of the Council of the Cremation Society. Intertwined with Smith's proposal was a suggestion that a limited liability company be formed to run the Woking crematorium, leaving the Society to concentrate on propaganda (*Cremation Society Council Minutes*, 22 July 1890) but the plan for a limited liability company to run Woking, proposed on 28 November 1892, did not get far; in the background there may have been some public concern that crematoria should not be operated for profit (White, 2003: 12–14) although privately run cemeteries had been a feature of British funeral life for over sixty years. The Paddington Burial Board's initiative had also stimulated the Society's London plans. In the autumn after the collapse of this project, the Society (*Cremation Society Council Minutes*,

23 October 1895) set up a committee, which included William Robinson, to look for two-acre sites within driving distance of Marble Arch (in London's West End) and to inform the Duke of Westminster about both Paddington and the new proposal. After two North London sites had been inspected the previous November, the Society agreed to form a company called The London Cremation Company Ltd in early 1900. The chosen site consisted of twelve acres of freehold farming land adjacent to Hampstead Heath. The company bought the site for £6000, of which £4000 was borrowed, and the Society purchased 2000 £1 shares. The new company was registered on 16 October 1900. Smith became Chairman, with John Swinburne-Hanham as Managing Director and William Robinson also on the Board.

Grainger has commented that crematoria, compared with cemeteries, made very specific demands on architects: in particular, they were 'a building type for which there was no architectural precedent. They were in that sense analogous to the early railway stations' (Grainger, 2000b: 61). In addition, given the atmosphere of contemporary Christian suspicion about cremation, it was important to present a building that was not unsympathetic to Christian sensibilities. The London Cremation Company had toyed with the idea of giving the brief to the architect Charles Voysey, the son of a founding member of the Society. In finally choosing Ernest George, they had the best chance of creating a style of crematorium blending grandeur and assurance, a place where 'committed supporters of cremation looked for a dignified but glorious departure, [and] sceptics might look for reassurance' (Grainger, 2000b: 63). Grainger stresses the importance of George's choice of Lombard-Romanesque in Golders Green. Gothic had for much of the earlier part of the nineteenth century been associated with church styles, and the turn of the century was a time of architectural reconsideration of church style. George recognised the importance of a building type for a crematorium which was sufficiently ecclesiastical in style to persuade religious people that cremation was an acceptable innovation and yet would not compromise their faith or tradition.

Grainger gives four reasons for Golders Green as the key point in cremation development in England. This was the first involvement in crematorium design of an architect of national standing, Ernest George (Grainger, 2006). George was already known to leading cremationists, having previously worked for William Robinson and Rosemary Crawshay's son, Robert. Secondly, Golders Green created a precedent, in terms of both architectural style and landscaping, which was to exert a profound influence on the design and planning of subsequent British crematoria. George introduced a series of important innovations, an alternative style, the porte-cochère as a feature, the design of the cloisters, the design of separate columbaria, the positioning of the catafalque, but most importantly perhaps, the circulation of mourners who entered through one door and left by another, into the gardens. The significance of the latter innovation would not be appreciated until the 1930s, when the number of cremations increased, making it necessary to keep groups of mourners apart (Grainger, 2005: 76).

Thirdly, it was the first crematorium in London, and unconnected with an existing burial ground. Thus, fourthly, Golders Green provided 'a new landscape of mourning which was to be the great legacy of the crematorium in the twentieth century'. The 'new landscape of mourning' was the particular contribution of William Robinson who took the opportunity to effect the ideas set out in his *God's Acre Beautiful* (1880), ideas further developed in his *Cremation and Urn Burial – or the Cemeteries of the Future* (1889). Robinson had proposed 'garden-cemeteries' in which 'no body in a state of decay should ever enter' (Robinson, 1889: 26, cited in Grainger, 2002b: 40) and in which urns for ashes would be buried. This would be a burying place in which there would be neither graves nor gravestones, only plaques and commemorative tablets, for which the columbarium and walls would provide the principal locations. It was a question of art, and cemeteries would become a new field for artistic effort.

> By the common consent of mankind 'God's Acre Beautiful' is most fittingly arranged as a garden, and as the place for urn-burials need not occupy more than a fourth of the space of a large cemetery the whole central or main part would be free for gardens and groves of trees...The cemetery of the future must be...the most beautiful and best cared for of all gardens. (Robinson, 1889: 5, cited in Grainger, 2002b: 40)

The six crematoria built before 1902 had either been denied the opportunity of landscaping, by being placed in existing cemeteries, or ignored the potential of their surroundings. At Golders Green, landscaping was considered from the start (Grainger, 2002b: 41). Whether considering either the Cremation Society's idealistic stance in the late 1940s when, in the context of a different public mood, it proposed that all new crematoria should be built on new sites and away from existing cemeteries, or contemporary public dissatisfaction with functional crematoria buildings in cemeteries filled with memorials, it is as well to consider the vision of the first generation of the cremation movement. The founders of Golders Green Crematorium had a vision which set a precedent too difficult for many local authorities to follow.

Golders Green Crematorium was opened on 22 November 1902. At the opening, Martin Smith said its aim was both practical and promotional:

> to extend the use of cremation...and also to furnish daily evidence that the process is simple, expeditious and reverent, absolutely free from all the painful and distressing incidents so often attributed to it by those ignorant of the process; in short, to popularise the use of cremation, to prove that it is a safe and economical method of burial, and that it can be carried on upon a pure commercial basis without fear of loss or disaster. (Smith, *Cremation Society Transactions for 1902* (1903): 27–35)

Golders Green was an immediate success for the cremation movement. Until the Second World War, it carried out more cremations than any other in the London area. By 1914 it had carried out over half the total cremations performed in the UK since 1885.

Progress of cremation in the United Kingdom between 1895 and 1914

Year	No. of crematoria	No. of deaths	No. of cremations	Percentage
1895	3	650,849	209	0.03
1900	4	670,126	444	0.07
1905	13	594,567	604	0.10
1910	13	555,515	840	0.15
1914	13	590,299	1,279	0.22

Source: Mortality Statistics from ONS and General Register Office, Scotland. All other figures from Cremation Society of Great Britain.

The first attempts to provide a crematorium began in the period before the legalisation of cremation. They required the pump-priming of private enterprise. There were three, partly overlapping, stages of development: first, the Cremation Society itself acted as the agent (Woking, Golders Green); second, local cremation societies were formed, usually with local initiative (Manchester, Glasgow, Birmingham); and third, local government authorities acted or combined to fund crematoria (Hull, Darlington, Leicester). One private crematorium was later sold to the local authority (Liverpool).

This book contends that funeral reforms have the best chance of success when they represent a benefit to a combination of interested parties, in particular the Churches, funeral directors, the owners of crematoria, whether private or public and the general public. In cremation's earliest stage, its advocates also sought combination of interests. Income for the first crematoria depended upon a number of sources. Private subscriptions were always helpful: the Society was helped at the outset by its Council members and, at key moments, by two of London's wealthiest land-owners, the Dukes of Westminster and Bedford. Private subscribers, however, preferred to back a winner. As for land, the economical strategy was to buy part of an existing cemetery, as at New Southgate, at Glasgow or at Liverpool. On the other hand, cremation fees produced the least reliable income at that time. Cremation was free for life-members of the Cremation Society. The result was higher fees generally which limited cremation to those who could afford it, although this was only one generally felt objection to cremation before 1918.

Not until 1911 (cremation's 27th official year) did the number of cremations exceed 1000 for the first time. Of these, 527 were at Golders Green and 125 at Manchester. Despite the Cremation Society's attempts to show that cremation could actually prove less expensive than burial, cremation was not at the outset a profitable activity for those who owned crematoria. A public shift of mood towards cremation needed to await a time when the non-Catholic Churches, local authorities and, above all, the working classes could be convinced of its practicality and its respectability. Following the Cremation Act 1902, five crematoria were built: Birmingham Perry Barr in 1903, Ilford (the City of London) in 1904 and Leeds, Bradford and Sheffield, all in 1905. Birmingham was built by a private company; the remaining four were all local authority owned and located in existing cemeteries.

At that point the first wave of crematorium building ceased. No further crematoria were built until 1922, after the First World War. The passing of the 1902 Act had the dual effect of checking the development of privately funded crematoria, and promoting that of public ones (Hussein, 1997). By 1914, seven of the thirteen crematoria were municipally owned. All these sites were in conurbations, with limited land at their disposal. As public crematoria were all situated within public cemeteries, the overheads were considerably lower. They could also charge lower fees to encourage the practice, setting different fees for residents and non-residents. Yet public responses were not enthusiastic. This proved highly frustrating to Sir Henry Thompson's successors.

Following Sir Henry's death in 1904, Sir Charles Cameron was elected President of the Cremation Society. Whatever his hopes, they were frustrated each of the seventeen years he held office. Despite the outstanding official progress – the Cremation Act, the Regulations, thirteen crematoria open by 1905, the middle- and upper-class clientele choosing Golders Green for their funerals – the 'extraordinary preponderance of members of the wealthy and intellectual classes' (*Cremation Society Transactions*, 1912: 12–15) – the total number of cremations increased only slowly. This compared ill with, e.g., Germany, where ten times as many cremations were carried out in a year (Council Report, in *Cremation Society Transactions* for 1912: 12–15), and France, with 94,000 cremations in Paris in twenty years (*Cremation Society Transactions* for 1910, AGM report, 17 March 1910: 12–13), where the majority of those cremated were paupers. From among the mass of the British labouring poor no response could be elicited.

Some analysis for this failure was attempted in various issues of the *British Medical Journal*, 5 March 1910, 25 February 1911 and 27 April 1912. As the Cremation Society saw it, there were three main obstacles to public acceptance of cremation: the religious, the sentimental and the forensic. Yet there were no solid arguments behind theological objections and the Catholic Church's position was based upon disciplinary, not theological, grounds (Devlin, 1911). The Society reprinted supportive quotations from the late Lord Shaftesbury and Bishop Gore of Birmingham, respectively conservative evangelical and Anglo-Catholic spokesmen. The forensic argument against cremation was sharper. Yet the Society argued continually that the destruction of forensic evidence was hugely reduced by the rigid system of checks exercised for cremation applications at, e.g., Woking and Golders Green (Herring, *Cremation Society Transactions*, 1914: 10). On 12 August 1913, *The Daily Telegraph* drew attention to the testimony of a doctor in Dublin that in the 1000 death certificates he had personally signed, he had seen the dead body in less than 2% of cases. Cameron comments on his report: 'in an enormous number of cases death certificates given by medical practitioners are filled in in the most perfunctory manner and too often on hearsay and without personal knowledge, so that the statistics of disease as compiled from them at the public expense are scientifically valueless' (Cameron, *Cremation Society Transactions*, 1914: 11).

This emphasised the continuing challenge of opening Pandora's box: the reform of death certification. Nothing had been done since the 1893 Select Committee *Report*, despite its comments that the present law on certification offered 'every facility for concealment of crime... In short, the existing procedure plays into the hands of the criminal classes' (Thompson, 1897, quoting the *Report*: x). The Society's case had not been helped by the notorious Barrow murder case where the defence counsel, Mr Marshall Hall, had adduced as one of his arguments that if Seddon, having poisoned Miss Barrow, had had her body cremated rather than buried, the traces of his crime would have been destroyed. While Cameron argued that Marshall Hall was extraordinarily ignorant of the comparative legal procedures necessary for burial and cremation, such a widely reported case probably helped perpetuate the forensic objection to cremation (*Cremation Society Transactions*, 1912: 13–14).

It was the failure to promote cremation as a benefit for the labouring classes that most concerned Cameron. The poor found particularly complicated the very death certification procedures which guaranteed the forensic advantages of cremation. 'The...procedure...involves a good deal of dancing attendance on officials who may not always have the suavity of manner and the readiness to oblige that makes the process easy. All this takes time, and to the poor...time means money' (*British Medical Journal*, 25 February 1911), but why did poor people not realise that cremation could be an economy? Burial Boards could bury paupers for sixteen shillings, excluding the cost of a coffin and its transport. The Society pointed out that, if cremation became popular, the cost would be ten shillings (*British Medical Journal*, 25 February 1911). Time and again, it is 'the mass of the poor' whose reluctance to break with burial traditions was deplored by cremationists. Why did they not wish to break free from the horrors of pit burial where 20% of Londoners were understood to be buried in 1920? Why did they not take into account that, far from their buried bodies resting undisturbed, disturbance was a serious probability. 'The mass of the population have to content themselves with temporary interment in graves of which their tenancy lasts only during the period necessary for their decay' said Cameron quoting Thomas Hardy's poem 'In the Cemetery' (*Cremation Society Transactions*, 17 March 1915: 11).

It is from the psychology of bereavement in the pre-1914 context of the urban poor that more precise factors may be found for the maintenance of traditional funeral customs. As to the demands of extended bureaucratic procedures and the extra expense of the crematorium process, it may be suspected that relatives, neighbours and undertakers themselves will have all taken this into consideration when making funeral decisions. It is possible that a risk of losing out on industrial insurance pay-outs may also have been involved. Such concerns, especially in the context of poverty, are hardly to be considered as entirely 'sentimental' factors.

'Sentiment' will certainly include the religious attitudes of ordinary people. 1908 represented the high water mark of Church membership numbers in the UK (Currie *et al.*, 1977). Thereafter Church strength steadily declined, not only in numbers but in the percentage of Church members per head of population. It is difficult to extrapolate religious beliefs of the public at large from those who are Church members; and the beliefs of Church members and of their leaders are themselves bound to diverge (Brown, 1981). Two 1920s heresy cases about denial of the resurrection of the body offer studies as to post-war changes in attitude and belief. For pre-war beliefs there were only occasional words of support from leading Churchmen or congregations. Bishop Gore, the leading Anglo-Catholic Bishop, was a consistent supporter:

> What I should desire . . . is that my body should be reduced rapidly to ashes, so that it may do no harm to the living, and then, in accordance with the Christian feeling, be laid in the earth – 'Earth to earth, ashes to ashes, dust to dust' – with the rites of the church. I do not see that there is any serious argument against such a practice, and, from a sanitary point of view, it has enormous advantages. (cited in *Cremation Society Transactions*, 1910: 12–13)

In 1910, Westminster Abbey decided to accept only cremated ashes for Abbey burial (the 1920 burial of the Unknown Warrior being the only subsequent exception). In 1912, the Pont Street, Chelsea, congregation of the Church of Scotland opened a new crypt chapel for the urn disposal of cremated remains. The Bishop of Rochester encouraged newly ordained clergy to permit only the burial of cremated remains (cited in *Cremation Society Transactions*, 1914, Council Report: 6).

Thus, up to 1914, public response was not enthusiastic. Not until the massive development of new land for urban housing (after 1918) would local authorities accelerate their efforts to promote the economical choice of cremation. Before 1918, cremationists' efforts were ignored or resisted by the majority of religious believers, funeral directors and, notably, the majority of local authorities. Commending the cremation movement's work, the *British Medical Journal* (25 February 1911) used unconsciously prophetic words, 'No campaign can be carried on without the sinews of war.' Yet the imminent Great War would expose the young male population to physical contact with dead bodies and their burial whereby their beliefs and perceptions – and, indirectly, those of their families – would be hugely altered.

5
The Development of Cremation, 1914–1939

The First World War effected changes in many spheres of life, including attitudes to death. In the new, post-war, environment the Cremation Society pressed its case through a number of different channels. These included its offspring, the Federation of Cremation Authorities,[1] Parliamentary legislation, local authorities and the Church of England, as well as many promotional activities. Through the Federation, it collaborated during the 1930s with the burials and funeral directing interests, emphasising cremation as a funeral reform. By 1939, whilst the UK cremation rate had only reached 3.5%, 54 crematoria had opened. The inter-war years thus laid the foundation for the future expansion of cremation as a municipal solution to the urban problems of the disposal of the dead. The period ended with a growing consensus on the part both of Government and of the burial and cremation interests to provide for less expensive funerals.

The war affected attitudes to the deceased and their destiny, funerals, grief, mourning and memorialisation (Fussell, 1975; Wilkinson, 1978; Winter, 1995). Threatened with sudden and violent death, soldiers learned to cope with death in superstitious, fatalistic, cynical and sometimes inconsistent ways. The religious interpretations of death into which servicemen had been socialised as children proved ineffective. During the war, Christian ethics had been subordinated to the national interest; after 1918, disenchantment with the Church's war-time role became coupled with the widespread rejection of the rituals associated with the Victorian way of death.

Of the effects of war experiences upon the British way of death, six will be discussed. First, the war served to reduce further belief in the resurrection of the body which was already in decline (Barrow, 1986). Before 1914, traditional assumptions of bodily resurrection from the grave lent cremation an atheist tone. What did the resurrection of the body mean now to the soldiers who cleared and buried the scraps of flesh from the barbed-wire entanglements? In the early 1920s H. D. A. Major, an Anglican theologian, and L. D. Weatherhead, a leading Methodist preacher and former Forces chaplain in Mesopotamia, were each accused by their denominations of heterodox views on the afterlife, particularly their denial of the resurrection of the body (Burge, 1922; Major, 1922; Weatherhead, 1923). The war generation realised that their beliefs in the afterlife of their dead ones had survived despite the absence for so many of a traditional funeral. If disposal of human forms in burial seemed to have no effect upon their afterlife prospects, was burial a necessary form of disposal for those who mourned them? Furthermore, the decline of belief in bodily resurrection left beliefs in the soul's immortality more salient.

The second change related to a revival of interest in spiritualism which, along with the partial revival of Church intercessions for the dead, indicated that the Protestant traditions of England were no longer sufficiently robust to support ordinary people as they sought to comprehend the mass bereavements in the war. The possibilities of communication between this world and the next, forbidden since the Reformation, became more attractive and plausible. The major qualification for Heaven had, traditionally and in the popular mind, been moral or due solely to the grace of God. Once these aspects were downgraded (Wilkinson, 1978), there was little to prevent automatic transfer. On the heterodox and spiritualist side, an otherwise para-doxical alliance had steadily grown between secularist and spiritualist views from about 1850. Barrow has demonstrated how spiritualism reconciled radicalism, socialism and religious concerns (Barrow, 1986). Winter has stressed that spiritualist attitudes among the soldiers did not so much create, as deepen, imaginative concepts of the spiritual world, growing for some decades (Winter, 1995). The War revived the previously moribund Society for Psychical Research, driving many mourners to spiritualism (Haynes, 1982; Hazelgrove, 2000).

The third change related to a dilution of belief in judgement and Hell. The doctrine of Hell was fading fast before 1900 (Rowell, 1974) and it proved irrelevant in wartime conditions (Fussell, 1975). Many clergy seem to have adopted the view that soldiers, having died in a good cause, went straight to Heaven, without passing through a process of judgement (Wilkinson, 1978). There were compensations. The War enhanced the practice of intercessions for the dead within the Church of England. Whilst this was an emphasis in the Anglo-Catholic movement in the late nineteenth century (Pickering, 1989), it challenged traditional Protestant scruples. Overall, the authority of all the major Churches concerning the end of life was reduced in diminishing the force of both their moral sanctions and their effectiveness in funeral and bereavement ministry.

A fourth challenge related to the privatisation of public forms of mourning and grief. For families at home, the actuality of death was at one remove because deaths had occurred in military hospitals and out on the ten fronts of the war. Families had just become accustomed to the new expectation that most children would outlive their parents. People learned to suffer the bereavement of family members without sight of coffin, corpse, funeral or, until peace in 1918, the grave. With so many dead husbands and sons, fewer people felt that they could now lay claim to the former social considerations extended to the bereaved. The wearing of mourning became too widespread to be distinctive. Paradoxically, this internalisation of grief was strengthened by the post-war publicity given to national and communal mourning, including the Two Minutes' Silence, the Cenotaph and the Tomb of the Unknown Warrior (Gregory, 1994). For Cannadine 'the key to the extraordinary success [of the Silence] was that it made public and corporate those unassuageable feelings of grief and sorrow which otherwise must remain forever private and individual' (Cannadine, 1981: 222).

A fifth change related to mourning behaviour, especially in the roles of women, one of the most visible consequences of changed attitudes to death and bereavement during the war. First, as early casualty lists mounted, mourning wear was increasingly seen on the streets, and individual widows no longer stood out. Secondly, the contrast of mourning wear with everyday clothes brought a re-evaluation. The *Illustrated London News* commented on the 1918 Royal Academy private view:

> Over all social functions war has thrown its blight... This year not one solitary costume was in any way remarkable. Where is there a person who is not suffering family and financial losses that make display and frivolous expense seem folly. (cited in Taylor, 1982: 267)

Furthermore, mourning clothes were considered to have a bad effect on morale. The face of grief was not to be shown to the men home on leave from the trenches. Thirdly, women have always been the major bearers of death and mourning ritual (Guthke, 1999). The war changed the role of women. Women of every social class were so busy in war work that they could not continue with the traditional periods of mourning seclusion. The war expanded women's horizons, for

The holocaust of young men had created such an army of widows; it was no longer socially realistic for them all to act as though their emotional and sexual life were over for good, which was the underlying message of mourning. And with the underlying message, the ritual too went into discard. (Gorer, 1965, cited in Taylor, 1982: 269)

The war provided liberating possibilities of new forms of employment and different attitudes to marriage and family responsibilities (Marwick, 1967: 317).

Lastly, wartime mortality had consequences for class-specific traditions of memorialisation, most clearly seen in the War Graves Commission (WGC). There had previously been no Army policy of noting and maintaining graves. Fabian Ware of the British Red Cross began to note the names and locations of British war dead (Gibson and Ward, 1989). He gained official support for the work of a Graves Registration Commission, setting precedents for a more democratic way of British death.

First, in keeping with public opinion, 'equality of treatment' should match an 'equality of sacrifice'. A War Office order of April 1915 reinforced this by a rule of 'no repatriation', partly 'on account of the difficulties of treating impartially the claims advanced by persons of different social standing' (Gibson and Ward, 1989: 45). In December 1919, the Minister for War, Winston Churchill, was asked to instruct the WGC to pay greater attention to the wishes of the next-of-kin, that is, to challenge the precedent of equality. However, in a Commons debate, 4 May 1920, W. Burdett-Coutts, MP, responded with a masterly speech in favour of equality of treatment and the WGC's principle was guaranteed (Longworth, 1985: 50–53). Democratic forms of memorialisation were thus further encouraged.

Secondly, Ware was concerned about the permanent care of the graves. By January 1916, he had established the National Committee for the Care of Soldiers' Graves (which was later renamed as the War Graves Commission) with the Treasury's financial support. Thirdly, front line soldiers were promised by senior officers that if they brought their dead comrades back to be buried in the cemeteries behind the lines, their graves would be maintained permanently. The WGC promised perpetual care with a marked grave for every soldier, whether or not identified. After 1918, war cemeteries were maintained to a high standard, with which local authority cemeteries could not compete. The significance of cremation as a less expensive mode of disposal became more apparent to local authorities.

During the First World War, the Cremation Society refrained from active propagation of its work; nevertheless, the number of cremations rose slightly, from 1222 in 1914 to 1947 in 1919. In 1917 HRH The Duchess of Connaught and Strathearn became the first member of the Royal Family to be cremated. The Society's finances were set on a sounder footing by the doubling of their capital, due to a legacy in the same year. The Society continued its tradition of seeking distinguished names for its Council and Committee and of publicising the choice of cremation by leading society figures. The Cremation Society's propaganda would make much, in the inter-war years, of the statesmen, churchmen and intellectuals who chose cremation, although this threw into relief the attachment of the working class to the burial tradition.

In 1921 Sir Charles Cameron was succeeded as President by the Duke of Bedford. Sir Thomas Horder, a Physician to the King, joined the Cremation Society Council in 1922, and for the next thirty years played an enormous part in the promotion of cremation (Horder, 1966). He was supported by Sir Peter Chalmers Mitchell, Director of the London Zoo. The Society thus paradoxically organised its radical and egalitarian policies for the disposal of the dead around the character of a voluntary society led by members of the establishment, a number of whose families – Cameron, Thompson and Swinburne-Hanham – had been among the pioneers. The Society engaged in a decade of vigorous promotion at local and national levels, but this did not reap rewards until the middle of the 1930s when local authorities increasingly opened crematoria. Grainger's research will help to calculate by how long changing attitudes to cremation preceded the take-up in practice, in different local and regional conditions (Grainger, 2005).

Progress of cremation in the United Kingdom between 1914 and 1930

Year	No. of crematoria	No. of deaths	No. of cremations	Percentage
1914	13	590,299	1,279	0.22
1915	14	643,884	1,410	0.22
1920	14	534,309	1,796	0.34
1925	16	538,348	2,701	0.50
1930	21	519,712	4,533	0.87

Source: Mortality Statistics from ONS and General Register Office, Scotland. All other figures from Cremation Society of Great Britain.

Under its new leadership, the Cremation Society decided to promote post-war cremation by building co-operation between the public and the private sectors. In 1921 the Council called a meeting of the existing Cremation Authorities with the objective of 'facilitating the working of the Cremation Act and Regulations and of quickening interest in cremation'. They met in London on 26 October 1922, with ten of the thirteen Cremation Authorities represented. The formal topics were: the promotion of, and deterrents to, cremation, the fee structure for certificates and forms of future collaboration. Meeting the next year in Liverpool, A. E. Piggott of Manchester Crematorium proposed the establishment of a Federation of Cremation Authorities (FCA), to act as a professional association for cremation authorities. This proposal was formalised in 1924 at the third conference.

The Federation of Cremation Authorities not only developed very quickly a life and identity of its own, but began to promote further co-operation with the cemetery interests. These had been promoted by the founding of the National Association of Cemetery Superintendents (1913). The Association's objective was to inform and advance the administration of cemeteries. Perhaps an indication of the growing acceptance of cremation, the Association changed its name in 1932 to the National Association of Cemetery and Crematorium Superintendents. A considerable step forward was taken when the FCA, supported by the Cremation Society, held the first joint conference with the National Association of Cemetery and Crematoria Superintendents in 1932.

The complex relationship between the Society, the Federation and the Association still awaits more precise disentanglement. This work will be important because the relationships between the three groups have not always proved easy and are very likely to have had an effect upon disposal policy over the decades. From the 1930s on, the growth of cremation threatened vested interests in the burial and undertaking groups because of the staff economies inherent in the cremation process. Furthermore, there was a division of labour involved: the Federation was composed of Cremation Authorities, i.e. employers and owners, whilst the Association was comprised of employees, whatever the level of their managerial responsibilities. The Cremation Society itself was in an ambiguous position because it was simultaneously the 'parent' of the Federation and, by its ownership of the Woking crematorium, a Cremation Authority in its own right, until the transfer of Woking to the London Cremation Company in 1937.

Meanwhile, the collaboration initiated by the Society from 1922 not only provided formal and informal avenues for networking and debate, but fostered a range of promotional activities, including lecture-circuits, advertising and pressure on local authorities. The conferences provided a platform for leading figures in death and funeral issues whose support cremationists sought – from the perspectives of public health, medicine, the Church, the law – and the resulting papers became promotional resources. In 1922–1923, the Cremation Society distributed a total of 60,000 leaflets to the public. In the 1924 General Election, a questionnaire was sent to all parliamentary candidates. Out of 330 replies, 290 candidates were in favour of reform of death certification and of cremation in industrial areas. Of this number, 96 were elected, including 62 Labour members (*Report of the Cremation Society Council for 1923*: 6–7). This may well have contributed to the enactment of the Births and Deaths Regulations Act 1926.

The target of the Federation's propaganda was the local government authorities. This was a time of change for local government. First, Labour majorities were being elected, often for the first time, and health and social issues were important, not least because of the enfranchisement of women in 1918. Socialist theories, part of the Labour Party's ideology, underpinned particular emphases on diminishing class barriers. Also, local government was tackling the problems of the rapid suburbanisation of the larger towns and cities. Most local authorities had to balance competing demands: the inter-war housing programme entailed massive use of urban land. Housing needs competed with those of cemeteries on local authority agendas. Cemeteries were too often regarded as the 'Cinderella' of public departments.

Throughout the inter-war period, cremationists reminded local authorities of the contrasting economics of burial and cremation: in 1926, local authorities lost an average of 18 shillings and 9 pence (94p) on each earth burial. P. C. Mitchell, the Cremation Society Chairman, noted that Blackpool had lost an overall £1700, Pontypridd £2000 and Sheffield £6000 in the year (Mitchell, *Cremation Society Transactions*, 1926: 16). Robertson, the Superintendent of the City of London Cemetery and Crematorium, commented in 1931 that 'the majority of municipally owned cemeteries are rate-aided, some of them to a very high amount' (Robertson, 1931: 20). As the employee of one of the nation's wealthiest local authorities, Robertson could afford to make such observations, yet all local authorities faced the choice of whether or not the disposal of the dead should be regarded as a public service. In 1899, 80% of Londoners had been buried in pits (common graves) (Herring, 1924: 70) and even though this proportion had dropped to 11% by 1938 (Wilson and Levy, 1938) sheer economics and difficulties in travelling to a crematorium meant burial not cremation was still the common choice: in 1924 pit burial cost eighteen shillings (90p) whilst cremation followed by scattering cost just under £10 (Herring, 1924: 72). Cemeteries, meanwhile, were suffering not only from the post-war inflation but from earlier neglect, during 1914–1918. Paradoxically, this issue helped to become what Rugg has called the inter-war 're-invention of burial' (Rugg, 2006). More local authorities began to consider the possibilities of budget economies by looking to cremation. The Cremation Society took initiatives to advise them. Meanwhile, new opportunities were offered for cremationists at national government level. In 1923, a parliamentary committee was formed to draft a bill for revised birth and death regulations (Rose, 1986: 122–35). The Cremation Society took steps to persuade the committee that burial and cremation legislation might be put on an equal footing. The Births and Deaths Registration Act 1926 was supplemented by the new Cremation Regulations 1930, issued by the Home Office. These all represented some easing of the certification requirements for cremation which had caused so much trouble, for example, to part-time undertakers (Rose, 1991). Post-war overseas tourism, together with the emergencies occasioned by large rail or air disasters, added pressure to the case for revised regulations (see below). So did the number of crematoria now open: 21 by 1930. That year, cremations first numbered over 4000 (0.9%).

When the war and the influenza epidemic were over, normal mortality resumed. Cremation's old opponents still remained: the Church of England and the Roman Catholic Church, the funeral directing business and local authorities. The Society sought to convince them all. It was enthusiastic but in no impatient haste, for no one believed that cremation would supplant burial within their own lifetimes (Frank Wilson, Buckinghamshire funeral director, personal communication, 1989). The Society maintained its original, legal, stance. Its primary objective continued to be to secure a legal framework more conducive to the choice of cremation. The Births and Deaths Registration Act 1926 placed burial and cremation on a more equal footing by insisting on a registration of deaths before burial. It was at last impossible to dispose of a body without a disposal certificate from a registrar or a coroner. The FCA pushed for further legal reforms, approaching the Home Office to suggest a consolidation of the Regulations.

Concerning Coroners, the FCA proposed that, where the cause of death was unknown, death certification might be adjusted to place cremation on a parity with burial: under the Coroners' Amendment Act 1926, coroners could now order a post-mortem and issue a death certificate if they thought an inquest unnecessary. It was also proposed that Coroners should be empowered to authorise cremation. Behind this request lay the events of the Sevenoaks rail disaster of 1927; some victims had left written instructions for cremation, but the adjournment of their inquests had prevented implementation. Where a jury was involved but there was no suggestion of criminal proceedings to be taken, the Coroner might authorise cremation before the jury had reached its verdict. The Meopham air disaster of 1930 also demonstrated the need for easing legislation for those victims who had previously indicated their choice of cremation.

Secondly, there was a shortage of doctors qualified to sign the cremation forms. When the 1903 Regulations were drafted, the underlying idea was that the Cremation Authority would be a local body, like the Burial Authority, which out of its local knowledge would appoint one or two leading local doctors to give the confirmatory certificate. The Home Office received two types of complaint: first, that the number of doctors officially listed to sign certificates was insufficient and, secondly, that the listed doctors were inclined to claim a monopoly and charge unnecessarily high fees.

The consolidated and revised Cremation Regulations 1930 enabled the Coroner to do for cremation what he could do for burial: issue a cremation certificate after a post-mortem and certification of cause of death but without an inquest (Regulation 8c). This measure simplified the bereaved's operation of choice in disposal. Regulation 9 now provided that certificate 'C' might be given by a registered doctor of five years' standing (not a relative or partner of the doctor signing certificate 'B'). This move enormously widened the choice of available doctors. By the revised Regulation 10, the Cremation Authority would no longer appoint medical referees, but nominate names for appointment by the Secretary of State, to whom the Authority would report.

Cremation was now increasing. There were several local building schemes in preparation.

Progress of cremation in the United Kingdom between 1930 and 1935

Year	No. of crematoria	No. of deaths	No. of cremations	Percentage
1930	21	519,712	4,533	0.87
1935	29	542,732	9,614	1.77

Source: Mortality Statistics from ONS and General Register Office, Scotland. All other figures from Cremation Society of Great Britain.

Lord Salvesen, whose persistence had contributed to the building of the Edinburgh (Warriston) Crematorium in 1929, summarised the obstacles to cremation in 1934. First, Regulation 4 of the 1903 Regulations stated that it was unlawful to cremate the remains of a person who had left written instructions to the contrary. Meanwhile 'relatives with impunity may, and often do, arrange for earth burial in spite of the most strongly expressed instructions for cremation' (Salvesen, 1934: 4). Rugg, in a personal communication, has suggested that in the early 1930s obstacles to cremation largely reflected the piecemeal and chaotic nature of burial legislation. Secondly, while burial authorities were allowed by the 1902 Act to provide and maintain crematoria, they had not been given power to use these when the disposal of remains became a charge on the public funds (Salvesen, 1934: 3). Thirdly, by the 1902 Act (S.5) crematoria must be built at least 200 yards from a dwelling house, although they could be nearer with consent. The regulation proved onerous for local cremationists: Edinburgh formed a Cremation Society in 1909, but could not find a site for twenty years. Fourthly, the 1902 Act protected clergy opposed to cremation. It allowed an incumbent to refuse to perform a funeral service in a public burial ground before, at, or after the cremation of a parishioner's remains. If he refused, no other clerk in holy orders could conduct the service without the consent of the diocesan bishop. This obstructed cremation choice for parishioners. Furthermore, crematoria were not to be built in the consecrated part of a burial authority's cemetery, leaving redundant Nonconformist cemetery chapels to offer suitable opportunities for conversion (Grainger, 2005: 158–171).

The Cremation Regulations 1930 gave the Cremation Society added energies. A journal, *Pharos* (now *Pharos International*), was aimed particularly at local authorities. Increased pressure was placed on the Church of England, through contact with its Bishops, to recognise the benefits of disposal through cremation. Through the Federation of British Cremation Authorities and the joint conferences with the cemeteries, the Society presented itself as a resource for local authorities and private companies contemplating investment in crematoria. To attract working-class support, a scheme of cremation assurance was set up in 1935. A lobbying agency, the National Council for the Disposition of the Dead, was established in 1932 to involve funeral directors and a wide range of civic organisations and charities in funeral reform.

The Catholic Church was challenged through the International Cremation Federation. In 1936, the Czech Cremation Society issued invitations to a meeting in Prague where it was agreed that a permanent international body would help to advance the cause of cremation. The International Cremation Federation was established in London in September 1937, with Jones as Secretary and Herring as Treasurer. The three principal aims were to secure the support of the Catholic Church, facilities for international transportation of Society members dying abroad and the establishment of a standard system of cremation law and regulations. Because of the Second World War, the contribution of the Federation to the cremation movement was principally a post-1945 phenomenon.

The policy of the Church of England on cremation had been laid down by the Convocation of Canterbury in 1911. When agreeing to conduct funeral services involving cremation, clergy used the Burial Service, the ashes being taken to represent the body. The ashes were interred in consecrated ground. At the outset, the practice of scattering was rare, probably because burial symbolically underpinned basic theological belief in the eventual resurrection of the body. During the 1930s there were reports of clergy discouraging scattering. In response to this practice, both crematoria and certain local churches encouraged the use of special 'gardens of rest' for the interment of ashes. Stoke Poges in Buckinghamshire sought to set a trend (Parsons, 2005c); this suggests that the scattering of ashes was a growing practice, one that was far more economical for all parties than columbaria.

Theology was also changing. The experiences of the First World War served to diminish general belief in the resurrection of the body and contributed to ferocious theological argument within the Church of England and the Methodist Church, focused on Major and Weatherhead. Modernists like Major eschewed the miraculous and accepted the progress of science (Hastings, 1987: 231). Modernists were anxious to find a faith for the times, and to prevent a drift into agnosticism. The Major and Weatherhead controversies were important because clergy were forced to consider the sense in which they believed, in their daily credal confession in 'the resurrection of the body' and to be on their guard that any cremation services were not inconsistent with their beliefs. Hence clergy were convinced that ashes should finally be buried and in consecrated ground. Bishops, more liberal in theology and moving among more establishment circles, seemed less troubled about cremation in general. In 1935 *Pharos* listed supportive quotations from twelve diocesan bishops, including Bishop David of Liverpool:

It is already agreed among the best educated Christians that the quickest, leanest and most seemly disposal of the dead is provided by cremation...in spite of prejudice against it which arises from a mistaken belief that in the resurrection the identical particles of the earthly body are reassembled and become the 'body that shall be'. (cited in *Pharos*, 2:1, October 1935: 18f.)

The *Pharos* editor elicited these replies in response to a written question: 'In your opinion, is there anything in cremation offensive to Christian opinion or contrary to Christian doctrine?' The Society actively sought agreement from bishops and forced them to debate the issue.

Certain bishops had already chosen cremation for their own funerals in the 1920s, like Bishop Mitchinson and Bishop Hicks. As the latter was Bishop of Lincoln, a change in attitude is evident since his predecessor's sermon in 1874 (Wordsworth, 1874). Bishop Charles Gore addressed the 1924 Wembley Cremation Conference. He gave his unequivocal support for cremation on both utilitarian – cleaner, healthier, more decent and more respectful – and theological grounds. The Nicene Creed spoke of the resurrection neither 'of the body' nor 'of the flesh' but 'of the dead'. Whilst a great many people still conceived of the Resurrection of the Dead as 'the re-collection of the material atoms and elements of the dead body at the end of the world; . . . they wish the body . . . so to remain that they can think of it as a still existing entity, and which they can conceive of as capable of being reconstituted'. Not only was such a re-collection impossible but it was irrelevant to the issue of burial and cremation, because cremation only effected what burial did but in a far speedier time (Gore, 1924: 3–5).

The inter-war Anglican Church energised its social concern. Lloyd disputed 'the popular delusion that bishops as a class took no interest in social welfare' (Lloyd 1966: 233). The Convocation of Canterbury directed the Church's particular concern to 'overcrowded and insanitary' housing conditions. With this perspective, the bishops' concern for hygiene over dead bodies kept in the home and for the reallocation of land for new housing and recreation is a positive reason for their encouragement of cremation. Parish clergymen also had social consciences. The Reverend D. T. Sykes of Kent described the humiliation felt by mourners first at the 'public reading time' and then at the grave, dug eighteen feet deep and already part-occupied. By comparison, one of the chief attractions of a crematorium service was that 'in death we have no distinctions of creed or class, age or sex' (Sykes, 1931: 5).

Clergy were increasingly uneasy about their role in the conduct of pauper funerals. McHale, a later Federation Secretary, has described the miserable 'public reading time' services as they had developed by the 1950s (McHale, 1991: 70). Whilst the first part of the burial service was read for all the mourning families simultaneously, the burials followed in order. The undertaker at the head of the queue had the satisfaction of the clergyman's first attention at the graveside. Salvesen had commented that smarter neighbourhoods built around an established cemetery were irritated by working-class crowds awaiting the 'public reading times' (Salvesen, 1934: 3), which involved queues of the bereaved, the rival undertaking firms, their horses and carriages all competing to be 'first in, first out'.

Whilst the Church of England reconsidered its attitudes to burial, local authorities were increasingly becoming convinced of the advantages of cremation. As an alternative form of disposal of the dead, it offered the prospect of enormous economic benefits, especially in cities: in 1935, whilst the national cremation rate was only 1.5%, the urban rate was 6.2% (*Pharos*, 1:2, January 1935: 18). Just as private crematoria made profits, municipal ones realised economies. Between 1935 and 1939 the number of crematoria grew from 35 to 54. As the period from decision to implementation could stretch from three to ten years, taking into account legislation requirements, councillors' preferences for cremation must have been formed long before their own crematorium was opened (Grainger, 2005). The public was still reluctant: by 1939 only 3.5% of funerals involved cremation; these statistics, however, could mask local class differences. In 1937, 18% of the funerals conducted by Kenyons, the London funeral directors, involved cremation, at a time when the national cremation average was just over 2%. Judging by Kenyons' clientele, it appears that cremation was preferred by those from a higher socio-economic background (Parsons, 2005a: 47).

The need for new suburban housing land collided with the need for new cemetery land. Local authorities' cemeteries were running short of grave-space; e.g., in 1936, Walthamstow Borough Council reported that only 20 private and 100 'public or third-class' grave-spaces remained. The new trend towards the single grave led to a slow decline in common graves said T. W. Davidge (*Pharos*, 1:1, October 1934: 10). Davidge was an architect with a concern for 'healthy homes' (Oliver *et al.*, 1981: 32–3). The claims of the insanitary dead increasingly competed with those of the unhealthy living. Medical Officers of Health were prominent proponents of the hygienic dimension in the disposal problem and were invited to address several 1930s Joint Conferences which many Councillors attended. Dr Jervis, the Leeds Medical Officer of Health, said:

> The main burial grounds, which were once on the outskirts, are rapidly being enclosed by new housing estates. At no distant date, those grounds will become insufficient . . . [there will be] a clash of two interests – those of the living and those of the dead. I make the former the most important . . . (cited in *Pharos*, 1:2, January 1935: 20)

The bereaved would benefit from more hygienic funeral practices, both in the home before the funeral and in the cemetery afterwards. They would also benefit from reductions in the cost of funerals. Councillor Wilson, of Wallasey's Public Assistance Committee, commented:

> month after month [he] had cases brought to his notice of people who had spent almost their last pound on funerals and headstones. Within a few months some of them were applying for public assistance. To the lay mind it must appear that some undertakers must measure the amount of their tenders by the amount of the insurance policy due. (*Pharos*, 2:4, July 1936: 5)

Yet only a combination of powerful interest groups could expect to take on the undertaking industry with any hope of success. Proposals for crematoria were not always welcomed by Local Councils. The interests of Housing and Cemeteries Committees, for example, clashed over use of vacant land. Alderman A. T. Pike, Secretary of the Garden Cities and Town Planning Association, blamed their difficulties on the requirement of the 1847 legislation, the so-called 'radius clause' of 200 yards. The answer was for the Planning Authority to control the land *around* a cemetery to ensure that development did not depreciate house values (Pike, quoted in *Pharos*, 2:1, October 1935: 12).

The problems were more acute for Councils locked inside urban areas, who had no undeveloped space of their own. In 1925, an editorial in the *West London Observer*, 24 April 1925, was quoted by the *Proceedings of the Fourth Cremation Conference 1925*: 44–6):

> London is fast becoming a huge, gaunt graveyard ... St.Pancras, St. Marylebone and Paddington, their burial spaces long since filled, are now compelled to send their overflow of dead bodies out to the suburbs for burial; while Kensington, having exhausted all available space in its new cemetery at Hanwell, now finds itself at loggerheads with the good people of Brentford, Chiswick, and Acton, who are protesting, and rightfully so, against the corpses of Kensington being brought out and dumped down in their midst, at Gunnersbury.

Kensington Borough successfully secured its site at Gunnersbury Avenue; and the western boroughs, after long and protracted preparations commenced the shared solution to their common burial problem when they opened the first joint-authority crematorium at Mortlake in 1939. Yet, overall, the metropolitan burial land shortage proved an increasing problem in the period between the wars. Pike commented on the

> undignified scramble for sites, preceded often by surreptitious prowling into the area of another Authority; emerging into the light of day only when a Public Enquiry into the loan application has been announced. (quoted in *Pharos*, 2:1, October 1935: 11–12)

As a town planner, Pike was persuaded that only unified control of the siting of cemeteries could disentangle local authorities from their dilemma. There was a strong case for unified control of cemetery sites and the attention of both politicians and town-planners was increasingly sought. Captain G. S. Elliston, MP, told the Royal Institute of Public Health in 1935: 'The London County Council wants a green belt. Currently our cities have a white belt of cemeteries' (quoted in *Pharos*, 2:1, October 1935: 6). Elliston was one of the first to formulate the alternative of 'playing fields or cemeteries', a theme repeatedly played over the next fifteen years by Lord Horder (Horder, 1936).

One possible escape from the impasse facing Councils was the shared solution: the appointment of joint boards or committees for a shared crematorium. As early as 1923 a number of south-west London authorities – including Acton, Ealing, Barnes, Richmond and Hammersmith – discussed a joint crematorium project. A revived attempt was made in 1931, led by Hugh Royle, Town Clerk of Hammersmith. Royle was to become a leading figure in the cremation movement throughout the 1930s and 1940s. The worsening national economic conditions – the UK came off the Gold Standard in 1931 – necessitated postponement of Royle's plan. The plan was revived in 1934 and the Ministry of Health advised a special Parliamentary Bill which was passed as the Mortlake Crematorium Act 1936.

In January 1939, Mortlake Crematorium was opened as the first Joint Board project. Sited in Hammersmith Cemetery, the Crematorium served a population of just over 325,000. It paid off all its debts within eleven years and proved an economic success for the local authorities involved. It was not only a precedent for combined local authority action but a sign that the public mood in urban areas was moving steadily towards cremation and a hint that cremation rates would rise with greater access to crematoria. The Second World War intervened and the Mortlake model could not be followed for several more years. Throughout the 1940s the economic situation meant that local authorities were unable to secure loans or receive permission for materials. Earlier in the 1930s, Sutton and Cheam, Carshalton, and Merton and Morden Councils had begun to examine a joint proposal in Sutton but Mortlake's pre-war success eluded them. *Pharos* followed all these negotiations meticulously, promoting joint action as a valuable model.

Elsewhere, local rivalries hindered combination. In 1934, Croydon Council contemplated a crematorium at its Mitcham Road Cemetery. The opposition group denied its necessity, pointing to neighbouring West Norwood where the crematorium was working at only 25% capacity. It was agreed that there were

> no social ties between West Norwood and Croydon. For Croydon people to go to West Norwood was like taking their dead to a strange country. (*Croydon Advertiser*, cited in *Pharos*, 1:2, January 1935: 18)

Furthermore, the Great Southern Land and Cemetery Company opened South London Crematorium in 1936, a little more than two miles away. The fact that Councils pursued their aim to have crematoria, despite the problems encountered, indicates that crematoria offered them opportunities for better use of scarce land, and financial resources, as well as enabling people to reduce their own funeral expense. These were common themes at the joint burial–cremation conferences of 1932–1939.

In October 1935, *Pharos* noted that whilst only 29 crematoria had then been built in the country, 38 more were currently being contemplated. Within the next four years, the cremation rate doubled: 25 more crematoria were opened, making the total number 54. Eight of these were in London: Streatham, Islington, Croydon, St Marylebone, Wandsworth, Enfield, Mortlake and Kensal Green. In the north were opened Harrogate, Leeds and Rochdale; in the Midlands, Birmingham, Cheltenham, Northampton and Oxford; in the east, Cambridge and Norwich; and in the south, Bournemouth and Weymouth. This pattern of development suggests that, whilst cremation's growth is correctly stated as numerically a post-war phenomenon, cremation's basis as a municipal solution to the urban problems of disposal was laid well before 1939 (Jupp, 2002).

Progress of cremation in the United Kingdom between 1935 and 1939

Year	No. of crematoria	No. of deaths	No. of cremations	Percentage
1935	29	542,732	9,614	1.77
1939	54	564,315	19,813	3.51

Source: Mortality Statistics from ONS and General Register Office, Scotland. All other figures from Cremation Society of Great Britain.

From 1930, cremationists developed new avenues of promotion and propaganda by initiating a series of joint conferences with the two interest groups judged the more critically opposed to cremation: the undertakers and the cemetery superintendents. In 1931 Herring accepted an invitation to address the British Undertakers' Association; this meeting initiated the alliance that developed into the National Council for the Disposal of the Dead. Of more lasting effectiveness was the joint conference format established in 1932 by the Federation of British Cremation Authorities and the National Association of Cemetery and Crematorium Superintendents. The latter had added the phrase 'and Crematorium' to their title that year. The joint conferences addressed a number of major issues, for example, on cemetery finance: were cemeteries and crematoria to be run at a profit or loss? If the latter, should not burial be regarded as a public service? Were town-planners, in the inter-war extension of suburbs, overlooking cemetery provision? How could new and economic models of cemeteries be developed, and would war-grave and lawn cemeteries help? How best might the disposal of cremated remains be provided for? How were social-class distinctions in burial to be reduced, with special reference to Sunday and 'public hour' funerals? How best might memorial facilities be reorganised, bearing in mind the cluttered landscapes of some cemeteries, the claims of class distinction, and the economies offered by the introduction of Books of Remembrance? What were the respective impacts of burial and cremation upon public health? What were the respective financial and aesthetic merits of burial and cremation? How were cemeteries best administered, given the complex relations between local authority departments, the status and training of cemetery superintendents and the legal situation which merited considerable reform? What progress was being made by the National Council for the Disposal of the Dead?

There were two undertones. Cremation, although growing, was not expected to become widespread even in the medium term. The number of local authority crematoria did not rise appreciably until after 1936, and private crematoria themselves had difficulties in securing investors, for example Charing in Kent (Grainger, 2005: 136–7). Again, the Buckinghamshire funeral director Frank Wilson told me in a personal communication (1990) that his father had been offered shares at Oxford Crematorium in 1939 but he refused, saying cremation would never become popular in his lifetime. At the first joint conference in 1932, when the burial rate stood at 98.8%, cremation was felt to have dominated the agenda, and thereafter a deliberate attempt was made to have a more balanced programme. The cremationists were felt to be a 'pushy' group. Herbert Jones, the new Assistant Secretary of the Cremation Society, used the joint conference to promote the cremationist agenda of the National Council for the Disposal of the Dead. He was a bold, but not always diplomatic, promoter of cremation. He became the Society's Secretary in 1937 and an increased pace and direction immediately became evident. The Society held a cremation-only conference at Oxford in August 1938 with international delegates; but its proposal for a second in 1939 was decisively outvoted, British delegates preferring the joint conferences to continue. A similar discussion had earlier taken place at the Federation's AGM in June 1938 when an Executive proposal for cremation-only conferences was heavily defeated. While the Society co-sponsored the 1939 joint conference, this tug of war over the Federation between the National Association of Cemetery and Crematorium Superintendents and the Cremation Society resurfaced after 1945 but with less satisfactory consequences.

The second undertone concerned burial reform and funeral costs, and focused on weekend funerals. Peter Benson, Superintendent of London's Tottenham and Wood Green Burial Board, argued in 1937 for a range of reforms (Benson, 1937: 34–47). He wanted to cut funeral expense for bereaved families by ending Saturday afternoon and Sunday funerals. His experience as Superintendent at Huddersfield was that, despite the arguments that mourners sacrificed wages in time off for week-day funerals, when bereaved families buried their dead at weekends they incurred more funeral expenses than the mourners lost in wages. The widow, instead of providing a funeral tea midweek for twenty, found it necessary – at a weekend – to provide for forty.

> The individual may have saved his wages, but unthinkingly he has added a little more to the expenses of the one least able to bear it. 'Burying them with ham', as the custom has been referred to, has caused more heartache and worry to the dependants left behind than all the small deductions for loss of time... Everything should be done to reduce the cost of funerals, especially in the poorer districts, where sums out of all proportion to the income are spent at these times. (Benson, 1937: 42,43)

If Saturday afternoon and Sunday funerals could be abolished, the first step would be taken to helping these bereaved families to help themselves. 'If Birmingham, London, Cardiff, and other towns can do away with Saturday afternoon and Sunday funerals, then... other towns can' (ibid.: 42–3, 46). By mid-1938, Carlisle, Chesterfield, Derby, Eastbourne and Hastings had all ended weekend funerals (*Journal of the National Association of Cemetery and Crematorium Superintendents*, August 1938: 12).

The Sunday funerals issue illustrates the relationship between mode of disposal, social class and family economics that, in urban and industrial areas, remained powerful up to 1939. The issue of weekend funerals, like those of common graves and industrial assurance policies, and inexpensive burial versus expensive cremation, reflected social class levels and the ability to pay. The characteristics of the society that catered for, and accepted, such social differentiation in the disposal of the dead were about to be changed – drastically – both by the experience of war on the home front and by the post-war election of a Labour Government committed to the dissolution of class barriers in a Welfare State. At the 1938 joint conference, a former Labour Cabinet minister, A. V. Alexander, sent a pro-cremation telegram listing several issues. The first was concern for 'reducing to the mass of our population the general cost of funerals', and the last, a Socialist concern for making, to a greater degree than heretofore delineated, the disposal of the dead a public service provision:

> There is a growing feeling with regard to the exploitation of the times of family bereavement in the interests of specific profits. I want, therefore, to see public ownership of cemetery and crematorium facilities, but I am also against any system of State Registration for Funeral Directors[2], which would, *inter alia*, involve a monopoly association being set up for the private profit of a few. (Alexander, 1938: 31–2)

In 1939, the newly ennobled Lord Alexander addressed the conference in person, reflecting the new mood of Governmental intervention in the disposal of the dead as a matter of social reform. Whilst this arose partly from the work both of Sir Arnold Wilson and of the National Council for the Disposal of the Dead, it also reflected the growing political consensus about government's role in social welfare based on the experiences of the Depression. It was echoed during the war by such left-wing groups as the Fabian Society and the trade operatives publishing the *Funeral Workers' Journal*. The growing consensus on welfare during the 1930s bore fruit in the 1942 Beveridge Report which recommended the Death Grant.

It was against this background that the National Council for the Disposal of the Dead had been founded. In 1932 H. T. Herring addressed the

British Undertakers' Association. He realised that alliances with the undertaking profession could effect greater public take-up of cremation. His proposal for co-ordinated work between the interest groups involved was accepted at the 1932 joint conference and by the Federation in November of that year. The Federation proposed an alliance between itself, the Cremation Society, the National Association of Cemetery and Crematorium Superintendents and the British Undertakers' Association. For reasons yet unclear, the Society did not involve itself formally – though Herring, Horder and Salvesen were active – in what became the National Council for the Disposal of the Dead. Undoubtedly, this Council was an organisation encouraged, if not formally established, by the Society to secure a more favourable climate for cremation, with heavier influence in obtaining parliamentary legislation by a combination of other interest groups (listed at *Pharos*, 1:4, 1935: 11).

In February 1933, the National Council for the Disposal of the Dead formulated four objectives: the revision and codification of the laws governing the disposition of the dead; the preservation of land amenities in the interests of the living; the improvement of the status of those concerned with the disposition of the dead; and the safeguarding of the public interest in all matters affecting the disposition of the dead. The first two aims were clearly supportive of cremation. The third object accepted sectional interests in the undertaking trade and in the National Association of Cemetery and Crematorium Superintendents by seeking higher professional status. The fourth was largely interpreted as securing lower funeral costs for families. The National Council attracted the initial support of Sir Arnold Wilson, a left-of-centre Conservative MP with a distinguished war record and experience as post-war Governor of Mesopotamia (Marlowe, 1967). Wilson offered to pilot Parliamentary Bills arising from the Council's objects. In January 1936, the Council became a corporate body with Horder as President.

Despite its laudable objectives and establishment support, the National Council for the Disposal of the Dead ultimately failed in its purposes. Its secretary, J. A. Barry, considered afterwards (Barry, 1939: 10–12) that, whilst revision of the law had been the prime object, this had proved too massive an undertaking and, after protracted discussion with the funeral directing interest, the National Council for the Disposal of the Dead decided to prioritise the British Undertakers' Association's long-standing interest in the State registration of undertakers, their parliamentary bill to this effect having been unsuccessful in 1925. 'The British Undertakers' Association, by concentration on a scheme of State Registration, may therefore discover the key to other problems' (*Pharos*, 1:2, January 1935: 15). The Association was asked to prepare a scheme (*Pharos*, 1:1, October 1934: 31) but it found a consensus difficult. Clearly, part-time funeral directors and smaller firms were indignant that larger companies should be empowered to create a monopoly by which new entries to the profession might be restricted; and some firms would lose work. Meanwhile, the British Undertakers' Association (BUA) dropped its trades union registration and changed its name to the National Association of Funeral Directors. *The BUA Monthly* (founded 1922) became *The National Funeral Director* in 1935.

The registration issue turned Sir Arnold Wilson from a supporter of the National Council for the Disposal of the Dead to its opponent. He accused the Council of making its priority the drafting of a Bill which was 'calculated to further the business interests of certain sections of the funeral trade' (Wilson and Levy, 1938: 165). Wilson wished to prevent the National Association of Funeral Directors from becoming a closed guild (ibid.: 158) which would hurt both new businesses and the, largely part-time, rural businesses (ibid.: 157, 160). He accused the undertakers and their allies of unnecessary price rises, e.g. in coffin furniture, of exclusive trade practices, e.g. in requiring carriage masters to join their association and, directing his attention to the private cemetery managers, of touting for business (ibid.: 155–7). In Wilson and Levy's view, Horder should be working to reduce funeral costs across the board, not supporting undertakers' interests.

In June 1938, Horder moved the Second Reading of his Funeral Directors (Registration) Bill in the Lords (*HL*, 2 June 1938, cols 853–66). His Bill proposed a Statutory Board to control training and admissions to a funeral directors register. The Board's Chairman and three other members would be appointed by the Minister of Health. In the debate, the Labour peer, Lord Strabolgi, declared his party's opposition, holding that the Bill would both create a monopoly and raise funeral costs. Behind the latter lay the issue of industrial assurance – he was not the only peer to have read Wilson and Levy's recently published book – which benefited both assurance companies and funeral directors. Labour wanted to provide a death benefit for all people insured under the National Insurance Acts and a commissioner under the Ministry of Health to monitor all funeral matters. The Bill was rejected. Five years' work seemed to have produced nothing. Horder graciously accepted defeat. J. A. Barry, Secretary of the National Council for the Disposal of the Dead, put a positive spin on the defeat by suggesting that the Bill's opponents had effectively shunted the argument back to the Council's prior objective:

> We ... [were helped] – all unwittingly – by the opponents of the Bill, to institute the enquiry which we have always considered would be the first step towards the fulfilment of Object No. 1, i.e. the codification and revision of the laws governing the disposition of the dead. (Barry, 1939: 11)

Thus the National Council for the Disposal of the Dead's support for the British Undertakers' Association's proposal proved to be its undoing. It could be argued that the National Council for the Disposal of the Dead's policy – and very probably the Cremation Society's – was to buy undertakers' support for cremation in exchange for state registration. Unfortunately for cremationists, it was probably the only policy the Council might have adopted with any chance of success; for the laws for the disposal of the dead were so complex that parliamentary time would never have been given to wholesale reform. As for piecemeal reform in favour of cremation, the Society had already gone as far as it could. Wilson and Levy, meanwhile, were now concentrating their attention on industrial assurance (Wilson and Levy, 1937) for despite appeals from many sides to discourage funeral expense, the mass of working-class people continued to invest in burial insurance (for a contrary view, see Roberts, 1971: 228).

The connection between ability to pay and the assurance arrangements which tied the investor to burial were pinpointed by Charles Cameron as early as 1920 (*Cremation Society Transactions*, 31 March 1920: 11–12). He pointed to the widespread commitment of the working classes to forms of industrial insurance in which, according to the Parmoor Committee of 1920 (Parmoor, 1920), 30 million people had invested. For two or three pence paid weekly, families anticipated a lump sum of £10–12 to be paid towards a funeral when death occurred. One witness to the Cohen Committee in 1933 offered a higher estimate, 'three or four shillings [15–20p] a week from the cottage homes of England' (cited in Wilson and Levy, 1938: 57; Cohen Committee, 1933). Parmoor had pointed out that, so high were the collection and management costs of industrial insurance, even members who maintained their payments received only six-pence-three-farthings [2.8p] for every shilling [5p] they had paid (Cameron, ibid.: 11–12).

Why did the working man seek funeral insurance? The Anatomy Act 1832 permitted unclaimed bodies of the poor to be used as cadavers for anatomists. This gave rise to intense fears on the part of the poor and, then, to the stimulation of existing Friendly Societies and newer insurance companies who sold burial assurance, called industrial assurance, to provide families with lump sums for funeral expenses and thus avoid the dreaded pauper's funeral (Richardson, 1987, 1989). This fear was the stimulus which drove people to enter policy agreements, however ill they could afford them (Wilson and Levy, 1938: 61; Strange, 2003).

For Wilson and Levy, the great majority of the eighty million industrial assurance policies in existence were life-of-another policies which were 'to a large extent illegal except in so far as they are intended to meet expenses attendant upon the death of the person whose life is insured'. Money was spent on clothing, hospitality and all those items which went to make a funeral a ·public show. The working man needed money at funeral time because, even if he had been able to save, cash reserves were often exhausted by the hospital, nursing and medical expenses of the person who had now died (Wilson and Levy, 1938: 59). Yet industrial assurance did nothing to reduce the actual costs of burial and funerals, interment or cremation, but had, in many cases, sought to enhance expenditure on funerals (ibid.: 59). Successive governments had ignored legislation for burial expenses despite the recommendation of a (Conservative) Royal Commission 1876. Wilson and Levy were convinced that, in the words of John Fischer-Williams, QC, to the Cohen Committee, 'if the stigma of the pauper funeral were removed, that would go a long way to cutting away the roots, or at any rate a part, of the system of industrial assurance' (cited in Wilson and Levy, 1938: 63).

When the Second World War broke out, Wilson joined the RAF and was killed in 1940. He did not live to see the result for which he aimed. Within eight years of Wilson's campaign, Prime Minister Attlee's National Insurance Act 1946, by introducing death benefits, broke some of the shackles of industrial assurance. By that time the war had changed the sentiments of many people about burial and funeral practice. It is not unreasonable to suppose that the investment by the majority of people in industrial assurance policies partially underpinned the 'sentiment' which, in the eyes of Cameron and other cremationists, tied them to burial with financial cords. Ironically, the Cremation Society borrowed from this tradition in providing free cremation for its subscribers and in its own system of Cremation Insurance (*Pharos*, 1:2, February 1935: 7–8).

Evidence about inter-war undertakers' attitudes towards cremation funerals is ambiguous. The *Undertakers' Journal* regularly included cremation copy, yet the joint conferences regularly spoke of funeral directors' lack of interest. Cremation's disadvantages for undertakers included its occupying employees, horses and hearses for a whole day, and cremations where the clients' instructions for simplicity and discretion ran counter to the conspicuous ceremonial which was the undertaker's best advertisement. Further, the legal certification required an additional expenditure of time. A letter in 1920 described in frustrated detail the hazards of completing the necessary certification on time (*Undertakers' Journal*, July 1920: 201). Cremation provided less work for fewer men (Parsons, 1997: 79–84). Part-time undertakers already interpreted their union's plea for reduced weekend working as an attempt to concentrate work into the hands of the full-timers. As for the allied trades, undertakers had always encouraged cemetery monuments (B. Smale, 1985: 105). The introduction of cremation might disperse with memorials almost completely.

Parsons, himself a former funeral director, judged that cremation was not at first a threat to the undertaking profession. Although cremation was recognised (in the late nineteenth century) as a contributor to funeral reform, 'the advocates of change were essentially mistaken over a subtle distinction; cremation was about disposal not funeral reform' (Parsons, personal communication). The undertaker's income was not affected as the undertaker-led staged procession was not necessarily modified. During the inter-war period, cremation presented undertakers with greater challenges. Parsons indicates that leading London firms like Kenyons, catering for the middle and upper classes, were conducting a far higher proportion of cremation funerals than the capital's cremation rate (Parsons, 2005a: 47). In 1925, 30% of all Kenyon's funerals were cremations; 20 years later, this had risen to 54%. This was at least twenty years before the national average reached 50%. In 1931 the British Undertakers' Association's J. R. Hurry denied that the majority of undertakers opposed cremation. Burial, he suggested, was its own best argument for cremation: he 'had seen as many as thirty bodies in a cemetery chapel on a Sunday afternoon, and with rain pouring down one must feel that there was a better method of disposing of the dead' (Hurry, *Proceedings of the Tenth Conference of Cremation Authorities 1931*: 29).

Yet cremationists felt that undertakers preferred burial. The coffin was one issue, for coffins that were to be burned need not be so elaborate or expensive. In 1930, A. W. Hildreth, of Darlington Crematorium, noted that, whilst the *Undertakers' Journal* gave the impression that most funeral directors were in favour of cremation, the undertaker made his profits out of the coffin: a coffin costing twenty-five shillings would be sold to the client for ten or fourteen pounds. The undertaker would not support cremation if his coffin only profited him three pounds (Hildreth, *Proceedings of the Ninth Conference of Cremation Authorities 1930*: 12). J. D. Robertson, the Superintendent of the City of London Cemetery and Crematorium, also reckoned most undertakers were opposed to cremation. 'The general run of undertakers are interested more or less in many other business activities in connection with their trade and cemeteries, all of which they feel would be bound to suffer if cremation became the norm.' The influence of undertakers over funerals meant that 'we cannot ignore [their] influence in a method of disposal which we are well aware is gradually taking a firm hold upon the community' (Robertson, 1931: 22). As long as traditional features of undertaker-led funerals included tailor-made coffins for the dead who were on show at home and horse-drawn funeral parades acting as business advertisements, cremation held few attractions for undertakers as a simpler, more discreet and less profitable mode of disposal. Within fifteen years the developing technologies of motor transport, refrigeration and embalming offered undertakers economies of scale that would make cremation increasingly attractive and profitable (Parsons, 1999). Meanwhile, a threat to 1930s undertakers came from an unexpected quarter. After 1918, several Co-operative Wholesale Societies – whose history has not yet been written – introduced a funeral service designed to undercut the specialist undertakers and provide a cheaper service for their members. Smale commented:

> Private membership [of the British Undertakers' Association] was therefore challenged by an apparently monolithic competitor and was therefore viewed with apprehension by the small businessman. (B. Smale, 1985: 154)

Pressure might be applied by the undertaker when a client suggested a preference for cremation, but there would be no cogent proof of this. The following letter, sent to me by Miss Rebecca Pickles (aged 81) in response to my letter in *Reform*, October 1988, illustrates how the undertaker was able to manipulate the next-of-kin into choosing burial against the deceased's wishes:

> My mother and father lived in Bradford, W. Yorks, with 5 children. They were both Christians (Congregationalists). Both believed in resurrection after death. My mother died in Jan. 1923. Before she

died, we often, during 1st World War, used to walk with mother in Schoolmore [*sic*] cemetery. From our house we could see the smoke rising from the chimney in crem: sometimes if we went near the wall-side of cemetery we saw graves had fallen in & mother would say to us, 'I shall be cremated & that won't happen to me.' We all knew she wished to be cremated. All tho' not many folk were then. However she went into Bfd Old Infirmary one Monday morning with a case, telling the neighbours, 'I'm just going off.' She had an operation, came round, then had a relapse and died Wednesday evening Jan. 17.23.

When the undertaker came & our aunties & uncles we found out that if 1 blood relation objected to cremation, they would not do it. Mother's elder brother & wife were going home, when he turned back to say, 'He could not let his sister burn' so objected. So she was buried. If she had written her wish down, there would have been no argument. Now I tell folk to write it down at the bottom of their will. My father did so. I am the last living 81 now. All since mother been cremated as I expect to be.

The mother was a Congregationalist, a denomination whose proprietorial interest in graveyards had ceased with the 1850s burial laws (although Nonconformists continued to sit on Burial Boards). She believed that cremation would make no difference to her after death, even though her theological beliefs were in the resurrection of the dead: she saw no inconsistency between the two positions. Whilst she may not previously have looked inside it, the crematorium was near her home. She had no worries about the unpopularity of cremation, only about the future neglect of individual graves in the cemetery. She left no written instructions but counted upon her family's co-operation with the wishes she had verbally expressed.

The events of the family conference are undetailed. Whether or not the corpse was laid out at home, the surviving relatives were present: there was a family conference in which the undertaker participated. Aided by the failure of the woman to leave written instructions, the family chose to accept the undertaker's word about the objection of one relative thus disregarding the mother's real and well-known intentions. The mourners were eventually led from their home to the cemetery by a procession watched by their neighbours. The public example of a working-class family adopting a quiet cremation had been avoided, and the neighbours were reaffirmed in their belief that whatever radical choice this Nonconformist Christian had proposed before her death, she would continue to follow tradition after it.

Innovations came near the end of this period. The undertakers developed the chapel of rest, the only non-domestic alternative to the notorious public mortuary. Although there had been a few chapels of rest prior to the 1930s, the first purpose-built funeral homes were opened in 1937, yet their real value to undertakers was not appreciated widely until after the new suburbanisation from 1945 onwards (Parsons, 1997: 88–9). Embalming also began at the same time, simultaneously a sanitary measure and an additional item of expense (Parsons, 1999). With the Second World War and the unavailability of 'Belgian Black' horses from Holland, the motor-hearse was increasingly adopted. This made the transport of relatives to the new crematoria situated on city bypasses far easier and more under the undertakers' control.

When the war broke out, the cemetery and crematorium movements were far better organised. They were laying plans for the future and improvement of their services, the need for which would be enhanced among the general public by their war-time experiences. The growing 1930s consensus for less class-specific and cheaper funerals was pursued during the war years by plans laid by both local and national government. The war helped to stimulate nearly all the major groups involved in burial and cremation to advance the benefits of the latter. By 1939, local authorities were steadily changing their attitude towards cremation and after the war their importance increased dramatically.

6
The Advance of Cremation: Wartime and Reconstruction, 1939–1952

Wartime and post-war reconstruction had a direct effect on the popularisation of cremation with both local authorities and individual families. The cremation rate rose from 3.7% in 1939 to 9.1% in 1945 and to 17.1% in 1951. In the war, the involvement of both service personnel and civilians contributed to the increased mood of solidarity and the enhanced sense of a democratic self-identity which shaped attitudes for a more classless and socialist society after the war. Together with the prospect of a welfare state after the war's end, this helped to cement a consensus for radical approaches to democratic social change. In this context cremation may be termed in retrospect 'the democratic way of disposal'.

The era of reconstruction was led by a Labour Government anxious to revive Britain's prosperity according to socialist principles. The new Health Service not only gave improved care to the sick, but also altered the context of dying: by 1959, more than half of all deaths took place away from the home. The use of land for housing, recreation and agriculture was a major concern, as was the mounting cost of the disposal of the dead. Following the Beveridge Report, the Government was concerned to make funerals less expensive. Together with the Church's change of policy, a whole range of institutions was involved in a reorganisation of practices and attitudes to disposal after the war. All these contributed to the shift to cremation.

The context of this change includes the civilian experience of death in war-time. The correlation between war-time experience of death and changing patterns in funeral choice needs greater investigation because of the paradox about overall mortality in the war. First, the civilian public enjoyed better health, part of the paradox that 'war saves lives'. Britain distributed a more limited food supply more equitably in wartime than in peacetime (Winter, 1986). Citizenship included a new bundle of rights, by which each member of the population was entitled to a fair ration of food and health care. The immediate effects were dramatic: by 1945, infant mortality had been reduced by a quarter, maternal mortality by one half (Smith, 1986).

Secondly, deaths directly caused by war were only half those of the First World War: 270,000 members of the armed forces were killed, and 60,000 civilians were killed, principally in bombing raids. Gregory (1994) has shown how Second World War deaths compared with the First. Civilian casualties were high in the early years because of air raids. That civilians were involved in risk from the outset contributed to the feeling that this was 'the people's war' (Calder, 1969). It was not until 1943 as invasions of mainland Europe began that land forces' casualties began to mount. Cannadine estimates that such losses were easier to bear because the Allies' war aims were perceived as more moral than in the First War. The pall of death did not immediately descend upon post-1945 Britain as it had a generation before (Cannadine, 1981: 233). There was no revived theme of the 'lost generation', partly because family members were usually posted to different fighting units, and partly because the country was led for twenty years more by men who were survivors of that 'lost generation'. No second Unknown Warrior was brought to London. There were few separate memorials, the names of those dead in battle often being appended to First War monuments (Davies, J., 1994). Armistice Day was celebrated in 1945 after six years' suspension, but in 1946 it was removed – and relegated – to the Sunday nearest 11 November and renamed Remembrance Day (Gregory, 1994). Set within the weekend, annual remembrance became an increasingly voluntary act.

The mood of patriotism was felt as increasingly anachronistic in the era of nuclear threat and among the 'baby boomers', who had experienced neither war, nor, increasingly, familiarity with death in their childhood. The implications of Hiroshima, the Holocaust and, from 1945, the nuclear threat, served to make global, rather than domestic only, the threat of death. The improvement in nutrition and health focused the prospect of death upon the elderly. Major diseases, cancer excepted, were steadily pushed back. The prospect of premature death was largely refocused upon accidental death, in mass traffic accidents, nuclear warfare or by terrorism. This distancing of the prospect of death was strengthened by the decline of visible mourning procedures and the removal of death from the home with the increased availability of hospital care for people nearing the end of their lives.

In anticipating the demands of war, both the burial and the cremation interests made preparations. The massive casualties in Spanish Civil War air raids intensified British concerns for which The Air Raids Precautions Act 1937 provided the financial framework. Circular 1779 (Ministry of Health, 28 February 1939) instructed local authorities on preparations for burying those who would die in air raids. Before the war, it had been expected that each night's bombing would kill 3000 people and injure another 12,000. In the event, the worst night's toll in London (10–11 May 1941) killed 1436 and injured 1792 (Longmate, 1973: 133). Rugg has traced the decision-making process whereby the Government decided to maintain the burial tradition, discounting cremation, whilst causing popular dissatisfaction by the details of their burial proposals (Rugg, 2004).

The Government redirected responsibility for disposal away from the Home Office to the Ministry of Health under the general heading of casualty services. Circular 1779 gave planning guidance to local authorities via Town Clerks; this included empowerment to requisition burial space. The cremation movement now pressed for a role for cremation in the national emergency. A delegation from the Society of Medical Officers of Health met with the Ministry and recommended the use of cremation, particularly on sanitary grounds, but without success. The pro-burial stance seems to have been supported by the National Association of Cemetery and Crematorium Superintendents, whom Town Clerks presumably consulted. The Association's report of May 1939 (cited in Rugg, 2004: 160–1) gave six reasons for burial: the number of crematoria was small (only 58) and that several major urban areas were without them; crematoria could not deal with the massive casualties expected (Bradford could perform just eight cremations a day, and Hull only five); there was plenty of burial space left; air raid disruption to the gas supply would impact upon crematoria; identification of war dead would be impossible after cremation; and that many of the public still opposed cremation on religious grounds. The Ministry stated on 13 May 1939, 'the Ministry do not favour cremation. The process is too slow and equipment would be entirely inadequate for dealing with any large number' (cited in Rugg, ibid.: 161).

Six months later, war having begun, the Cremation Society and the Federation of British Cremation Authorities together renewed pressure on the Home Office in a letter of 3 November (text in *Pharos*, 5:6, December 1939: 8). They asked the Home Secretary to exercise his existing powers under the Cremation Statutory Rules and Regulations

1930 paragraph 14, pointing out that the burial policy of Circular 1779 went against the wishes of people who had stated a preference for cremation. Whilst Town Clerks were empowered to make an order for the burial of a casualty, they were not allowed to grant the Certificate E for cremation. As Certificates B and C could not authorise cremation, there being no 'last illness', it was effectively ruled out unless relatives paid for a post-mortem. Thus the Federation argued for a modification of the 1930 Regulations whereby Town Clerks could issue an amended Form E for people for whom cremation was desired. On 2 July 1940 the Home Secretary amplified Defence Regulation 30 by means of an Order in Council. This dispensed with the need for medical certificates (save that of the medical referee for the crematorium) in cases of deaths registered as being due to War operations (*Defence Regulations No.30 Deaths occurring in consequence of War Operations,* text in *Funeral Workers' Journal*, August 1940: 91). This brought the Regulations governing the cremation of civilian war victims into line with those for burial, a considerable simplification of the cremation procedures.

The Ministry's policy on burials was not without tensions for 'the State attempted to subsume individual burial preferences within wider communal imperatives' (Rugg, 2004: 154). The State sought to impose shroud-burial and mass graves on unidentified victims. It encouraged mass burials, facilitated timber supplies for coffin-making, and warned that private burials increased labour costs. Mass burial following heavy casualties offered practical and economic advantages, but 'there remained a deep-seated resistance to the notion that families should pass funerary matters over to statutory authorities' for there were far too many echoes of pauper burial (Rugg, 2004: 167). The practical necessities after especially traumatic raids overwhelmed the normal decencies expected in peacetime. Wartime pressures on burial may thus have further precipitated the shift to cremation. Rugg offers two relevant clues. First, by seeking to restrict family control in funerals, the State may have stimulated individual families to seek greater control and personalisation through cremation, where funerals were necessarily individual – as well as indoor – occasions. Secondly, 'the acute emergency provided by the war constituted a context in which families could further distance themselves from the fact of mortality, by turning over to the State the responsibility to deal with funerals' (Rugg, 2004: 172).

Rugg's paper provokes a question which only further and detailed research can answer. If, in 1939, local authorities, bearing the major responsibility for the disposal of the dead, still largely favoured the burial tradition, what factors led to the war-time growth of cremation, not only among individual families – the proportion of whom choosing cremation grew from 3.8 to 9.1% – but among local authorities, of whom 200 were planning for cremation facilities by 1945? For the former, further research into family funeral histories is required.[1] As for the latter, the shift of national mood is plainly discernible in the key interest groups involved, a critical matter which this chapter will later explore.

The first casualty of the war was a training pilot flying out of RAF Hendon. His fatal crash on 3 September 1939 was followed by cremation at Golders Green. In November 1940, Neville Chamberlain, Prime Minister at the outbreak of war, died and was cremated. This was the first cremation of a Conservative premier; Ramsay MacDonald, the first Labour Prime Minister, was cremated at Golders Green in November 1937. Whilst none of these funerals was representative of those who died in war-time, they were symbolic of the increasing trend. The reasons for this correlation need full and separate investigation, but there are clues. The following table reveals the sharper rise:

Progress of cremation in the United Kingdom between 1939 and 1945

Year	No. of crematoria	No. of deaths	No. of cremations	Percentage
1939	54	564,315	19,813	3.51
1940	56	654,312	25,175	3.85
1945	58	550,763	42,963	7.80

Source: Mortality Statistics from ONS and General Register Office, Scotland. All other figures from Cremation Society of Great Britain.

The outbreak of war had brought almost all crematorium building projects to an end: Sunderland's crematorium was left a shell, prone to vandalism, for nearly ten years. Two local authorities, Stoke and Kettering, rated their crematoria projects as of sufficient priority to merit completion (1940). The Downs, Brighton, was a private initiative (1941). Canley, Coventry, which in 1941 required only a fortnight's work to complete, was finally opened in January 1943. Of the four opened during the war, Stoke-on-Trent had 101 cremations in 1940 and 578 in 1945; Kettering had 29 in 1940 and 88 in 1941, with 205 in 1945; the Downs, Brighton, had 311 in 1941 and 822 in 1945; Coventry had 163 services in 1943 and 311 in 1945. Thus the rise of the national cremation rate (from 1 in 25 funerals in 1939 to 1 in 11 in 1945) occurred with the addition of only four more crematoria.

Whilst cremationists commented that each new crematorium created a new demand for its services (e.g. *Pharos*, 7:1, February 1941: 2) cremations seem to have risen more sharply in the areas prone to bombing. In 1941, cremations at Mortlake in Richmond, Surrey, averaged one for every three burials and Croydon, South London, averaged one for every five (*Pharos*, 8:1, February 1942: 5). Southampton Council decided that for Local Authority funerals for civilian war dead, cremation was to be substituted for burial without cost (*Pharos*, 7:1, February 1941: 7). In Camberwell, south London, cremations rose from 191 in 1939 to 450 in 1942, first overtaking burials in February 1943 (*Pharos*, 9:2, May 1943: 7). The same issue reported that, in the winter quarter of 1942–1943, the number of Barnes people cremated at Mortlake represented one quarter of the Borough's deaths (*Pharos*, 9:2, May 1943: 7). Such statistics hint that there must have been a shift among working-class families as well among the middle classes. The AGM of the Federation of British Cremation Authorities in June 1941 was told that cremation numbers had risen because of the new Regulations whereby medical certificates were dispensed with for the cremation of air raid victims (*Pharos*, 7:3, August 1941: 7). The correlation between death from air raids and burial/cremation choice needs much more critical attention and evidence. London was certainly the area most affected by bombing: in the four months from 7 September to 31 December 1940, London suffered 13,339 deaths. i.e. 22% of the total civilian war deaths of 60,595 (Longmate, 1973: 133).

But what was it about war deaths that may have helped more people to decide against burial? A Durham correspondent wrote to *Pharos* about the effects of high explosives dropped on a cemetery behind his house, 'The results were loathsome, an indescribable chaos of human remains, some of which were even thrown over the cemetery walls by the blast' (*Pharos*, 9:1, May 1943: 1). The funerals following air raids provided other forms of trauma. Hull's air raid of 9 May 1941, for example, was followed by the burial of two-hundred victims in a shallow trench grave. The burial service was timed for seven in the evening and passes for mourners to attend were allocated: just one close relative for each victim. Such practices, despite other attempts to militarise or personalise mass burials, were not popular for 'in the measures taken to control the funeral and its costs and contain any action that might be taken by the family to personalise the event, the state essentially configures the civilian war dead scheme as pauper burial, despite all its attempts to achieve the opposite' (Rugg, 2004: 23).

Similar clues are provided in an account by T. D. Dalglish, the Clydeside Cemeteries Superintendent, following the Clydeside air raids of 13–14 February 1941 (Dalglish, 1944). In that two night raid, 35,000 of Clydebank's 45,000 inhabitants were made homeless. All but seven of its 12,000 houses were damaged (Calder, 1969: 210). A short time before the raid, Dalglish had taken the precaution of having a large number of graves dug at Dalnottar Cemetery. After the raid, private interments began on Monday 17 February and continued throughout the week, the coffins being brought by lorry. Later on the Monday afternoon (the 4 p.m. departure from the mortuaries suggests dusk may have fallen by the time funerals began), the unidentified bodies, and the identified bodies which were unclaimed for private burial, were brought together from the mortuaries for common grave burial. A Union Flag was provided for each victim, and the Secretary of State for Scotland and other local officials were present. Both senior parish ministers and parish priests were invited 'as it was impossible to state which denomination each victim belonged to'. On the Wednesday, air raid victims who had died in the local hospital or bombed-out houses were buried, often as charred remains.

Several characteristics of the appalling experience of air raid bereavement may be identified: the trauma of the bombing experience and consequent sudden death on a mass scale; the shared ceremonies which the sheer weight of numbers involved, along with the restricted resources available, reducing the pre-war traditional procedures; the innate class-structures of Glasgow with some priority given to those whose families had purchased a private burial; for every family, the participation of Protestant and Catholic clergy will have been a unique departure from tradition in a sectarian-minded community; the trauma for families used to waking their dead in their own homes now having to attend funerals where remains could be both unidentified and incomplete; and the necessarily bureaucratic arrangements denied most families the opportunity of a say in the funeral arrangements. With all these arrangements made for a community where the Superintendent had had the foresight to make adequate preparations, one wonders what it was like for those communities where preparations had not been in hand. The Clydeside experience of communal burials hints at a deeper resonance. For months afterwards people came to the cemetery to enquire where loved ones were buried.

When informed that so and so was buried in the Communal Grave, they somewhat resented it and many demands were made on me to have the bodies lifted and interred on their own private ground. However, that was impossible, and when it was explained that the dead had received burial by the Minister, etc., the people were quite satisfied. I think these people thought that 'Communal' burial was a kind of 'Pauper' burial, and I would impress that point on you all in case you have at any time to experience it. (Dalglish, 1944: 11)

Dalglish's account is likely to be representative of a number of industrial cities following air raids.

Certain town councils promoted cremation by price adjustment: Southampton reduced its fees (*Pharos*, 7:1, February 1941: 2); Blackpool equalised burial and cremation fees (*Pharos*, 8:2, May 1942: 9); and the Mortlake Crematorium was so profitable, it levied no precepts on its constituent boroughs from 1943 (*Pharos*, 11:1, February 1945: 11). A very much larger number of authorities took steps to assess how cremation might help their plans for post-war reconstruction. The war-time pages of *Pharos* chronicle the progress of discussions at local authority level which resulted, by the end of the war, in over 200 local authorities putting in applications for crematoria. It was the war-time context that stimulated local government all over the country to invest in crematoria.

After the war, Benson offered two major reasons why public opinion had shifted towards cremation. 'Perhaps this was caused by damage caused by the enemy in cemeteries – but it seems much more likely that the pioneers of cremation were reaping the rewards of their work' (Benson, *Journal of the Institute of Burial and Cremation Administration*, 15:3, August 1948: 21). The country-wide surge of interest of local authorities suggests other critical factors were involved. Clarifying the relative strengths of these will require a thorough analysis of the Local Council decision-making processes in a representative sample, an analysis comparing Councils which followed through their initial explorations and made formal applications to the Department of State. This will require separate research probing the changes in attitudes to disposal and to cremation, in particular the changes which began in the 1930s. In the pages of war-time *Pharos* can be traced ninety of the two-hundred English local authorities which prepared plans for crematoria in their post-war reconstruction. These were examples of communities whose geography made land particularly scarce and for whom cremation represented economies both of space and of financial investment. Some of those ninety had to wait many years for their crematorium (like Peterborough, which finally opened in 1959). Some never followed the project through. Others never received permission. Others decided to combine with neighbouring authorities. A more precise chronological account of how local authorities were persuaded to advocate and provide for crematoria must await research into individual crematoria projects. Grainger's gazetteer will provide an essential basis for this task (Grainger, 2005).

More than any other individual, Lord Horder was responsible for the successful promotion of cremation during the War. He succeeded the Duke of Bedford as President of the Cremation Society in 1940 and was also its Chairman. His biography reveals him to have been extremely active in a variety of government work (Horder, 1966). He travelled the country on business both for the government and for the British Medical Association. He was in an almost unique position to press cremation's case with local political leaders. For example, when Coventry Crematorium had been opened on 23 February 1943, the ceremony was followed by a town hall meeting with an address by Horder. After the usual themes of cremation as a funeral reform, hygienic for human remains and healthier for mourners ('whose health resistance may have been reduced by long periods of anxiety'), with dual certification a virtual guarantee against crime, he stressed his personal theme of 'cemeteries or playing fields?' with special attention to the problems of post-war social reconstruction. 'To the municipal authority, faced with the problems of post-war reconstruction, and harassed by the lack of available acres, cremation offers a practical proposition' (Horder, *Pharos*, 9:2, May 1943: 2–3).

Undoubtedly, war-time experiences drew the attention of local authorities to the mounting difficulties in responsibility for the disposal of the dead, attentions that had been partially apparent in the inter-war years. The aspirations of cemetery superintendents, stimulated by increasing professional contacts throughout the 1930s, emphasised how fragmented and confused was municipal cemetery administration, where responsibilities were often distributed among competing committees. Government oversight was exercised principally through two departments, of Health for burial and of the Home Office for cremation. The legal position was even more complex than as presented by the cremation movement, the 1940 edition of Fellows' *Law of Burial* referring to 175 statutes, 120 of which were enacted before 1902 (Fellows, 1940).

There were different regional customs (Gorer, 1965) and wide variations in fees, including the historical differential charges levied by local councils and parishes for residents and non-residents. The left-wing Fabian Society in its *Funeral Reform* (Clarke, 1944; a 1943 Fabian article on 'Funeral Reform' was reprinted in the *Journal of the Institute of Burial and Cremation Administration,* 1944: 6–9) gave examples of fees charged by local authorities (between £1 and £3 for the common grave and £5 to £10 for the private grave (in London)); by crematoria (between two and eight guineas); by Churches (between 2/6 [12½p] to four or five pounds, with one Burial Board having 'a scale with at least a dozen different fees for the Religious Service according to the grave site and the time of the funeral'); and by doctors for cremation certificates (ranging between 10/6 [52½p] and five guineas [£5.25]) as well as their fee for countersigning Form A. 'Sentiment' was still strong: cemetery and crematorium staffs were well aware that bereaved families were being encouraged to overspend on funerals. When C. L. Hilton told the 1947 Cemeteries Conference that common graves should carry the lowest charges, a voice from the floor said that the reduction would still not prevent the family buying £100 worth of flowers (Hilton, 1947).

Some cemeteries and crematoria had struck bargains with undertakers to attract funerals. In October 1944, the Managing Director of the (then private) Aberdeen Crematorium was imprisoned for stealing 1044 coffin lids, some of which he had sold on to a local undertaker (*Pharos*, 10:4, November 1944: 2–3). The case embarrassed the cremation movement. The editor of *Pharos* commented that if public confidence in cremation were to be sustained, the highest standards of cremation must be maintained. Chairing the Cremation Society's AGM in June 1945, Sir George Elliston announced that the Society and the Federation of British Cremation Authorities had drawn up a Code of Conduct with a view to 'preventing a recurrence of other unfortunate incidents' (*Pharos*, 11:3, August 1945: 2). This prompted, some months later, the drafting of a *Code of Cremation Practice* which, with periodical revision, has been effective until the present day (see below, p. 143).

The war-time Coalition Government launched an enquiry into undertaking charges through its Central Price Regulation Committee (1943) and criticism of the profit motive in funeral directing was voiced more loudly after Labour was elected, with calls for undertaking to be nationalised (Allighan, 1947). This increased hopes that the Beveridge Report, in recommending a Death Benefit of £20 'would cut at the root of industrial assurance' and make industrial insurance schemes redundant. In 1944, the National Association of Cemetery and Crematorium Superintendents published its *Memorandum on Planning for Post-War Reform in the Disposal of the Dead.* This covered administration, finance, training and wages, town planning, cemetery and crematoria design and the role of disused burial grounds. It argued for the consolidation of all

Parliamentary legislation and the centralisation of services for disposal at local level. The Cremation Society had broadly parallel objectives for the post-war period, including the reduction of cremation costs, the standardisation of medical fees and the revision of cremation law (*Pharos*, 10:3, August 1944: 2–4). Thus stimulated by the general atmosphere of planning for post-war reconstruction (Garrett, 1943: 18), the cemeteries and cremation sectors committed themselves to reform (Batten, 1945; Eeles, 1945). Meanwhile, one of the major funeral interest groups, after years of war-time discussion, announced a change of direction. The Church of England had opposed cremation vigorously in 1874. In 1944 it announced its support for cremation.

In 1937, the Dean of Westminster, Dr Wesley Norris, petitioned the Lower House of the Convocation of Canterbury to make up its mind on cremation. As Chairman of the Central Council for the Care of Churches, Norris also sought a decision on policy for the disposal of ashes in parish churches. When clergy presided at cremations, were they offending the consciences of Christians who believed in the resurrection of the body? When the Prayer Book spoke only of the burial of the body and its burial in consecrated ground, was it lawful to scatter ashes, and was it lawful to bury or scatter them when the crematorium had no consecrated ground? In 1938 a joint committee of the Upper (Bishops) and Lower (Clergy) Houses of the Convocation of Canterbury was set up.

From 1937 until 1944, the Convocation discussed in both its Upper House and Lower House its theological and pastoral response to the growing requests for Christian cremation, complicated by the conditions of a nation at war. The Bishop of Norwich confirmed that the War had forced the Church to reconsider the cremation issue (*Chronicle*, Lower House, 20 May 1942: 231). For many clergy, this was a new experience: 'young chaplains and young curates were often asked to take a cremation service and they had not the slightest idea how to do it' commented the Archdeacon of Taunton (*Chronicle*, Lower House, 20 May 1942: 258). Increasing demands for cremation were forcing the Church of England to take a policy stand, one way or the other.

On 23 January 1942, the Revd C. E. Douglas persuaded the Lower House to form a small committee to consider proper forms of prayer for the cremation service. He recognised that some clergy thought there should be no prayer, while others used unauthorised forms (*Chronicle*, Lower House, 23 January 1942: 146). Personal interest was behind Douglas's request; twenty years earlier he had criticised Bishop Barnes for no longer believing in the resurrection of the body (Burge, 1922). Since 1924 he had been Proctor of the Convocation of Southwark and cremations at his local crematorium had risen to 400 per annum in the two previous years. The Lower House committee presented its report on 20 May 1942. The principal issue was whether any form of prayer was necessary for cremation. The main evidence came from the (Anglican) chaplain to a crematorium, who conducted between 200 and 300 cremations a year. In 99% of cases, he reported, ashes were scattered by the Superintendent in the unconsecrated ground of the Garden of Remembrance, 'privately and without prayer of any kind' (*Convocation of Canterbury. Lower House. Report*, 1942, No. 635: 1).

> It is clear that mourners desire and expect some form of prayer at the time of cremation and that, if incineration is not to be regarded as a substitute for burial, such form must be different from the order for the Burial of the Dead. (ibid.: 2)

The committee was thus faced with a situation where bereaved families regarded cremation as an *alternative* to burial, where they were content to let the service in the crematorium chapel be the last ritual word, and where they preferred the ashes to be scattered at the crematorium, rather than arrange for a subsequent service for the burial of the ashes on consecrated ground. The Church of England was thus confronted with a practice it would now be difficult to prevent.

Douglas was opposed to any suggestion that cremation be regarded as an alternative to burial. This would require a specific form of prayer for crematorium use which ought to avoid borrowing from the Burial use (*Chronicle*, Lower House, 20 May 1942: 249). The Dean of Gloucester disagreed: cremation should be regarded as an acceptable alternative to burial in the ground, like burial at sea: 'Was it any less Christian to commit the body to the flames in the name of God?' (*Chronicle*, Lower House, 20 May 1942: 251). He

> confessed he loathed the idea of cremation ... At the same time, he loathed himself still more for loathing the idea of cremation, because he thought that to loathe cremation was unscientific and antisocial and therefore unchristian. (ibid.: 251)

Canon Boughton supported the Dean of Gloucester. It was 'not right to regard cremation simply as a preparation for burial' (ibid.: 255).

A related issue was the point at which the funeral ceremony was completed. The Church's tradition had been to contain the whole action of burial within an envelope of Christian liturgy. But when did a funeral service for cremation cease – with the committal of the coffin to the cremator or with the scattering or burial of the ashes? Looking back from 1973, Friar commented that the general public felt overwhelmingly that the former was sufficient (Friar, 1982). Cremation as currently conducted meant that the Church neither had the last word, nor took charge of the remains by disposing of them in or upon consecrated ground. Canon Scott-Moncrief noticed that the action of cremation split the unity of both the liturgy and the body. The discussion, he said, had been based upon

> whether or not cremation was the end of the mortal remains of the dead person. It was the end of the body as an organism, but it was not the end of the mortal remains, as the ashes were still left. (*Chronicle,* Lower House, 20 May 1942: 257)

His personal practice was to persuade the relatives to bring back the ashes to be buried in consecrated ground. The Lower House voted to ask the Upper to give direction as to a form or forms of prayer for use when a dead body was to be cremated.

On 25 May 1943, the Upper House debated the report of the joint committee (*Convocation of Canterbury. Joint Committee. Report*, 1943, No. 627c). Introducing the report, the Bishop of Guildford referred to the crucial difference that had appeared between the two Houses:

> The line taken in the Lower House was that cremation was the preliminary to burial, while the Upper House rather held the view that cremation was a form of burial itself. It appeared that the only way to clear up the point was frankly to admit both points of view. (*Chronicle*, Upper House, 25 May 1943: 27)

The Bishops were clearly agreed that cremation was a permissible alternative to burial.

> As members of the Church of England, concerning ourselves with our own people, we are of the opinion that there is no objection to cremation, and that on social and hygienic grounds there is much to commend it, provided that due safeguards for decency and reverence are exercised. We attach no theological significance to the practice... We express our conviction that the practice of cremation does not in any way affect the Church's belief in the resurrection of the body. (*Chronicle*, Upper House, 25 May 1943: 28)

Such statements hint at the grounds on which the Bishops approved of cremation. First, the Bishops expressed no incompatibility between the Church's belief in the resurrection of the body and cremation. Secondly, cremation was to be recommended on social and hygienic grounds. Thirdly, Church members were already choosing cremation, and they did not find it incompatible with their beliefs. Fourthly, if people requested cremations, then the Church ought to accept their wishes. The trend, then, was being set not by a Christian theology of death but by the preferences of the bereaved:

> They (the Bishops) ought to think more of the convenience and wishes of the mourners, provided they did not ask for what was clearly unreasonable. (*Chronicle*, Upper House, 25 May 1943: 27)

The Bishops sought to recognise that three forms of cremation service were currently practised, and each should be acknowledged: the Burial Service in the Church, followed by cremation; cremation followed by the full Burial Service at the Church, the casket containing the ashes being treated in exactly the same way as the coffin; and the whole Service at the Crematorium, followed by either the interment of the ashes or the scattering of them, omitting to say whether consecrated ground was necessary. As for prayers, the Bishops concluded they should be left to the discretion of the clergyman, with the exception of the words of committal. These should be an adaptation of the Burial Service: i.e. 'Commit his body to be consumed by fire; commit his ashes to the ground, earth to earth, dust to dust'; or 'Commit his ashes to their resting place.'

As for scattering ashes, the Bishops of London, Salisbury and Guildford all thought ashes should 'not be permanently retained in unconsecrated grounds or buildings' (ibid.: 34). The only option then left for scattered ashes, therefore, was the Garden of Remembrance at the crematorium. The Bishops, unlike their clergy, did not want the Church to have custody of cremated remains. Yet the problem of scattering would not go away. Prayer was traditional at the act of interment, but where was it best placed at the scattering of ashes? For the committal of a body in a crematorium and the disposal of the remains involved *three* movements: the committal as the coffin passed (as on rollers) from the mourners' presence in the chapel, the insertion into the furnace, and the interment or scattering of the ashes. Cremation involved three separate stages and burial only one, a tri-section of the funeral service, which Lampard later commented the Church had never fully addressed

(Lampard, 1993). At what point was the committal prayer most appropriate? At the Bishops' next meeting, the Bishop of Guildford confessed that behind the forms of words for committal lay the division of opinion between the two Houses (*Chronicle*, Upper House, 26 May 1943: 76). The amended motion proposed that scattering should normally be done in a garden of remembrance, and 'if desired with prayer which may include the appropriate words of committal' (ibid.: 79). The motion was carried by thirteen votes to nine, a clear division between the two Houses on scattering.

The Lower House debated the issue again on 13 and 14 October 1943. Canon Edmond moved the acceptance of the Bishops' statement, including the phrases, 'we are of opinion that there is no objection to cremation' and 'We attach no theological significance to the practice' (*Chronicle*, Lower House, 13 October 1943: 234). The 'theological significance' was a critical issue in the Lower House. Douglas took exception to Edmond's statement that cremation did not affect the Church's belief in the resurrection of the body and produced an amendment:

> Provided that there be no intention to deny the Church's belief in the resurrection of the body, cremation of a dead body is lawful as a preparation for Christian burial in consecrated ground according to the order in the Book of Common Prayer. (ibid.: 261)

Douglas thus sought to defend three positions: the traditional theology, the traditional mode of disposal (for which cremation was only a preparation, not an alternative) and the final disposition in consecrated (i.e. Church-controlled) ground, but he lost by twenty-nine votes to twenty.

The debate on permissible types of service reactivated the divisions between the two Houses about ashes. The Revd W. R. Johnson thought scattering was not reverent disposal (*Chronicle*, Lower House, 14 October 1943: 307):

> Whatever one might think of cremation, the scattering of the ashes introduced another idea. If the ashes were kept together they were, at any rate in theory, the ashes of a particular person and represented that person's corporeal life. When the ashes were scattered an idea of dissolution of another kind was introduced. (*Chronicle*, Lower House, 13 October 1944: 266)

For the Archdeacon of Dudley, scattering discouraged sentiment, in particular 'the practice followed by some people of sitting beside a grave. Some people spent nearly all Sunday morning in that way' (*Chronicle*, Lower House, 14 October 1943: 313). Yet if clergy were forbidden to scatter ashes, then Convocation would have committed itself to the idea that 'the physical remains are the actual component parts of the resurrection body' (ibid.: 313). Three months later, the Lower House agreed to challenge the Upper House with Douglas' earlier amendment (*Chronicle*, Lower House, 21 January 1944: 120–1).

When the Bishops met on 24 May 1944, they discussed a slightly different form of words, as agreed by the meeting of the Joint Committee on 1 March. These words were clearly different in meaning from those agreed by the Lower House in January, the principal change being that: cremation of a dead body is lawful as a preparation for Christian burial *or* disposal in consecrated ground (*Chronicle*, Upper House, 25 May 1944: 184).

The Bishop of Birmingham, the modernist Dr Barnes, wanted to remove the preamble 'provided there be no intention to deny the Church's belief in the resurrection of the body':

> Belief in the resurrection of the present flesh had vanished; and if anything of that kind were put before our younger people who so often had had a scientific training, they were not so much indignant as amused. (ibid.: 185)

'The resurrection to eternal life' was the form he would like to see:

> Three-quarters of a century ago many people did actually believe that 'on the resurrection morning soul and body meet again'. We still sing the hymn but are careful to explain in teaching young people that the belief is not to be taken seriously. (ibid.: 186)

The Bishops unanimously agreed to omit the preamble, 'That provided there be no intention to deny the Church's belief in the Resurrection of the body' which left the first paragraph reading:

> Cremation of a dead body is lawful as a preparation for Christian burial or disposal in consecrated ground. (ibid.: 187)

The Bishops' intention was further clarified with the reiteration of their phrase from the previous year:

> For the avoiding of all scruple and doubtfulness it is declared: 1. That the practice of cremation has no theological significance. (ibid.: 189)

And what of the parishioners who still held scruples? The Bishop of Coventry thought 'they seemed to consider too much the people who had scruples – a particular minority – and to frame their policy in relation to them. The mass would be the sober-minded people who did not have scruples' (ibid.: 188). The final cremation debate on 11 October in the Lower House saw a critical Douglas chide both Dr Gorton about scruples and Bishop Barnes who had supported Dr Major twenty years before. But Douglas had clearly lost his case.

When cremationists assessed the debate, they were attracted most of all by the phrase that the practice of cremation had 'no theological significance'. Canon Rogers' words gave most satisfaction:

> The words adopted by the Upper House would convey a great deal of comfort to ordinary people and would convince them that if they wished to have the bodies of their relatives cremated their consciences need not be at all troubled in the matter. At the present time, when people were so much concerned about what was happening to the bodies of their loved ones, blown to pieces by shells and possibly having to be cremated on the battlefield, the clear statement adopted by the bishops would bring relief to people's minds. (*Chronicle*, Lower House, 19 October 1944)

There was no doubting the Church of England's new position. The doctrine of the resurrection of the body had been demoted. The substitution 'resurrection to eternal life' merged symbols and carried the suggestion that the future of the spirit was more important than that of the body. There was no reference in the debates to Saint Augustine's judgement that the mode of disposal did not affect the destiny of the dead themselves. The debate had been about the Church's authority and the position of mourners. The new position implicitly acknowledged that the choice and convenience of the bereaved was more important at funerals than the doctrine of the Church. This was, after all, the Protestant position carried to a further stage: for if there was no ultimate risk to the soul, then the funeral was of no consequence for the deceased and should therefore be utilised principally for the benefit of the bereaved. The new position was also a direct consequence of the 1850s' burials legislation. When the Church of England had surrendered control of the bodies of the dead, it gave up its control and monopoly on presidency at funerals, doctrinal interpretation, legislation and burial ground landscape (Jupp, 2001).

On 26 October 1944, the Archbishop of Canterbury, Dr Temple, died. After his funeral service in Canterbury Cathedral on 31 October, he was cremated at Charing Crematorium. His ashes were buried in the Cathedral Cloister Garth. Twelve months later, Temple's predecessor, the Archbishop in the Abdication Crisis (1936), also died and was cremated. Anglicans still hesitant about the legitimation of cremation could not have been set any stronger examples[2]. A new era had begun in the British way of death.

As suggested earlier, certain key interest groups moved during the War towards the acceptance and facilitation of cremation. The Church of England was the first. Meanwhile, many local authorities laid plans to upgrade local services after the war for the disposal of the dead. The wartime demands clearly contributed to the pressure for reform (Garrett, 1943), evidenced in the National Association of Cemetery and Crematorium Superintendents' *Memorandum* (see also *Journal of the National Association of Cemetery and Crematorium Superintendents*, February 1944: 6–9). The 1944 Memorandum sought burial law reform and greater co-ordination at local level. The disorganised nature of cemetery responsibility was indicated by the variety of committees to which different councils entrusted it, like the Baths and Washhouses Committee, or the Libraries, or the Markets, Housing or Public Health. Cemeteries became the 'Cinderella of the Department...There is no glamour or publicity in a cemetery' (Hilton, 1947: 12). The number of burials in common graves was going down.

Behind it all, the cost to local authorities of cemeteries had escalated, an issue which cremationists had regularly predicted. Burials nearly always involved local authorities in a loss. By 1950, the annual loss of £1 million calculated by Lord Horder in 1946 had grown to £1.75 million; the Secretary of State for Planning and Local Government, Hugh Dalton, accepted the results of P. H. Jones' survey showing that in 1950, of 559 local authorities making returns on burials, 555 were operating at a loss. In some areas the loss was more than £10 on each burial, e.g. Aldershot, Witney, Surbiton, Slough, Warwick, Sleaford, with Ventnor the worst at £15 9s 11d [£15.49p] (Dalton, 1951: 3ff.; for statistics cited, see Jones 1951: 2–4). Cemeteries took 500 new acres each year. With 200 local authorities applying for permission to build crematoria even before 1946, the era of popular cremation could not be far away.

The Cremation Society anticipated the post-war era with a sense of optimism. For seventy years, it had sought to persuade the public that cremation was in its best interests, especially in terms of expense and health. In 1945, the new Labour Government set out to make the most efficient use of British resources in a mood that seemed designed to put the disadvantaged first. This re-evaluation of traditions and resources was auspicious for the cremation movement.

The cremation movement was now in a strong position to exercise its influence. First, the Secretary of the Federation of British Cremation Authorities, Halvor Piggott, retired because of illness in 1945. From May of that year, Herbert Jones, the Secretary of the Cremation Society, took over Piggott's role in addition to his own. This amalgamation of roles was more easily made as in 1941 the Federation's office was bombed, and its shared residence with the Society had stimulated close co-operation. Secondly, the Cremation Society's Council represented to the Federation's Executive the need to draw up the Code of Cremation Practice (Cremation Society Council's Report for 1945, *Pharos*, 12:2, May 1945: 4). A text was adopted on 20 September 1945 (for text see *Pharos*, 11:4, November 1945: 2) and its provisions were highlighted in instructions distributed to funeral directors (ibid.: 3). Quickly adopted by the majority of Cremation Authorities (*Pharos*,12:1, February 1946: 1, 8), the Code was designed to improve ethical standards and to re-assure the public in the light of the Aberdeen coffins case. It was a key part of both Federation and Society strategy which Jones' dual secretaryship could lead. Thirdly, the Society published a third edition of *Cremation in Great Britain* as early as December 1945, distributing 500 copies free to public libraries. Fourthly, Society and Federation co-operated to form a new organisation, the Cremation Council of Great Britain. This enabled a more unified approach to be made to government departments to promote cremation. Fifthly, with a leader of national stature like Lord Horder and with Lord Beveridge among its new Vice-Presidents, the Society continued to exploit its many influential contacts.

The National Association of Cemetery and Crematorium Superintendents was first off the mark with a post-war conference, at London in September 1945. The Society held its own first post-war conference nine months later. Lord Horder surveyed the situation: many more local authorities had begun to consider cremation as a post-war policy to benefit their rate-payers and to fulfil their public health obligations, especially when land resources were so scarce. Councils were concerned for the new housing and for education, so Horder's pre-war motto 'Cemeteries or playing fields?' was now increasingly used (*Pharos*, 12:3, August 1946: 2). On burial law reform, Horder said:

There comes the need for modern legislation in keeping with the spirit of the age ... [and he added that] There is reason to believe that the Home Secretary is alive to the need for revision. (ibid.: 4)

Horder pressed the economical advantages that cremation offered to the bereaved. Horder also had his eye on town and road planning. Motor-driven funerals immeasurably strengthened the hand of local authorities when they sought new planning sites for crematoria.

Horder had developed strong contacts with political leaders over the years. He knew Aneurin Bevan well, and was currently locked in the British Medical Association's battle with Bevan's Ministry of Health over the proposed National Health Service (NHS). He arranged that both Bevan and Fred Marshall, the Parliamentary Secretary to the Ministry of Town and Country Planning, be invited to speak at the Society's conference. The support of Marshall's Ministry was critical, not only because 200 local authorities were applying for permission to build crematoria, but the cremationists needed the relaxation of the 200 yard rule; all actions pertinent to a Socialist Government favouring both funeral reform and planning legislation within a welfare state. When Bevan spoke at the 1946 Cremation Society's Conference, he warned the audience that the building of houses had first claim under current building restrictions. Speaking as a Minister, it was not for him 'to express favour for one form of burial as against another, especially when the subject is beset with sacerdotal enthusiasm'. Nevertheless, his personal choice was quite clear:

> Cremation is a much more speedy and hygienic method of disposal than burial. It substitutes a comfortable chapel for the service to that of the graveside, and as I have been a victim of some burial services on the Welsh hillsides I very deeply appreciate that point. (*Pharos*, 12:3, August 1946: 6)[3]

Commenting on the 1946 conference, Jones sounded the Society's new policy note. The pre-war joint conferences with those interested in the promotion and maintenance of burial would cease. Henceforth cremation-only conferences would be an annual feature. Jones wrote:

> Nothing could be clearer than that to revert to the old-time system of joint conferences in conjunction with the burial interests would be folly in the highest degree. (*Pharos*, 12:3, August 1946: 3)

With hindsight, this was a strategic miscalculation based on an underestimate of the increase of cremation. As will be described below, this separate policy lasted only five years. In 1950, the Federation resumed a joint conference arrangement with the Institute of Burial and Cremation Administration (the name which the National Association of Cemetery and Crematorium Superintendents had adopted in 1947). In the longer perspective, the growth of cremation was the effect of local authority policy and investment on which the Institute and the Federation were allies, representing both employees and employers. After 1950, the Education gradually developed its own identity again whilst, with the popularity of cremation, the Society's major work of promotion cooperated with local authorities' service provision.

Anecdotal evidence suggests that the irascible character of Herbert Jones – for five years dual secretary of the Society and of the Federation – was responsible in part for exacerbating tensions between the Society and the Federation, particularly over issues of training, conferences and policy. For example, the Federation, containing large numbers of elected Councillors, considered that crematoria could best be accommodated inside cemeteries, whilst the Society advocated the ideal of crematoria on separate sites despite the severely limited land resources available. Jones was an inveterate and highly knowledgeable promoter of cremation, but during 1945–1949 he held too many reins in his hands. He was also outspoken in his long-standing antipathy to burial, arguing, for example, that after 1945 came 'a flood of progressive ideals and a natural desire for improvement in all departments of life. Local Authorities which had shown little interest in the subject [of cremation] came to see that the burial system was an anachronism in an age of progress' Jones was addressing the Cremation Society Conference in 1949, at a time when the burial rate was still 80% (Jones, 1950: 5–8).

The antagonism had other bases than personal antipathies. Their rivalry focused, first, on there being arguments over the training of burial and cremation staff. Practical arguments about conference arrangements became more public. In November 1946 (*Pharos*, 12:4, November 1946: 10) the Federation's AGM instructed its Executive to arrange a joint conference with the Institute, but on 26 November the Federation's Executive decided on a cremation-only conference in 1947, at Cardiff. This was the pattern for 1948 and 1949 also, but both conferences witnessed scraps between the opposed positions; in September 1948 the Institute invited the Federation, the Society and the Cremation Council (see below) to a joint conference in 1949 (*Journal of Burial and Cremation Administration*, 15 (4): 16) but this invitation was refused (*Journal of Burial and Cremation Administration*, 16 (1): 9).

In 1949, Benson's attempt to move a resolution for joint conferences to be resumed in 1950 was discouraged by Hugh Royle, from the chair.

At the Federation AGM one month later, the Executive's proposal for a cremation-only conference was overthrown by the members. Rugg has commented (personal communication, 2005) that this indicates that Federation members, many having day-to-day experience of the public's needs, knew that burial and cremation facilities should be provided in tandem. The outcome of the Federation's AGM was the prompt resignation of Herbert Jones as its Secretary, followed by that of Royle as Chairman. With Jones' departure from his key Federation role, the Federation and the Society began to take separate roads towards the promotion of cremation. They continued to work together through the Cremation Council until the passing of the Cremation Act 1952. In the summer of 1952 the Council was disbanded.

On 20 September 1945, when Jones had been Secretary of the Cremation Society and of the Federation of Burial and Cremation Authorities for four months, the Federation had agreed in principle to a fusion with the Society. The Cremation Council was set up as a joint Federation/Society instrument to 'act as the central authority for the Cremation Movement, and to be the vehicle of approach to Government Departments' (*Pharos*, 12:1, February 1946: 10; *Pharos*, 12:2, May 1946: 4). From 1945 up to 1952, the Cremation Council was very active in tackling the Government. Despite Bevan's personal encouragement and his interest in joint applications, his Ministry of Health rejected every crematorium application from local authorities from 1945 to 1947, very largely on grounds of financial stringency. For example, by December 1945, the Ministry of Health had turned down applications from Accrington, Weston-super-Mare and Oldham. During 1946 it rejected applications from Darlington, Exeter, Liverpool and Manchester. This was discouraging to the large number of local authorities who had included crematoria in their post-war reconstruction plans.

In 1947, frustrated by the Ministry of Health's successive rejections, the Cremation Council adopted a new policy. It chose fifteen authorities with the most pressing claims. It submitted to the Ministry a memorandum passed by the Cremation Conference in 1947. This was at Cardiff where Dr William Price's last surviving daughter Penelopen was a welcome guest (*Pharos*, 14:1, February 1948: 4–6). The request was denied. The Council tried again, reducing its list from fifteen to five. Discussions with the Ministry followed. In December 1948, the Ministry gave limited permission: six authorities could submit building proposals: Kingston-on-Thames, Blackburn, Grimsby, Southend-on-Sea, Bolton and Sunderland. In addition, Ashton-under-Lyne and Dukinfield

Joint Burial Committee was invited to submit an application to convert a cemetery chapel into a crematorium.

This long-awaited decision signalled a new government policy of encouraging local authorities to phase in cremation to supplement burial, albeit by authorising expenditure and resources at a very restrictive level. The log-jam was broken. It was not a speedy process: Sunderland was only opened in 1951. In 1949–1950, the adaptation of cemetery chapels for cremation was permitted at Hartlepool, Middleton, Northallerton, Oldham and Skipton. In 1951, permission was given to South-West Middlesex, Halifax, Wolverhampton and Portsmouth/ Gosport. Any concern that rate-payers' money would be wasted was dispelled by endorsement from the public. The number of cremations continued to grow.

Progress of cremation in the United Kingdom between 1945 and 1952

Year	No. of crematoria	No. of deaths	No. of cremations	Percentage
1945	58	550,763	42,963	7.80
1950	58	574,297	89,558	15.59
1952	63	558,994	107,699	19.27

Source: Mortality Statistics from ONS and General Register Office, Scotland. All other figures from Cremation Society of Great Britain.

Insufficient credit has been given to Bevan as a promoter of cremation. As Secretary of State for Health, Housing and Local Government, he held, in one pair of hands, control of the very Ministries whose support was most critical in the promotion of cremation by local government. In statements formal and informal he would have been able to galvanise local and national support for cremation on grounds of better health, better stewardship of land resources, family purses and local government budgets. Furthermore, as an atheist brought up in and representing a Welsh industrial constituency moulded by Nonconformist culture, he had no personal convictions or interest to encourage him to uphold Christian traditions about burial, despite the Nonconformist tradition of his constituency's culture.[4]

Bevan's support for cremation was paralleled by that of the Home Secretary, J. Chuter Ede, who in September 1947 set up an Interdepartmental Committee to examine the regulations on cremation. This seems to have been a response to concerted action from several directions. First, on 29 June 1945, Sir George Elliston, Horder's successor as chairman of the

Cremation Society Council, and Herbert Jones met with senior officials at the Home Office to discuss amendments to the Cremation Act
1902 and the Statutory Rules and Orders 1930. They were informed that
the Secretary of State had already called for suggestions for revision of
the latter (Cremation Society Council Report, *Pharos*, 12:2, May
1946: 4). Secondly, on 10 October 1946, the Cremation Council
decided to write both to Bevan and to Ede, the letter to Ede on 8 November
carrying a Memorandum; but even before that date it was learned that
an Inter-Departmental Committee was in process of formation and
by whom the Memorandum would in due course be considered (see
Pharos, 14:1, February 1948: 4–6, which includes a copy of the Memorandum). Thirdly, the government's intention was again reflected in the
paper of Gary Allighan, MP, to the Institute of Burial and Cremation
Administration's conference in 1947 (Allighan, 1947). His proposals for
the municipalisation of the funerals industry met with such a positive
response that a motion was passed:

> That this Conference urges the Minister of Health to set up forthwith
> a Commission of Inquiry to investigate the conditions existing in
> the essential public service for the disposal of the dead.

As the Home Secretary constituted his Cremation Committee on 1 May
1947, the Institute's resolution, in the event, proved unnecessary. Its
significance lies in the fact that it revealed that Local Authorities
around the country were broadly in favour of combined national and
local governmental action to secure cost-effective reforms in the
disposal of the dead.

Four departments were represented on Ede's committee: the Home
Office, the General Register Office, the Ministry of Health and the
Department of Health for Scotland. Austin Strutt, Home Office representative, told the Cremation Society conference in 1951 of the origins
of the committee (Strutt, 1951). One was the 1940s' rise in cremations.
A second was public concern about malpractices at crematoria (like the
Aberdeen case). Despite the voluntary code of practice adopted by the
Federation, the Government considered that if cremation was to grow,
then it should be regularised. The principal recommendations, as
published in 1950 (Cremation Committee, Cmd. 8009, 1950), were
that, first, the siting, establishment and approval of plans for all
crematoria, public or private, should have prior official approval. This
would require the amendment of the 1902 Act. Secondly, inspection
of crematoria had been somewhat haphazard hitherto. Now that 'the

establishment of crematoria is developing as a local authority service' (ibid. Cmd. 8009, para. 11) there should be more local supervision. Thirdly, crematoria practice should involve greater care for coffins. Each coffin should be cremated separately. There should be no interference with the coffin once it had arrived at the crematorium, save for one exception: metal fittings might be removed from the coffin before incineration. The ashes resulting from each cremation should be kept separate. Fourthly, staff recruitment should be improved. Lack of skill had been evidenced by complaints to the Inter-Departmental Committee in respect of parcels of ashes sent to relatives but lost in the post. Fifthly, the committee recommended the extension of the 1902 Act, which stipulated that the wishes of any person known to have left written instructions forbidding his cremation should be honoured. Cremation should also be prohibited when the deceased 'was known to have held views or beliefs inconsistent with cremation' (ibid. Cmd. 8009, para. 16). This clause safeguarded the Catholic position.

It was a sixth recommendation that caused the most difficulty for the committee. This concerned certification; the committee recommended that Cremation Certificate A (deceased's prior consent) should be dispensed with but, to save the trouble of legal amendment, where the application for cremation was not to be made by the next-of-kin or a relative, an assurance should be given that the deceased had concurred. On Certificate B, the committee recommended an amendment to permit certification by the doctor *to the best of his knowledge and belief* if he had visited the deceased within fourteen days prior to his death.

Certificate C, the confirmatory medical certificate, proved a contentious issue. Sir Henry Thompson had first proposed the confirmatory certificate to allay suspicions that cremation might hide forensic evidence. Nevertheless, the need for the second certificate and the increasing and varying costs of certificates had severely irritated supporters of cremation. In the committee's Report, there was a clear division of opinion between the professional and trade bodies whom the committee had invited to give evidence. The abolition of Certificate C was recommended by the Cremation Council, the Cremation Society Council, the Proprietary Crematoria Association, the Association of Municipal Corporations, and the Society of Medical Officers of Health, all clearly supporting local authority interests' in crematoria.

These groups alleged that in the majority of cases both the confirmatory examination and the certificate were treated in a perfunctory manner. Secondly, the charge for the certificate constituted a deterrent to a family to apply for cremation. (There was no standard charge for certificates which therefore varied from doctor to doctor). Thirdly, there was no case in which the enquiry necessitated by the confirmatory certificate had led to detection of crime in fifty years. Arguments for the retention of the certificate were made by the Director of Public Prosecutions, the Coroners' Society and the British Medical Association (BMA). The Coroners' Society wanted no relaxation of the arrangement which, for it, prevented the concealment of crime by cremation. The BMA affirmed that the necessity for two certificates was 'sound and in the public interest' (ibid. Cmd. 8009, para. 38).

The committee recommended the retention of Certificate C. It knew it restricted applications for cremation, it judged it unnecessary as a safeguard, but concluded that it was 'an essential item in the system'. The medical profession, with the Coroners, had clearly won their argument. Strutt explained a little of the context. At the very start of the committee's work, a doctor in Southport had sought to murder his wife and to conceal his murder by cremation. After police enquiries had commenced, he committed suicide and the doctor who conducted the post-mortem also committed suicide. This made it 'absolutely impossible [for the Committee] to proceed on the basis that experience over a long period of time showed that Certificate C was no longer necessary' (Strutt, 1951: 21).

In the new post-war era, funeral directors were also taking stock, and contemplated the advantages of cremation to their profession. The war had had a crucial effect on the undertaking industry. The war and post-war austerity proved successful where both Wilson and the National Council for the Disposition of the Dead had failed. The funeral director George Rose described the post-war changes in the funeral directing service in his home city of Nottingham where the undertaker traditionally performed his funeral work as a sideline (Rose, 1991). In 1939, there were 300 undertaking firms in Nottingham, most of them wheelwrights, joiners, painters and decorators. When 'one of the six funerals a year took place, all other work stopped. The french polisher was called, and the trimmer for the coffin interior. A hearse would be borrowed and the top hats dusted down'. By 1950, only 30 funeral directors remained, one tenth of the number in 1939. Slum clearance meant that there was no longer the population for a neighbourhood firm to serve. Bereaved families' perceptions also changed. 'Before the war, for example, a ride in a motor car was a novelty. When all families had access to some sort of car, hearses had to be smartened up.' The upward shift in business rationalisation and professional self-image change also phased out another traditional undertaking service, the layer-out. 'This woman ruled the neighbourhood, as a midwife at birth and at death when she dealt with the corpse. She herself called out the street, organising hospitality, a collection and ensuring that traditional courtesies were arranged' (Rose, 1991; Adams, 1993).

It seems to have been the Co-operative Societies which stimulated the general upward change in funeral directing. When they improved their premises and their facilities, every competitor had to follow suit. No one has yet attempted a business history of the Co-operatives' contribution to the funeral industry; this would hugely illuminate the rationalisation of funeral directing which predated the acquisition policies of the Great Southern Group in the 1970s and of Hodgson in the 1980s (Hodgson, 1992; Parsons, 1999). The growing pressure to compete with others increasingly challenged smaller firms. Housing conditions in the post-war era also played a part. On the new housing estates, where people were able to invest more in privacy and comfort with through living-rooms and central heating, it became impractical to keep a dead body at home. This coincided with the hospitalisation of the dying from the 1950s onwards. This shift of care for the corpse was also commercially encouraged by the funeral director (Howarth, 1996; Bradbury, 1999). A south-Midlands funeral director indicated that his business improved tremendously from the advantages of refrigeration and the chapel of rest.

> When someone was laid out at home, I had three men flat out making the coffin to fit and take round. That was a lot of overtime to pay. Once I could persuade people to let me take the corpse off their hands, I could make the coffin in my own time, and cut my bills. And I didn't have to persuade them too hard. They were really very relieved not to have the burden of having someone in the house all the time to look after their [dead] Dad. (Frank Wilson, personal communication, 1992)

This aspect of the distancing of death, then, was not only the work of hospital staff: it was also an agreement between the funeral director and the bereaved family.

The amalgamation and take-overs steadily continued in the funeral directing industry (Parsons, 1999). This enabled, for the surviving firms, the more efficient use of two particular resources, providing shelter for the corpse and the replacement of horses by cars. As regards the former, an increased concern for public health was one contributing factor, but the advantages of a chapel of rest did not dawn on the funeral trade until the mid-1930s. Refrigeration techniques, developed before and during the war, enabled the funeral director to offer shelter for the corpses between death and funeral. This, combined with the development of embalming techniques, enabled a process whereby the funeral director took charge of the body, with the realisation that control of the body was fast becoming the key to funeral rituals, and to the funeral director's enhanced role (Parsons, 1999).

The motor vehicle, introduced in 1905, was originally used for the collection and long-distance transportation of bodies. Motor driven funerals became a necessity during the Second War. The car was cheaper and easier to care for than the horse; with its greater speed, 'the pace of the funeral procession was quickened and the time required for each ceremony reduced' (Howarth, 1997: 132). It fuelled the fashion for simplification of the funeral and the distancing of disposal. It made the conveyance of coffins and families to crematoria a much more economic proposition, enabling funeral directors to conduct more funerals each day. Chapels of rest, motor hearses and facilities for cremation were all combined to simplify and streamline the traditional British funeral; and bereaved families with, increasingly, other demands on their time contributed to the process. It was during the 1940s that funeral directing companies realised the commercial advantages of cremation.

The post-war Labour Government, pursuing its welfare programme, introduced new benefits for bereaved people in 1946, seeking to liberate them from reliance upon industrial assurance. The Fabian Society detailed the pressures exerted by 60,000 part-time salesmen selling burial insurance on the doorstep (Clarke, 1944). Whilst people were not thereby entirely freed from financial anxiety following bereavement, it was significantly reduced by four types of benefit from national insurance: widows' benefits and Death Grants, with guardians' and children's special allowances (George, 1968). Under the pre-war national insurance scheme, widows received ten shillings [50p] per week, irrespective of age, employment or age of children. The 1946 benefits were designed to meet the varying needs of widowhood at different ages and in different circumstances. The scheme recognised that widowhood, sudden or anticipated, inevitably involved financial, social and emotional adjustments. It therefore paid the widow a higher rate for the first thirteen weeks, and thereafter, following Beveridge's recommendation (Beveridge 1942: 64), encouraged return to work. Allowance was made for widows with dependent children and those too old – over fifty – to adjust to work outside the home.

The Beveridge Report (1942) recommended a national insurance benefit for funeral expenses. The Death Grant was, for an adult, £20 in 1948 and paid to everyone. It was raised twice, to £25 in 1958 and to £30 in 1967. Thereafter, the value of the Death Grant was allowed to decline so that it no longer fulfilled its original aims. In 1987 it was replaced by other Social Security Death Benefits. Its aims were modest but it relieved some pressure from funeral expense and industrial assurance. It was designed partly to end the shame of the pauper funeral whose decline was accelerated in the increasingly affluent society of the 1950s. The conditions of the pauper funeral were, however, steadily removed by the break-up of traditional neighbour-hood communities and by the increased prosperity of the post-war years, as Rose testified for Nottingham (Rose, 1991). The Death Grants await their own history. Their introduction helped to reduce class divisions in British funeral behaviour, to which the provision of crematoria was immeasurably to contribute.

The Cremation Act 1952 was the fruit of the Interdepartmental Committee on Cremation Regulations. The Cremation Society asked a member of its Council, Joseph Reeves, MP, to promote a Private Member's Bill for cremation. The resulting Act was very largely Reeves' work (Reeves, 1952).

Reeves consulted Home Secretary Ede, who gave his promise that, if the Bill obtained a Second Reading in the Commons, he would guar-antee the necessary parliamentary time. The second Labour administra-tion (1950–1951) had a fragile majority. A Private Member's Bill offered the only chance of parliamentary time. Reeves began his preparations but the Labour Government fell and a Conservative Government was returned. Reeves had to start again with the new Home Secretary, Sir David Maxwell Fyfe, who intimated his support for the Bill. Reeves then carefully chose his day as early as possible in the new Parliament: 30 January 1952, the second day of the first session following the Christmas recess. The Government was only three months old. Reeves hoped by this stratagem to ensure that his Bill led the field, ahead of other Private Members' Bills.

The new Prime Minister, Winston Churchill, announced he would tell the Commons of his conversation with US President Truman, followed by the Chancellor of the Exchequer battling with a financial crisis, both now booked for 30 January 1952. Reeves had to argue his Bill in the ten-minute space between Prime Minister and Chancellor. The Commons Chamber was full and somewhat annoyed when Reeves was called. Reeves spoke for just five minutes and received the consent of the House.

The committee stage was eventually set for 1 April. To enable the approval of building of crematoria, Reeves kept his amendments of the 1902 Act as brief as possible. They included enabling local authorities to establish crematoria either singly or in combination; reducing the radius clause to 100 yards; abolishing Statutory Declaration 'A' (which had obstructed cremation applications by the requirement to arrange and pay for a statutory declaration); authorising the Home Secretary to set maximum fees for doctors' cremation certificates; amending the definition of a 'burial authority' to apply to any local authority or combination of them (previously, only those authorities which were already Burial Authorities could so apply); ensuring that all sites and plans for crematoria were approved by the Ministry of Housing and Local Government. These amendments, if passed, would enable local authorities to overcome limited land resources and thus help bereaved families.

In March there was an unforeseen obstacle when amendments were tabled by Gilbert Mitchison, MP for Kettering. His main concerns were, first, that only local authorities should be empowered to build and run crematoria (thus excluding both County Councils and private companies); and, secondly, that the two hundred yard rule should be retained. It had been the preference of the Interdepartmental Committee to reduce the radius clause, but this would have involved amendments to the 1902 Act, whereas the Committee's remit was in respect of the 1903 Regulations (Reeves, *Proceedings of the Cremation Society Conference*, 8 July 1952: 20).

Reeves discovered that these amendments had come from the Federation which had thereby resiled from the recommendations it made to Home Secretary, Ede, in 1947. He learned that a number of Town Clerks had written to Mitchison claiming, amongst other things, that the two hundred yard rule should be kept principally because of smells. According to Pharos, Mitchison 'claimed to represent the views of the Association of Municipal Corporations' (*Pharos*, 18:2, May 1952: 3). Reeves did his best to counter these objections but his room for manoeuvre was limited as only one morning was allowed for the committee stage. The Committee rejected the building restriction (thus ensuring the private sector's involvement) but retained the two hundred yard rule by two votes (Reeves, 1952).

The Act received the Royal Assent on 26 June 1952, the Government having provided for a three month period thereafter to pass the revised Regulations (for the text of *The Cremation Act, 1952 Statutory Instruments 1952 No. 1568* see *Pharos*, 18:4, November 1952: 6–7). The passing of the Act was, in retrospect and in comparison with its predecessor fifty years before, relatively easy. The stage was now set for the development of cremation, chosen by one fifth of the population for their funerals in 1952. The 1950s and 1960s saw an unparalleled and accelerated rise in the provision of crematoria.

7
The Popularisation of Cremation in England, 1952–2000

In the 1950s and 1960s the cremationists' 75-year campaign came to fruition. Between 1952 and 1970 the cremation rate rose from 19.27% to 55.41% and the number of new crematoria rose from 63 to 206, the vast majority being built by local authorities. The huge increase in building brought crematoria within most urban families' reach. In 1964 the Vatican relaxed the Catholic ban on cremation. The influx of Hindu migrants from the Indian sub-continent further bolstered religious support for cremation. After 1970 the onward pace of cremation slowed but it passed 70% during the late 1980s. In the increasingly consumerist culture in the 1990s, public attention turned to improving the quality of funerals. The cremation process was particularly affected by the Environmental Protection Act 1990, in an increasing context of ethical issues around death. The government became interested in a wide range of death issues, in the active participation of which the cremation movement entered the twenty-first century.

There are indirect correlations in this period between the rise in the cremation rate and the decline in church adherence. Behind the secularisation characterised by declining church attendance lie such issues as new opportunities and life chances as changes in educational provision, career choice – especially for women – leisure options, greater prosperity with the wider availability of consumer goods and the sexual revolution, all of which promoted a more hedonistic way of life. This was a bias towards immediate consumption rather than postponed gratification which had characterised religious guidance over long centuries of limited life and health chances.

In this shift of values, new attitudes to death, the corpse and funeral practice are revealed. The work of Davies (Davies, 1990,

1997c; Davies and Shaw, 1995) and the current Sheffield research into changing habits in the disposal of cremated ashes will hopefully answer some of these questions (Kellaher *et al.*, 2004). Was there a taboo about death (Walter, 1991a)? And if so, what was its contribution to the choice for cremation? Did it encourage simpler forms of funeral and memorialisation? Detailed studies of families' funeral histories will help.

The Cremation Act 1952 gave local authorities many of the powers needed to help further crematoria projects. The identity of the Federation of British Cremation Authorities was reasserted by the break with the Cremation Society and with the renewed joint conferences drew strength from regular consultation with the cemetery interest. In 1988, Ernest Turner, then Secretary of the Federation, criticised the Cremation Society's post-war action in adopting a negative stance towards local and national government:

> After 1945, when the cremation figures began to grow, the Cremation Society decided that the time had come to sever all connections with organisations having anything to do with cemeteries and burial, because it thought that such associations were detrimental to the cause. The Federation took the opposite view, believing that the public were more likely to be weaned than bulldozed... (Turner, 1988: 86)

Such differences should not be exaggerated: the pages of *Pharos* and the Cremation Society's *Conference Proceedings* reveal through the 1950s and early 1960s much evidence of continued and dynamic co-operation between Local Councils and the Society, to which Jones fully contributed. In 1957 Jones was congratulated for successfully persuading the Ministry of Housing and Local Government to redefine the radius clause. Now, whilst crematoria, lodges, chapels and grounds for the scattering of ashes fell within the 1902 Act Section 5, other areas of the site did not. This had the effect of freeing up councils' planning decisions for cremation projects, especially in urban cemeteries. When Jones was succeeded as Secretary in 1963 by Kenneth Prevette, there were over 170 crematoria. The Society, like its sister organisations, the Institute and the Federation, maintained good relationships with national government, particularly with the Home Office. The private sector seemed content to leave the initiative to local authorities and did not rush to seek new sites.

Progress of cremation in the United Kingdom between 1952 and 1970

Year	No. of crematoria	No. of deaths	No. of cremations	Percentage
1952	63	558,994	107,699	19.27
1955	82	580,509	141,353	24.35
1960	148	588,032	204,019	34.70
1965	184	612,247	271,130	44.28
1970	206	638,834	353,957	55.41

Source: Mortality Statistics from ONS and General Register Office, Scotland. All other figures from Cremation Society of Great Britain.

Meanwhile, suburban development and the relaxation of building restrictions, together with the adoption of motor transport by funeral directors and the spread of car ownership among the general population, ensured that the two hundred yard rule was not the major problem previously feared. In 1952, over 20% of funerals involved cremation. An increasingly prosperous and healthy society could afford to turn its attention to money-making and spending. This helped to fuel new opportunities for social and geographical mobility that, combined with the shedding of restraint, poverty and traditional class barriers, helped to switch the attention of many people towards more hedonistic lifestyles which, with increasing good health and longevity, distanced the prospect of death (Martin, 1978a).

Institutional Christianity was unable to compete with the prevailing fashionable liberal morality (Hastings, 1987; Davie, 1994). It was at once insufficiently authoritative to combat less orthodox Christian sects and largely welcoming to the other traditional major religions which accompanied immigration from the Old and New Commonwealths. Paradoxically, the policy of co-existence undermined its own position, encouraging a growing sense that all religions were the same and could be taken, or left, as a matter of ethnicity, leisure pursuit or personal choice; the Christian religion was of less authority when offering interpretations or solace at a time of death (Wilson, 1966: 92–3). Once Catholicism accepted cremation in 1963, the mode of disposal of the dead was decreasingly of denominational importance for people born in a Christian culture. With the growth of Islam and Hinduism, for whom burial and cremation were the respective rules, urban local authorities knew they had to offer both forms (Friar, 1968; Cribb, 1980), and the choice of disposal became a matter of ethnic custom or personal choice. As an issue for controversy, the religious factor in disposal became almost irrelevant.

During the 1950s, cremation was solidly established as a public service, funded by local authorities. By 1960, one third of funerals involved cremation and 148 crematoria had been built. Overtaking burial could not be far away, even though on two long-standing issues – dual medical certification and the Roman Catholic position – there was little progress in the 1950s. Nevertheless, the financial benefits for local authorities of the rising cremation rate had become apparent, and the Joint Board principle made a substantial contribution to building development.

Progress on crematoria building was initially slow. During the 1940s and 1950s several combinations of local authorities sought to follow the successful precedent set in 1939 at Mortlake, following either Joint Board or Joint Committee procedures (Glossop, 1947). No post-war Joint Board Crematorium experienced as many difficulties as the South-West Middlesex Crematorium, first proposed in 1942. Three neighbouring authorities reached agreement on a parliamentary Bill by December 1945 and earmarked a site to prevent interim housing development, which would trigger the 200 yard rule. The Act received the Royal Assent on 18 July 1947. In December 1947, the Ministry of Health agreed to the site purchase but would not authorise building. Meanwhile, three other authorities sought to join the project, requiring a second parliamentary Act, passed in 1950. The final architect's plans were passed and tenders received; the Ministry hesitated again and finally permitted tenders to be invited but only for half the building project. The Ministry again delayed the start, twice, until it finally gave permission in November 1952. With only half the proposed buildings, the crematorium opened in 1954, to serve a total population of 600,000. The South-West Middlesex Crematorium development had experienced the most trying problems and in the worst economic circumstances (Jamieson, 1954). The joint principle proved both a warning and a model, eighteen joint crematoria being built over the next twenty years. Joint projects enabled poorer or less populous communities to share a facility and, meanwhile, the more that crematoria produced an excess of income over expenditure, other local authorities were encouraged to find the finances to build their own.

Throughout the 1940s and early 1950s, the Cremation Society and the Federation of British Cremation Authorities, for all their enthusiasm and effort, were repeatedly delayed or rebuffed by the Ministry of Health, the Ministry of Housing and Town Planning or its successor, the Ministry of Housing and Local Government. In June 1953, Jones advanced a national plan (Jones, 1953b). This proposal may seem to have been long overdue, but during the war so many crematoria had been projected that such a plan seemed unnecessary and during 1945–1951 national resources were so limited that it was impractical. The more relaxed 1950s provided the first practical context in which a plan could be proposed to harness the pro-cremation impulse of local government in a practical way. Jones noted that by 1953 the cremation rate exceeded 20% and the pressure for housing and recreational facilities had forced a more utilitarian and less sentimental assessment about the disposal of the dead; yet an understanding that the Minister responsible would allow an annual number of crematoria to be built had not been honoured. Among examples cited, Halifax and Huddersfield each sent 700 cremations a year to their nearest neighbouring crematoria in Leeds and Bradford; and Slough's population had risen from 10,000 in 1914 to over 70,000; yet none of these had a crematorium of its own; and the second generation of new towns offered the cremation movement a new opportunity to press the land-saving advantages of cremation.

The Society approached the Ministry of Housing and Town Planning with a memorandum for a national policy based upon population requirements. Encouragement was given to Huddersfield and Slough and to projects for the West Country and for Kent (White, 1954). Nevertheless, several years elapsed before these promises bore fruit: Huddersfield was not opened until 1958, and Slough until 1963; Truro and Torquay were both opened in 1956, but Exeter had to wait until 1963.

Of the two long-standing obstacles to cremation choice, the death certification issue was persistently pressed by the cremation movement. Certification procedures were a hindrance and an expense. First, funeral directors reported that Certificate A, requiring a statutory declaration, involved the expenditure of both time and money in contacting a person authorised to administer the oath; it deterred families from pressing for an original cremation choice. (This was a decade in which the majority of homes still had no telephone.) Secondly, there being no standard fee, doctors charged varying fees, and these had increased since the Cremation Act 1952 had been passed. It was regularly claimed by the cremation movement and by medical referees that the attention given to the dead body by the second doctor was so perfunctory an inspection as to be useless. Dr Francis Camps, the Home Office pathologist, made regular visits to the Joint and Society conferences. His favourite examples included doctors' failures to notice one case of stabbing and another of strangulation, and of doctors placing their own signatures in the space intended for 'cause of death'. Seventy-five percent of all certificates refused by Registrars proved to have been completed incorrectly by doctors (Camps, 1969: 52). These arguments were regularly rejected by the British Medical Association. Jones (1953a) surveyed selected regions, revealing variations of between two and four guineas for certificates. Reeves passed these to the Home Office and raised Parliamentary questions. The Home Office, clearly unwilling that the Home Secretary should prescribe the maximum fee level as he was entitled to do, passed on a new communication from the British Medical Association that the latter had itself informed doctors that a suitable fee for either certificate was two guineas (£2.10) with travelling allowances. Despite this being a long-running issue, the paradox was that the cremation rate continued to rise and indicated that the confirmatory certificate was no longer such a great barrier to cremation choice. The steady shift in location of death to hospitals and other institutions increased the availability of doctors. The increased rationalisation of funeral directing procedures made the certification more of a matter of routine; the cost of certificates seems to have been increasingly overlooked by the public in the more prosperous climate of British society. Nevertheless, for practical or symbolic reasons, neither the cremation interest nor the British Medical Association was willing to jettison its position on dual medical certification. Following further pressure from Reeves, the Home Office offered a Working Party representing the interested groups. These included the Home Office, the Ministry of Health, the Department of Health for Scotland, the Federation of British Cremation Authorities, the Cremation Society, the Proprietary Crematoria Association and the Institute of Burial and Cremation Administration.

This working party first assembled in 1959 but, meeting only twice a year, its progress was slow. There was no meeting of minds on medical certification between the cremation movement on the one side and, on the other, the British Medical Association, the Association of Municipal Corporations, the Association of Crematorium Medical Referees, the Director of Public Prosecutions and the Police. A decision by Ministers was required. In the Cremation Regulations 1965, the government retained the second medical certificate. Defending the Home Office decision, G. I. de Deney told the Cremation Society Conference that, regarding doctors' procedures, he was 'not going to be drawn into a detailed discussion of whether criticisms are valid that it [Certificate C] was completed in such a perfunctory manner'; yet these criticisms were a substantial part of the cremationists' case for the abolition of Certificate C. On the forensic issue, there were about 150 murders each year in the UK. 'We have little or no evidence to suggest that any considerable number of homicides do escape detection' but 'if we made any relaxation which had the effect that only one murder was committed that wouldn't otherwise have taken place the Home Secretary would then be subject to most serious criticism' (de Deney, 1964). Hindsight suggests a political context: the Conservative Government had already encountered considerable criticism in its search for a solution to the increasingly loud calls of the anti-capital punishment reform lobby (Potter, 1993). The Labour Government of 1964–1966 fulfilled a manifesto pledge for the abolition of capital punishment. This was not the appropriate climate in which to press for the abolition of Certificate C.

The working party made progress on some other matters. It had not previously been lawful to cremate unidentified remains nor the remains of anyone known to have left a written note to the contrary. Facilities were eased for the cremation of remains given for anatomical research and of unidentified remains. Funeral directors were particularly grateful for the shift of the decision as to whether to cremate away from the person who had just died to the next-of-kin. A funeral director, Mr Roberts, described his earlier problems arranging funerals among the retired community along the South Coast:

> We have an application for cremation from a person probably dying in Bognor where there are no relatives, either in a boarding house or a home, and the relatives come down, we will say, from Birmingham, Nottingham or the Midlands, who is the Executor to make the application? We can find nobody who can vouch for him, so he has then to take Application Form A right the way back up to the North, post it off to us with a delay of probably two days before we can get these papers to the crematorium. (Quoted in *Proceedings of the Cremation Society Conference* 1959: 31)

In 1963 the British Medical Association published a report on Deaths in the Community (BMA, 1963). This argued that the existing law failed to ensure that causes of death were established with sufficient accuracy and hinted that murders might still go undetected. The Home Office set up a committee under Judge Norman Brodrick. The new Labour Government was pledged to abolish capital punishment and it was presumably important to ensure that murders might not go undetected.

The Brodrick Committee took six years. The exasperation of the cremation movement is evident from the successive reports of both the joint and the Cremation Society conferences. The Report, when finally published in 1971, pleased both cremationists and funeral directors. It considered that the British Medical Association had been unduly alarmist: and that the threat of undetected murder was totally non-existent. Among its recommendations were that statutory forms A, B, C and F should be abolished; that the office of Medical Referee should disappear; and that a certificate for disposal issued by a registrar of deaths, or by a coroner in the event of an inquest, should be sufficient authority for either burial or cremation. Brodrick said that his committee had not taken lightly the recommendation to equalise certification for burial and cremation. The Committee believed the threat of undetected murder as a result of deficiencies in the present law was exaggerated. The Committee was convinced that its proposed new legal safeguards would be more effective, although they would result in more post-mortems (Brodrick, 1972).

The cremation movement's satisfaction was short lived. The Brodrick Report was never fully discussed in Parliament and never became law. The reasons have never been explained, but pressure from the British Medical Association is often mentioned by cremationists.[1] Both Federation and Society switched their criticisms to the rising costs of the dual certification, but by 1971, the cremation rate stood at over 60% of all funerals. The practice of cremation had been taken up by the majority of the British, despite the benefits and disadvantages of the secondary certificate. This raises the intriguing judgement that the certification issue may have become in the 1960s something of a traditional and symbolic concern for the cremation movement: it had posed inconvenience for funeral directors and superintendents, but once cremation became the majority choice its administration became routine. Until the murders by Dr Harold Shipman became public knowledge in 1999, the certification issue remained dormant for thirty years. Nevertheless, it is the public who still has to pay the increasing costs of dual certification, estimated at £35 million in 2000.

In 1964 a significant religious change facilitated the further expansion of cremation. On 2 May the British *Sunday Times* broke the news that the Roman Catholic Church had relaxed its 1886 ban on cremation. The decision was apparently taken the previous year when the Pope circulated a confidential letter to bishops, but secrecy was imposed by the Holy Office.

The new Catholic stance was largely the result of an initiative by the International Cremation Federation. The war itself had an indirect effect. Post-war reconstruction promoted the swifter popularisation of cremation in European countries, notably those where Catholic hegemony was weaker, in societies either newly Communist, or where post-1918 political boundaries had strengthened areas of Protestant culture. The growth of cremation in post-1918 Austria and Czechoslovakia made the International Cremation Federation all the more anxious to effect change in other Catholic territories after 1945 (Jupp, 1993b). The International Cremation Federation's Congress at The Hague in 1948 wrote to Pope Pius XII, but unsuccessfully (*Pharos*, November 1963: 9ff.). In 1954, Herbert Jones, in his dual role as Secretary of both the Cremation Society and the International Cremation Federation, met the papal nuncio in Paris, Cardinal Roncalli. On 28 October 1958, Roncalli was elected to succeed Pius XII as Pope John XXIII. On 25 January 1959, Pope John announced new initiatives. One was the revision of the Code of Canon Law, last revised in 1917. A second was the calling of a Vatican Council.

Cremationists were anxious to seize the opportunities offered by these two initiatives. At the International Cremation Federation Congress at Stockholm in 1960, Dr Michelfeit, President of the Austrian Cremation Society, successfully proposed a solution based on the Catholic distinction between divine law and human law (Thurston, 1936: 1–2). The former, the *Jus Divinum*, was unchangeable, being understood to have divine origin. The latter, the *Jus Humanum*, was the creation of the church; it could be tailored to the requirements of different dioceses when it became the *Jus Singulare*, a category particularly relevant in times of plague or in missionary contexts as in India or Japan.

The International Cremation Federation believed that the arguments behind the Vatican's 1886 decision no longer applied. First, the Federation proposed cremation for aesthetic, sanitary and economic reasons. Secondly, it claimed always to have refused to have recourse to ideological, religious or political motives. Thirdly, it claimed never to have adopted a hostile attitude to any Church. The Federation felt it important to disassociate itself from former Masonic and other anti-Catholic movements. Dean Rald, a Danish Lutheran minister and President of the Federation, presented the case for cremation as one of individual choice for the mode of disposal which was to do with neither doctrine nor dogma:

> The Christian message of resurrection and eternal life...will not be less trustworthy or realizable in the world of faith whether our perishable bodies are destroyed by twenty years in a grave or in one hour by fire...Our Christian faith is entirely independent of the attitude practical reasons make us adopt to the matter of cremation. (Rald, 1962: 16–17)

Rald and Michelfeit met with the Vatican's Cardinal Bea. He left them with the impression that cremation was an issue to which the Catholic Church no longer attached much importance. Rald and Michelfeit changed their strategy, encouraging individual Cremation Societies to approach national Catholic leaders. By September 1962, letters had been sent to 270 Bishops throughout the world urging them to consider removing the ban. Optimism grew when the Council's Disciplinary Committee placed the issue on the agenda of Canon Law revision. The Vatican Council's decision was approved by Pope Paul VI on 6 July 1963, becoming public news ten months later.

The Church's Instruction recognised that cremation was not in itself an assault upon the Christian religion, although it had been an instrument wielded by those who wished to deny the resurrection of the body and the immortality of the soul:

> The burning of the body, after all, has no effect on the soul, nor does it inhibit Almighty God from re-establishing the body again. Cremation does not, in itself, constitute a manifest denial of the above-mentioned doctrines. (*Acta Apostolicae Sedis Official Commentary*, 24th October, 1964, Section III, 5:13, 822–3, cited in *Pharos*, February 1965: 15)

Yet an association was still to be maintained between care for the dead body and belief in its resurrection. Thus the Church continued to encourage the burial tradition:

> The greatest care must be taken to see that the custom of burying the bodies of the faithful must be preserved intact. Therefore the Bishops should see to it that... Christian people should maintain the present custom of burial and not abandon it unless driven by necessity. (ibid., cited in *Pharos*, February 1965: 15)

Canons 1203 (2), that cremation was forbidden, and 1240 (1) that those requesting cremation should be deprived of ecclesiastical burial, now only applied when cremation was decided upon as a denial of Christian teaching, for propaganda purposes, or out of hatred for the Catholic Church and the Faith. The whole effect was the easing of the ban on, not outright acceptance of, cremation. This was evident in the penultimate paragraph:

> In order, however, to prevent undue damage being done to the feelings of the Church's tradition in the minds of Christ's faithful people,

and in order to demonstrate unmistakably the Church's opposition to cremation, the rite of Christian burial and the accompanying public prayers may never be held at the crematorium itself, nor may the cortege be accompanied even without ceremony. (ibid., cited in *Pharos*, February 1965: 16)

In this new situation, the Cremation Society invited Cardinal Heenan of Westminster to suggest a Roman Catholic priest to join its Council. Monsignor John McDonald was nominated; he became the Cardinal's adviser on cremation and played a vital role in promoting cremation among English Catholics and resolving tensions when they arose. For Catholics in the UK, two issues emerged, the first being financial. Now that cremation was permitted, it could put pressure on Diocesan budgets. The Catholic Bishop of Salford complained to Monsignor John McDonald that Salford's Catholic Cemetery began to lose money after the relaxation of the cremation ban (McDonald, personal communication, 1991). Whatever the reasons, no Christian Churches in Britain have yet built their own crematoria, unlike the Lutheran Church in Sweden (Jupp, 1993b: 133–45).

The issue for mourners was that of the ban on Catholic clergy accomsdpanying the coffin to the crematorium. McDonald's paper at the Cremation Society conference in 1965 'caused something of a hulla-baloo' (McDonald, personal communication; extracts from the discussion following his paper are reprinted in 'The Catholic Church and Cremation', *Pharos*, November 1965: 81–2). This led to a conference resolution to Cardinal Heenan, the leader of the Catholic Church in England and Wales. The resolution read:

That (a) owing to the absence of a Roman Catholic priest at the crematorium, and the concern and sorrow caused to the relatives at a moment when they most need the comfort of a priest, and (b) since many Roman Catholics in perfectly good faith, and in the natural and understandable belief that any clergyman is better than no clergyman, accept the presence of a minister of any denomina-tion when they reach the crematorium before the final stage. The Authorities of the Church be respectfully requested to permit the presence of a priest in the crematorium chapel which would be appropriately prepared for the occasion. (cited in *Pharos*, November 1966: 91, 93)

Prevette, the Cremation Society Secretary, in submitting the conference resolution to the Cardinal, deliberately stressed the fact that families were so unwilling to let their loved ones go to their cremation without prayer that the prayers of 'any minister would do' (McDonald, personal communication). McDonald took the resolution to Cardinal Heenan who took it to the Pope. On 9 July 1966 a new Instruction was approved by the Congregation for the Doctrine of the Faith. On 23 September instructions were sent to all priests in England and Wales: 'Hitherto a body to be cremated was not accorded Christian burial. At the request of the Hierarchy the Holy See has relaxed this rule for England and Wales. You may attend the crematorium and conduct an appropriate ceremony' (cited in *Pharos*, November 1966: 92–3).

The take-up of cremation by British Catholics was neither immediate nor speedy. In 1975, there were only 11,319 Catholic cremations in Britain, far less than a quarter of the number of Catholic funerals (McDonald, 1975: 388). There was clearly official resistance, with a number of bishops failing to issue the Instruction (Defoe, 1971: 643; Russell, 1965: 37). By 1983, McDonald commented that there were 'many Catholics who still do not know the position of their church with regard to cremation' (*Pharos*, November 1983: 147). Nevertheless, liturgical provision was made fairly early. In December 1967 an Order of Service for use by Catholics at a crematorium in England and Wales was published, followed by a revised version in 1973 (also approved by the Scottish bishops) which included a service for the burial of ashes. Pastoral Directives were issued in England in August 1969 (McDonald, 1975). There were still no guidelines yet for the disposal of cremated ashes. McDonald's own preference was for the burial of ashes as burial symbolised more nearly

the belief in the resurrection...God by His almighty power can bring back the body from ashes as easily as from dust...but the Christian faith of the doctrine of the resurrection of the body is more clearly symbolised by burying what remains in a tomb or in a grave and then awaiting...the resurrection. (McDonald, in *Pharos*, February 1975: 38)

It is likely that Catholic clergy, when first conducting cremations, would instinctively follow the traditional line. Indeed, when Monsignor McDonald died in 1992, Cremation Society Council members attended his funeral at Westminster Cathedral and, later, found themselves standing around an open grave.

Catholic cremations in the UK did not accelerate until the 1980s. Cremation liturgies are set out in the *Order of Christian Funerals* (1990). The Catholic Church has followed the Anglican 1944 decision, that is, with cremation assumed into the funeral liturgy as an alternative to burial. Cremation has its place in the Rite of Committal, following celebration of the full funeral liturgy with the dead body present (Rutherford, 2001). The politico-religious situation in the UK was neither that of competitive pillarisation as in the Netherlands (Keizer, 2005) nor of a country throwing off its right-wing, Catholic-dominated past in a drive for modernisation as in Spain (Chulilla, 2005). Yet in the UK the Vatican's decision was critical for attitudes towards cremation generally. By removing its ban, the Catholic Church further contributed to the removal of the religious factor in the British mode of disposal, as far as Christianity was concerned. The Orthodox and Caribbean Christian minorities, like Jews and Muslims, could follow the dictates of their religious traditions and their ethnic culture. For the vast majority of Christians in Britain, cremation was, from now on, a matter of personal choice.

The period 1971–1988 proved, in retrospect, a quieter one for the cremation movement in general. The cremation rate moved beyond 60%. The opening of a new crematorium became a more rare event. The 'taboo' upon death discussed by Gorer's article 'The Pornography of Death' (Gorer, 1965) was consistent with the professional profile adopted of cemetery and crematorium staff. The discretion of local government arrangements for the disposal of the dead was exemplified by the comment of 1969's President of the Institute of British and Cremation Administration, 'In these islands, I feel, we have the finest funeral system in the world, with the impact of death on the community not too apparent. I want it to stay that way' (cited in *The Observer*, 13 July 1969). The public's corresponding lack of interest in funeral issues was instanced by Lord Stoneham:

> The modern development of cremation has been a silent revolution, one of the sincerest tributes that can be paid to your movement is that the public hear so little about it. We must realise that there would be nothing to gain and much to lose by making the subject of the disposal of the dead one for more general public attention. (Stoneham, 1967: 13)

Progress of cremation in the United Kingdom between 1970 and 2000

Year	No. of crematoria	No. of deaths	No. of cremations	Percentage
1970	206	638,834	353,957	55.41
1975	218	645,876	394,909	61.13
1980	220	644,684	420,717	65.26
1985	222	654,701	443,687	67.77
1990	225	629,629	438,066	69.58
1995	229[+]	649,635	445,574	68.59
2000	243[++]	611,960	437,609	71.51

Source: Mortality Statistics from ONS and General Register Office, Scotland. All other figures from Cremation Society of Great Britain.
[+] The first crematorium in Northern Ireland was opened in 1995.
[++] Includes Arnos Vale, Bristol, which closed in 1998.

The day-to-day issues faced by staff were reflected in their conference proceedings and professional journals. Naturally, many of these reflected the concerns of local government, whose reorganisation was recommended in the government's Maud Report: cemeteries and crematoria seemed to have been overlooked as J. W. Roberts said, 'It was ludicrous and in the worst possible taste that cemeteries should be grouped with Baths and Wash-houses – they should be with Health' (Roberts, 1967: 37). There were fears about the status of superintendents, the comparatively low rates of pay, the shortage of recruits, and the failure of local authorities to insist on training programmes – all issues clearly related – as well as the introduction of work study and incentive bonus schemes. In 1979 there was a strike by cemetery workers in Liverpool (Blackwood, 1979). This was a reflection of the worsening national economic situation, with growing inflation under the Wilson, Heath and Callaghan governments from 1964–1979, and the international fuel crisis resulting from the Middle East conflict of 1973.

This situation brought increasing concerns for greater efficiency and lower maintenance costs; for cemeteries, these increased development of lawn cemeteries, with the removal of grave curbs. Despite the growth of cremation and the inflow of funds, cemeteries and crematoria still felt they were rated unfairly. Despite the amount of land saved by cremation, cemetery land was still an increasingly rare resource; Gayner was one of the first to propose the re-use of old graves (Gayner, 1970). In crematoria, the Book of Remembrance and the rose bush were now the most popular (and most profitable) memorials, and there was a new interest in the contribution memorials might make to helping bereaved people (Clegg, 1988). Meanwhile, old burial grounds were a continuing problem (Dunk and Rugg, 1994). In disused cemeteries, problems of maintenance grew, especially of old memorials, long neglected by their own families, and often damaged with the increase of vandalism (West, 1996). There was the growing issue of the exhumation of ashes, when families moved house and wished their dead to be relocated with them, and in old cemeteries where permission had been given to redevelop a section for road-widening or property development. Planning authorities made strange decisions: Southend-on-Sea crematorium objected that its borough proposed to develop adjacent land as a football stadium, dog-racing track and weekday trading market (*Resurgam*, 1989: 78).

Given the energy crisis, the efficient use of fuel was a regular topic, especially with the introduction of natural gas and, later, with commercial attempts to develop cheaper electricity. The first post-war generation of cremators had posed problems of smoke and noise; whilst these had largely been cured, the deterioration in cremator installation and maintenance in the 1970s brought demands for higher standards from and greater competition among manufacturers. Music, car parking and traffic management, and relations with clergy and funeral directors were regular items, together with occasional anxiety that the wrong body had been buried or cremated. The disposal of cremated remains seems to have been solved by the development of Gardens of Rest, encouraged from the 1930s; 15% of cremated remains were taken away by relatives, but little significance was accorded this at the time.

In 1989 P. W. Cribb wrote his last editorial after thirty years as editor of *Resurgam*. He regretted the general downgrading of the status of the cemetery and crematorium superintendent. This was not conducive to recruiting, or retaining, the best officers. He also regretted 'the apparent disregard for the public on the part of so many cremation authorities. It seems that in many cases the convenience of the public is the last consideration and their nuisance is barely to be tolerated' (though this applied to other departments too). Whilst there were model services, 'we have cemeteries and crematoria which close for long periods at Christmas and other holidays, offices which are open only at inconvenient times, out-of-hours bookings are not accepted and there is a general air of "take it or leave it"' (Cribb, *Resurgam*, 1989: 90–1). It was not that the managers themselves entirely neglected their clients: attempts to understand families' changing needs had been, from the 1960s on, a regular feature of Conference agendas with, for example, the funeral customs of immigrants (Friar, 1968), changing social attitudes to cremation (Thomas, 1976) and the psychology of grief

(Hinton, 1972) all being indications of a greater interest in the needs of bereaved people and of an open ear to current research from outside the funeral services.

During the 1980s, the social culture of the nation began to change under Thatcherite financial regime which meshed with the corresponding principles of the consumer movement initiated by Michael Young and his Consumers' Association (Dench *et al.*, 1995). In 1991 the Office of Fair Trading published a report on funerals which, while mostly criticising funeral directing procedures, levelled the phrase 'conveyor belt' at the cremation process. K. C. Briggs, President of the Federation, was well aware of crematoria where 'Twenty-two services a day through one chapel cannot serve the best interest of the bereaved' (Briggs, 1989: 22). The interest of the general public was also aroused by the increasing media attention to people bereaved in the series of human and natural disasters in the later 1980s which gave people permission to speak more freely about dying, death, funerals and memorialisation. The 1990 disaster Hillsborough football (Walter, 1991b) was a major factor in this process, further stimulated by the circumstances of the death and funeral of Diana, Princess of Wales (Walter, 1999b). Roger Arber who became secretary of the Cremation society in 1982 led the society's contribution in the new stages of cremations development and was also elected as Secretary General of the International Cremation Federation in 1990.

Meanwhile, the spread of television from the late 1950s stimulated an increased market for visual representation in which death played its part. The Northern Ireland troubles began again in 1968; real and violent deaths became a staple feature of print and media journalism, alongside fictional ones. In the early 1980s the public became rapidly aware of the spread of HIV/AIDS. Whilst there were few signs that the public taboo about death was beginning to break down (Walter, 1991a), the media were able to exploit any scandals at cemeteries and crematoria.

Three incidents in the late 1980s may be seen as a harbinger of a new era in which cemetery and crematorium service, consumer expectation and media interest came into sufficient proximity to bring death matters up to a far more public exposure. First, in Merthyr Tydfil, South Wales, it was discovered in 1987 that cemetery staff, faced by a shortage of burial space, had covertly dug up coffins after burial and relocated them in the cemetery to make room for fresh interments. Secondly, in June 1987, *The People* headlined an article 'Gold from bodies sold as scrap' which helped to reveal that some precious metals left in the ashes at four UK crematoria were being sold for charity. Thirdly, in

February 1988, Westminster City Council sold off three cemeteries to a private developer, for a total of 15 pence. Westminster City Council had hoped that the new owners would balance the maintenance costs by the opportunity to rent or sell off the cemetery lodges, but, following a public outcry, the Council had to re-purchase the Cemeteries for a much higher sum.

Death was found to be increasingly newsworthy, especially as the late 1980s brought a series of unrelated disasters: the Heysel football stadium, the Hungerford shootings, the Lockerbie bombing, the *Marchioness* Thames disaster, the Bradford football stadium fire, the Piper Alpha oil rig fire, the sinking of the cross-channel ferry *The Herald of Free Enterprise* and the Hillsborough football disaster. Walter was one of several sociologists to assess the significance of public and press reactions to Hillsborough (Walter, 1991b): ordinary people were beginning to express emotions more publicly and the media seemed to have adopted a monitory mode, 'the policing of grief' (Walter *et al.*, 1995; Walter, 1999a).

The economic climate of the Thatcher governments brought a new discussion of the relative costs of burial and cremation. The first was the *Audit Commission Occasional Paper 8*, 1989. Entitled *Managing Cemeteries and Crematoria in a Competitive Environment*, the paper was concerned to achieve the reduction of costs and an increase in revenue for a local authority service whose principal objective was the 'dignified disposal of the dead' (Audit Commission, 1989: 9). Cremation was far more economical than burial. Crematoria made a slight profit and saved 200 acres of land each year. Burial cost local authorities £40 million each year. Cemeteries occupied 16,000 acres of land, principally in and near urban areas. Whilst seeking to leave the disposal decision with individuals and families, the paper made suggestions as to how savings might be implemented and income increased. Cemetery staff costs amounted to 56% of expenditure. The Local Government Act 1988 required compulsory competitive tendering. This legislation affected maintenance standards (regularity of grass-cutting, economies in horticulture) and maintenance methods (more mechanised gravedigging, the continued encouragement of lawn grave sections and the removal of kerbstones) and the reduction of overtime (with the discouragement of Friday afternoon and Saturday funerals). Cemetery income covered 28% of expenditure. As for crematoria, staff costs amounted to 39%. The Audit Commission's first recommendations on more cost-effective burial at first seemed likely to encourage among the bereaved just those elements of status in grave-choice and expenditure on memorials that were prominent 160 years previously. Its stimulus over the following years – before it was succeeded by the Best Value regime – was to increase the cost of burial. The Audit Commission Report, however, made no reference to the environmental threat which was to dominate the cremation service for the next decade.

The Environmental Protection Act (EPA) 1990 proved even more influential. As indicated earlier, the reform of funerals and the British way of death were partly promoted, by Dr George Walker and his supporters from 1839, as part of a public health agenda. The *Health of Towns* and *Interment* reports and the 1850s burial Acts were the result of a shift in the frame of reference of the British way of death. In 1874, cremation was also proposed as a more sanitary way of disposal than burial. In the second half of the twentieth century, public health concerns were amplified by an environmental focus. In 1956 the Government introduced the Clean Air Act, following the Beaver report upon industrial pollution: London smogs passed into history. The chemical industries produced hazards of their own. Legislation like the Disposal of Poisonous Wastes Act 1972 signalled an increase of government concern about the environment (Bartlett, 1991). In 1988–1989 environmental pollution became a major political issue. Within a year, increasing government pressure in a European context led to speedy legislation, the Environmental Protection Act 1990. This brought sudden and enormous problems for the cremation service. The environmentalist campaigning group, the Friends of the Earth, published an *Environmental Charter* which recommended cremation be discouraged in favour of burial. The cremation process had not then been singled out as a significant polluting process (Wilson, 1991) but local authorities, as the major provider of cremation services, had to act responsibly and speedily.

The EPA came into force on 1 January 1991. The regulations required massive alterations or entirely new equipment with new or higher chimneys, staff retraining, continuous monitoring equipment and the requirement of a secondary cremator chamber for the most effective elimination of pollutants. The challenge to Cremation Authorities was given the acronym BATNEEC, 'best available techniques not entailing excessive costs', whose joking alternative was CATNIP, 'cheapest available technology not involving prosecution' (David Smale, personal communication). The response of crematoria to the demands of the EPA was led by the Federation, especially through its successive Secretaries Peter Wilson, Jon Luby and Bernard McHale. The cost of the conversions required by the EPA, for the, then, 225 crematoria in the

UK, was estimated at £70 million (Horan, 1991; Wilson, 1991), a figure revised upwards by Bernard McHale, Federation Secretary, as £120 million (McHale, 2001: 20). Most of these costs were passed on to families. Funeral costs escalated during the 1990s.

As for the cremation process, pollutants had two sources: the human body and the coffin. Both affected funeral directors' procedures and supplies. Artificial body parts needed attention before the funeral, with pacemakers being removed. The EPA challenged existing coffin manufacture: 90% of UK coffins were then made of chipboard, its bonding including synthetic resins and cellulose lacquer. An upgraded chipboard was required to reduce the formaldehyde content by 66%. Metal and melamine were now unacceptable. Coffins had often been lined with PVC sheeting which, when ignited, gave off black smoke and the toxic gas, hydrogen chloride. The EPA outlawed the use of PVC, bitumen and pitch. The interior fittings of the coffin were now to be made of fibre, either cellulose or synthetic: polyester and acrylics were no longer acceptable. This required some sensitive advice to families where youngsters had died and, as football fans, might otherwise have been cremated wearing their football strips.

The EPA galvanised the funeral industry and cremation facilities. Cremation Authorities were set the task of meeting the requirements of the EPA by 1 April 1998, for which no local authority had expected to budget. There was unexpected help when, on 2 August 1995, the Conservative Government published a Private Finance Initiative (PFI) which offered incentives to local authorities to sell off certain assets, including crematoria. Only the Cooperative Funeral Societies and the American-owned Service Corporation International (SCI) had the capital available to acquire them. There was critical reaction from consumer groups. Michael Young, now Lord Young of Dartington, spoke against the PFI in the Lords (Young, 1995). In the event, only two public crematoria passed into the private domain. Ian Hussein, Institute Secretary in 1996, attributed this to two major factors: the operating surplus produced by crematoria for local authorities, and the fact that most local authorities were then controlled by Labour, for whom the privatisation of a sensitive public service would invite criticism (Hussein, 1997).

In 1988, unaware of the imminent EPA, the editor of *Resurgam* stoutly maintained that crematoria should remain within the public domain (*Resurgam*, 31: 3, 1988: 53). In 1996, Hussein conceded that a mix of private/public partnership was now the way forward (Hussein, 1997). In the event, crematoria authorities completed the EPA's modernisation programme by 1998. Despite some public concern at the outset, the increased costs represented approximately £30 for each cremation, an average increase of about 10% on that portion of the funeral bill that covered the cremation. It seemed that the whole experience affected the confidence of local government authorities as the owners and managers of the majority of crematoria. The development of locally owned crematoria continued to slow down. The numbers of privately owned crematoria increased: they had few burial losses to offset, and in 10% of cases were now connected to funeral directing businesses.

The environmental challenge deepened, with a specific concern about mercury. The government's concern with mercury had formally begun with the 1992 Convention for the Protection of the North East Atlantic, thereafter called OSPAR as it merged the former Oslo and Paris Conventions on sea- and land-based pollution. One of the key drivers in the UK Government's strategy was the target date of 2020 for cessation of the use of specified hazardous substances. One property of mercury as a hazardous substance is that it does not degrade either in the air or in the sea. Mercury emissions from crematoria were identified as a significant source of mercury pollution, for which there were no international controls. Within OSPAR, consideration of each hazardous substance was given to a lead country; mercury was handed to the UK. A significant proportion of mercury emissions came from the cremation of the mercury contained in dental amalgam. Whilst the proportion of the UK population with dental fillings was steadily declining, the age-profile was such that, by 2020, the dominant pollutant would be mercury because British industry as a whole would by then have reduced its own pollution in mercury and other elements to a low level.

The cremation movement would have to commence a second stage of installation of filtration and gas-cleaning. Some estimates spoke of costs approaching nearly £200,000 per crematorium, nearly double what Cremation Authorities had to raise in the 1990s for the EPA. The Federation of British Cremation Authorities and the Cremation Society co-operated in funding an independent survey of mercury emissions, as they believed the government's estimate was too high (Edwards, 2001). McHale, as Federation Secretary, organised a seminar in March 2000 for Cremation Authorities to discuss the issues, followed by a survey of Cremation Authorities which revealed that, in the light of the projected costs of new technology, up to 23% of crematoria might be closed by their local authorities on the ground of costs.

As Local Councils would be taking their decisions separately, this raised the possibilities of two particular spectres. First, specific neighbouring local authorities might close both of their crematoria, thus depriving population clusters of a cremation service. Secondly, a regional system of crematoria might be established with local chapels for the funeral service and cremation taking place at large sites some distance away. This would create such distances between crematoria and local 'chapels' used for families' funeral services that the British way of death would be dramatically altered, with results so far uncalculated. The Federation and the Society began a new era of active co-operation in the cremation interest, awaiting the government's response to the results of its survey.

Public dissatisfaction with aspects of the funeral system gave rise to a number of agencies which sought to reform funeral behaviour, whose general aim was to transfer more of the decision-making process back into the hands of bereaved families and away from the professionals. Some took as their guide Walter's *Funerals and How to Improve Them* (Walter, 1990) and Spottiswoode's autobiographical *Undertaken with Love* (Spottiswoode, 1991). In 1992 Young set up the National Funerals College, a project to stimulate better funeral practice. It published *The Dead Citizens Charter* (National Funerals College, 1996, 1998; Jupp, 1997b) promoting the rights of dying and bereaved people. Given the context of John Major's Conservative Government's Charter policy to empower the public to exercise rights to better services, the charter concept commended itself to the Institute of Burial and Cremation Administration. Ken West, the reforming Superintendent of Carlisle Cemeteries and Crematorium, and Ian Hussein together pioneered the Institute's *Charter for the Bereaved* (Institute of Burial and Cremation Administration, 1996, 1998). This met with some initial opposition from within the cemeteries and crematorium system and from funeral directors, but has proved particularly effective because it came from service providers. The Institute's development of an associated 'Charter mark' system steadily helped cemeteries and crematoria to achieve higher standards of service, partly supported by the Labour Government's 'Best Value' project for local authorities, a successor to the Conservative Government's Compulsory Competitive Tendering (CCT) process.

Similar concerns for consumers acted as a further catalyst for re-alignment within the funeral directing industry. Until 1989, there was only one major funeral directing trade association: the National Association of Funeral Directors. From 1972 the Great Southern Group extended into both crematoria and funeral directing. A series of acquisitions in the 1980s by the media-aware entrepreneur Howard Hodgson (Hodgson, 1992) raised his company to the status of a multinational by the acquisition of Kenyons and the French firm Pompes Funèbres Generales. Smaller independent family firms resented the growing dominance of the bigger players and in 1989 a number broke away from the National Association of Funeral Directors to form the National Society of Allied and Independent Funeral Directors. The largest funeral directing group, the Co-operative Funeral Societies – conducting one-quarter of the nation's funerals – broke away from the National Association of Funeral Directors in 1994, claiming it dealt inadequately with clients' complaints. Their new trade association, the Funeral Standards Council, immediately set up the Funeral Ombudsman Scheme and appointed a consumer rights lawyer, Professor Geoffrey Woodroffe, as the UK's first Funeral Ombudsman. This Scheme steadily won over funeral directing groups with both the Society of Allied and Independent Funeral Directors and Service Corporation International eventually joining it. However, the Ombudsman could only deal with complaints from members of associations who were themselves members of the Funeral Ombudsman Scheme; and the existence of a Local Government Ombudsman meant that local authority-owned cemeteries and cremato-ria did not feel the need to join the Scheme. These two factors limited the number of annual complaints, which never rose above 200 (Funeral Ombudsman Scheme, 1994/1995–2001). This was a paradox which bred its own tensions: the Funeral Ombudsman Scheme had difficulties pleading the necessity for its existence when it could not increase the number of complaints and thereby reduce its costs. Simultaneously, it was in funeral directors' interests to handle clients' complaints in-house rather than to have them dealt with at national Ombudsman level. In 2002 both the Society of Allied and Independent Funeral Directors and the Funeral Standards Council withdrew on grounds of cost from the Ombudsman Scheme, which then could not continue.

The Consumers' Association published the first edition of its guide-book *What to do when someone dies* in 1967 (Harris, 1967). The Association reported on funerals first in 1961 and then in 1982, 1992 and 1995. Information and transparency were key issues. Their researcher Colin Brown noted that as the majority of deaths are now those of the elderly and take place in institutions, the vast majority of families are totally unaware of funeral procedures and the funerals market, with no idea of what standards to expect.

many people are totally in the hands of the funeral industry right through from the GP or hospital, police, maybe coroner, funeral directors, clergy, cremation or burial staff, monumental masons, the whole lot. The consumer feels totally in their hands. People had no idea what the boundaries are between their legal, medical and personal rights and obligations, and their responsibilities. They don't know what is standard practice.... A funeral is a distress purchase by distressed people who are not equipped for the task and...therefore...not a conducive environment for complaint. (Brown, 1995: 165)

Similar themes were taken up by *The Economist*: 'The funeral industry thrives on the acumen of its managers, but also because of three features of the market: ignorance, sentiment and taboo. Without them, its profits would decompose faster than its corpses' (*The Economist*, 4 January 1997). The work of the Consumers' Association was also taken up by the Oddfellows' Friendly Society, which began to publish bi-annual reports of UK funeral costs (The Oddfellows, 2000). Cemetery and crematorium authorities were aware that while funeral directors were the main agents for the bereaved family, criticisms could also be aimed at them.

Consumer attention was enhanced by greater government attention as British funerals gained an international ingredient. Young's project, The National Funerals College, was launched at a seminar on 11 June 1994 on 'The Future of Funerals: options for change' (Young, 1994). The preceding week, the Great Southern Group was approached by the US funeral firm, Service Corporation International (SCI). By the end of August, SCI had acquired both PHKI (the acronym of the combined companies, Pompes Funèbres, Hodgson and Kenyon International) and the Great Southern Group, thereby now owning 15% of the British funeral market. SCI paid over £300 million for its stake in the UK funerals market and needed to make a return on its investment. It opted for a high-media profile, but attracted thereby the greater attention of its competitors. Within months, it was reported to the Monopolies and Mergers Commission (MMC), the claim being that its dominance in certain regions constituted an unfair trading position. The Commission's report (MMC, 1995) ordered SCI to sell on a number of its businesses. Some of these businesses were bought by Co-operative Societies who had themselves attracted the attention of the Commission earlier (MMC, 1987. Even a Conservative government was unwilling to court criticism by declaring the Co-operative Societies (conducting 25% of British funerals) to be in a monopoly position. Many commentators shared a concern about 'vertical monopoly' or monopsiny, the process whereby the same business exercised an indirect monopoly by owning several links in the supply chain: in this case, funeral directors, cemeteries, crematoria, memorials. SCI had learned from the experience of US funeral directors, when the American way of death was criticised by Jessica Mitford in the 1960s (Mitford, 1963, 1998). US funeral directors had responded with an emphasis on customer choice and service (Fulton, 2000). There was concern among consumer groups that 'vertical monopoly' would become more widespread in the UK, especially as local authorities were increasingly willing to invite private crematorium companies to assist with crematorium provision.

The UK situation brought into greater prominence the rising sales of pre-paid funeral plans. On one hand, these were of the essence of informed choice; on the other, all funeral directors realised that they led to increased market share. The government responded with two reports, *Pre-Paid Funeral Plans* (Office of Fair Trading, 1995) and *Pre-Paid Funerals: A consultation paper* (Department of Trade and Industry, 1996). The government's two main concerns were the financial risk to funeral directors and the mis-selling risk for consumers. The Conservative Government and its Labour successor from 1997 both declared their preference for self-regulation, and pre-paid plans became a new component of the UK funeral market. Meanwhile, SCI pioneered greater staff training, emphasised consumer choice and recruited some of the leading funeral directors and crematorium superintendents. SCI (UK) did not increase its stake in UK funerals beyond 15% and underwent a management buyout to become Dignity plc in 2001.

Given the pace and the publicity of these developments, the context was right for the leaders in the cemetery and crematorium services to press for other reforms from within, some of which affected cremation procedures directly: revisions to the Code of Practice, the disposal of foetal remains and a longer-term challenge, the revival of burial.

The *Code of Cremation Practice*, first drafted in the winter of 1945–1946, had been enshrined in the 1951 Report of the government's Inter-departmental Committee. Brendan Day, manager of Cardiff's cemeteries and crematorium, considered that whilst the code should not be amended simply on financial grounds, financial stringencies coupled with rising fuel costs were causing problems which could be eased by a change to the code. Day proposed that Section 3 (b), 'on the day when the cremation service takes place . . . the coffin and its contents shall be put into the cremator exactly as they have been received on the catafalque and cremated', should be amended to allow cremations to take place up to a maximum of 24 hours following the service. Day argued that the rising costs of fuel and of pre-heating the cremator when there were few cremations as well as the costs of installation and maintenance of the new cremators required by the EPA would be eased by timing cremations for more fuel-efficient periods. Day reckoned that the public would accept the change and one of his supporters argued, on moral grounds, that the consumption of fuel and the emission of waste gases was now more serious than maintaining a code which in itself had spurious value (Day, 1995: 151).

The Federation debated the issue during 1994–1995. The major arguments against change were the conviction that the very existence of the Code had been effective for the public's adoption of cremation; that the public expected the cremation to take place on the day of the committal service, and that the British public would not accept the change (*Resurgam*, 38:4, 1995: 220–1). Day's amendment was rejected. Nevertheless, the environmental issue has thrown up continuing challenges for cremation of which the foetal remains issue is only one.

Whilst just over 600,000 people die each year in the UK, about 170,000 pregnancies never reach term or survive birth: reproductive loss, which involves both medical and social terminations, represents levels of anguish and sadness for prospective parents (Kohner and Henley, 2001). Until the end of the nineteenth century, the deaths of children and infants were commonplace. Some of the elderly people interviewed in the Fens in the early 1990s (Jupp, 1993a, b) recalled times when still-births merited neither funeral nor passing-bell. One recalled running an errand for his mother, taking a dead baby to the sexton for burial in an adult's coffin; another pointed me to a neighbour's garden where he knew a baby had been buried eighty years before. Given a century of far better diet and medical treatment, both infant- and maternal-mortality rates have dropped sharply. Pregnancy and child-raising have increasingly involved larger investments of parental time, education and money. Issues of medical ethics and patients' consent have become important. The passing of the Abortion Act 1967, with successive adjustments of the stage at which foetuses may be legitimately terminated, has meant that the numbers of terminations in hospitals have hugely increased. Before the EPA, it was the procedure in many hospitals to dispose of non-viable foetuses in the hospital sluices or incinerator. Prior to the 1980s, most burial and cremation authorities were largely unaware of this issue (Howlett, 1997: 53). From 1990, the EPA enforced change in hospital procedures. A television programme compered by Esther Rantzen stimulated overnight a great public concern for mothers who did not know where their still-born children had been buried (Jon Luby, personal communication). Over the last twenty years, systems of support for parents suffering reproductive loss have been widely developed, including the Stillbirth and Neonatal Death Society (SANDS) and the Foundation for the Study of Infant Deaths (Kohner, 1992).

After the EPA, the work of disposal of foetal remains passed very largely to local authorities' cemetery and crematorium services. The Institute of Burial and Cremation Administration first drafted a set of guidelines in 1985 (IBCA, 1985: 70–71). From 1990, cremation authorities were presented with an increasing demand for their services, yet they lacked a legal framework for guidance. Whether it was a result of the EPA, the issuing of directives as to the disposal of clinical waste, the endeavour to control hospital finance budgets more directly or the work of and publicity attracted by those organisations established to offer help and guidance to newly bereaved parents, considerable pressure had been placed on cremation authorities to accept 'bulk' disposal of unidentified human remains. Crematoria were concerned not only for proper documentation, but to ensure there was sufficient care and guidance for parents over disposal choice (Luby, 1992: 154). Parents should be sensitively informed that, after cremation, there would be no visible remains. For crematoria there were problems posed by the Code of Cremation Practice – especially for those situated nearest to major maternity hospitals. The Code prescribed that coffins be charged individually into the cremator. This was impracticable for individual foetal remains, although some crematoria authorities put twenty-four sets of remains together, but on separate trays, for cremation. Cost was also a significant factor. A number of crematoria were willing to break the Code quietly for the sake of hospitals, for others the Code was paramount. The IBCA pushed for communal cremation.

Angela Dunn, Bereavement Services Manager at Liverpool, researched the issues for the Institute of Burial and Cremation Administration (Dunn, 1997) and drafted a new code with the Royal College of Nursing 2001. The Institute and the Federation failed to agree on the implications of the old Code for the new situation, the latter being reluctant to break with the clear requirement that individual coffins should be cremated separately. The Federation Executive came to realise that the numbers of foetal remains had risen so high that individual cremations were impossible; it consented to multiple cremations (*Resurgam*, Autumn 2001, 44:3, 134). The Institute and Federation could not reach agreement as to where the limits on confidentiality might confidently be drawn.

An associated issue was stimulated by public reaction to disclosures about the Bristol and Alderhey Hospitals (White, 2001b: 16). In each hospital it was discovered that large numbers of samples of human tissue, having been collected in post-mortems, had lain unused in storage, often for several years. Press attention focused on the remains of foetuses and children, the critical reaction of parents, the value of the research and the moral responsibilities of researchers, together with the problem of appropriate funeral services for the body parts. For parents, the most important issue was that they had not given consent for the retention of their babies' organs. The concern of burial and cremation authorities focused on the practical disposal of the tissue blocks and slides within which particles had been retained as part of the post-mortem process. The government appointed its Chief Medical Officer Professor Sir Liam Donaldson to advise them (*Retained Organs Commission*, 2002).

Towards the middle of the 1980s, the Institute of Burial and Cremation Administration became aware that so much attention had been given to cremation legislation and procedures that more needed to be given to cemeteries. Within many cities having significant portions of people from Muslim, Orthodox Christian and Caribbean culture, the necessity of providing burial space continued. Meanwhile, Nicholas Albury founded the Natural Death Centre. It began vigorously to promote 'natural' and 'green' burial, which drew press attention and proved an economic opportunity for Councils wishing to address voters' environmentalist concerns. The Centre's *The Natural Death Handbook* (Albery *et al.*, 1993) provided access to radical styles for arranging funerals. These included cardboard coffins and woodland burials. Fresh initiatives were meanwhile being taken within the funeral service sector to promote burial. Partly in response to the formation of the Association of British Burial Authorities (ABBA) by Sam Weller, the former Campaign Manager for the Memorial Advisory Bureau, a complementary Confederation of Burial Authorities (CBA) was launched in 1994 and sponsored by the Institute of Burial and Cremation Administration. The CBA and the ABBA helped ensure that burial issues were given more attention not only among the funeral services but with local and national government.

If burial were to continue as an available alternative to cremation, solutions to the shortage of available and accessible burial land were necessities. In 1993, Hussein, then Superintendent of the London Borough of Newham's cemeteries, offered 'A proposed solution for extending the life of existing cemeteries' (Hussein, 1993). His survey of existing burial space in London estimated the rapidly approaching time when London boroughs would have no space. Would cremation then be compulsory? How might boroughs continue to offer burial and cremation options to their multi-cultural populations? Hussein proposed the re-use of old graves. He persuaded seventy local authorities to fund a survey to assess public attitudes towards the concept. This was published as *Re-using Old Graves* (Davies and Shaw, 1995). Its survey of 1603 people in London, Nottingham, Sunderland and Glasgow revealed that 60% of people would support re-use, provided that the graves had not been used for periods of between sixty and one hundred years. Hussein, meanwhile, was supported by the London Planning Advisory Committee which won an award for *Planning for Burial Space Needs in London* (London Planning Advisory Committee, 1997). This study has contributed substantially to the theme of shortage of burial space upon which press attention has focused.

An unexpected impetus came from within the Labour Government, elected in 1997. Andrew Bennett, MP, was the co-chair of the Parliamentary Select Committee for Environment, Transport and Regional Affairs (ETRAC). Bennett was concerned to encourage urban regeneration and realised that cemeteries, with their communal, historical, environmental and cultural significance, if restored and maintained, could play a significant part in an urban renaissance (Bennett, 2000). The report *Cemeteries* was published in March 2001 (ETRAC, 2001). Bennett appreciated that the advent of modern cremation had not only saved land but extended the life of the limited burial space available; he was convinced that the British public needed to be offered the choice between burial and cremation. Yet cemeteries were very poorly served by burial authorities; as the Press Notice ran: 'The problem of under-funding has been exacerbated by poorly-trained staff, confused legislative responsibility, and neglect by both central and local Government' (ETRAC, 2001). The Home Office responded to the Report's criticisms by establishing a Burials and Cemeteries Advisory Group (BCAG), to assess the law and procedures in burial and to advise on legislation for the re-use of old graves. It is too early to predict either this Group's recommendations or parliament's willingness to take them up; thus it is not yet possible to predict whether there will be a revival of burial or government support for it.

In January 2000, Dr Harold Shipman of Hyde, Cheshire, was convicted of the murder of fifteen patients. It was subsequently concluded that he was responsible for over 200 murders. Shipman was widely understood to have shown unparalleled betrayal of the trust of his patients. Among the first of successive government responses Professor Richard Baker undertook a clinical audit of Shipman's practice, finding that in 57% of 282 cases in which one of Shipman's patients had died and for whom Shipman had signed the death certificate, the circumstances of the death were highly suspicious: 'the public cannot be expected to have confidence in a system that fails to detect the murder of a large number of patients over a period of years' (*The Times*, 20 July 2002). Baker found that whilst Shipman and his colleagues regularly acted as each other's second signatory, Shipman was much more meticulous than they in completing form C. Following representation from victims' families, Dame Janet Smith was appointed to chair a public inquiry commencing in 2001. She commented that the death certification system requiring a second doctor to sign 'provided no safeguard at all' (ibid., 20 July 2002).

Thus, thirty years after the Brodrick Report's 1971 judgement that undetected homicide was not a major concern and its recommendation for the abolition of Certificate C which the British Medical Association had resisted, here was a scandal that showed both that secondary examination and certification (upon which the BMA had successively insisted for the sake of security) could be abused and was perfunctory (as cremationists had regularly claimed). The Home Office pathologist Professor Michael Green, recommending far better policing of forms B and C, proposed full-time medical referees (Green, 2000). In the subsequent series of government investigations, the cremation movement played an active part, for example, pressing the government to introduce a medical examiner system. This was not a new proposal, as Stephen White, a Cremation Society Council member, pointed out:

> the Cremation Society's view had for a long time been that the procedures for certification and registration should be sufficiently rigorous as to render unnecessary any distinction being made between burial and cremation. (White, 2001b: 23)

During research on the Society's earlier activities, White discovered that the founding fathers had adopted a second Declaration, seventeen years after their pioneering Declaration in 1874. With their parallel concern for reforming death certification in the 1890s, they had adopted a second Declaration in 1891 to 'move the Government to appoint a local officer in every district, to make a more searching inquiry into the cause of death in *every* case'. This argued for a long consistency on this issue (White, 2001b: 23). Meanwhile, the Shipman case proved to have opened a Pandora's Box of death issues, challenging certification, registration and Coroners' procedures which, in 2000, were a long way short of resolution.

8
Conclusion

Over a long perspective, responsibility for the disposal of the dead in Britain has passed from the local and personal to the distant and institutional. It has passed from families, neighbours and parish clergy to medical professionals, funeral directors and local government authorities. The growing preference of cremation to burial in the twentieth century is part of this process. This process is not ineluctable, as 'natural death' and funeral reform movements in the late-twentieth century indicate. Nor is cremation a final stage in disposal, as the founders of the Cremation Society appreciated. Promoting an alternative to burial, they framed their Declaration 'until some better system is devised, we desire to adopt that usually known as cremation'.

Cremationists would claim that while the system can be improved, cremation has benefited English society. First, it broke the monopoly of the burial tradition and widened consumer choice. Secondly, it has helped to reduce the economic costs of funerals for which reformers from George Walker to Arnold Wilson had campaigned for over hundred years. Thirdly, it has contributed to what may be termed the democratisation of death, by offering simpler alternatives to older forms of funeral and memorialisation which were redolent of class distinction. Fourthly, it has sought to promote better public health and to reduce environmental pollution. Fifthly, it has enabled alternative use of 6000 acres of urban land (Audit Commission, 1989) for housing and recreational use. Sixthly, it has developed ceremonial facilities that can be sensitive to the ritual traditions and requirements of faith and secular groups and are not hostile to religious or secular interpretations of death or the after life. Seventhly, it has provided a system for the respectful disposal of the dead which fits with the requirements of a socially and geographically mobile society.

It is a coincidence that cremation was first advocated in the very decade in which English patterns of mortality were on the cusp of change. Since the 1870s, patterns of mortality in the UK have radically altered (Mitchison, 1977; Tranter, 1996). One quarter of all nineteenth-century deaths were of infants dying before their first birthday. The death rate of these children fell from 154/1000 in 1900 to 75/1000 (1925) 30/1000 (1950) and 8/1000 (1990). In the 1870s life-expectancy also began statistically to increase. Between 1919 and 1990 life-expectancy increased from 58.8 years for males and 67.5 years for females to 73.00 and 78.5 respectively. Increases in life-expectancy for the over-45s began after 1950. Better diet and health provision compete for the primacy in effecting this change.

The implications for the disposal of the dead are, first, that death is now what happens to the old, rather than to the young. In the first half of the twentieth century, falling death rates were largely due to the reduction of communicable infectious diseases. By 1950, the primary causes of death had become non-communicable, degenerative conditions like heart disease and cancer. This means that both the care of people in old age and their disposal after death are usually tasks for children or relatives who are middle-aged, economically independent and frequently living at a distance.

Secondly, the death of children has become, correspondingly, exceptional. Fewer than 4000 males and 2000 females die between their first and nineteenth birthdays (DHSS Mortality Statistics, 2001). The trauma of such bereavement is partly because, in an age when so many parents limit their families by contraceptive methods, pregnancies and child-rearing now represent a considerable investment of time, money and emotion. The consequent attention given to the funerals of the young has been extended most recently to the rituals chosen to mark the deaths of the still-born. The public concern about retained organs and the government's strategy to reduce youth suicides are extensions of this new attitude.

Thirdly, death is no longer a frequent experience in the family. Longevity and general health have increased, whilst family size has been reduced and maternal deaths have severely declined. For every 100 mothers who died in childbirth (usually at home) in 1900, only four died (in home or hospital) in 1960. Yet children's lack of personal familiarity with death was, albeit paradoxically, increased by the 1939–1945 war conditions, a process augmented by the post-war concern of parents that children should be shielded from talk of death and discouraged from funeral attendance.

Fourthly, death now usually takes place in institutional settings. The Department of Health and Social Services (DHSS) annual reports indicate that the proportion of people dying at home first dropped below 50% in 1958–1959. Between 1969 and 1987, home deaths dropped from 42 to 24% (Seale and Cartwright, 1994). By 1997, only 20% of all deaths in England and Wales took place at home. Other locations were: NHS hospitals/nursing homes 54%, private hospitals and non-NHS nursing homes 10%, other communal establishments 8%, hospices 4% and others 4%. In institutions the majority die without relatives present. The next-of-kin have thus been progressively distanced and disenfranchised from personal care for their dying relatives. This has been increased by the process hypothesised as the shift whereby biological death is preceded by social death: where the dying person's involvement in social life is increasingly restricted by the withdrawal of others from that social life, in anticipation of the expected death (Glaser and Strauss, 1965; Mulkay and Ernst, 1991; Seale, 1998). The relatives' part in this has been characterised by the Fultons (R. Fulton and J. Fulton, 1971) as 'anticipatory grief'. The distancing process continues through funeral arrangements because dead people are only very rarely returned to their own homes. The wake has passed into history.

Fifthly, institutionalised death is now followed by institutionalised disposal. Modern death certification and registration procedures, together with the involvement of funeral directors (Howarth, 1996; Bradbury, 1999) and the municipal organisation of disposal (Naylor, 1989) have largely removed the active participation of the family from the processes between death and funeral. This lack of participation can be compounded by the decline of the nuclear family and the increasing geographical isolation of extended family members, both of which affect funeral attendance and bereavement support. Since the 1960s, a number of bereavement support groups, both statutory and voluntary, have been organised to serve the needs of people whose ability to come to terms with their bereavement has been vitiated by the lack of relatives or friends living in sufficiently close proximity.

Since 1939, the specific role of the local community in funerals has changed specifically in laying out the body, viewing it and attending the funeral. The layer-out (Roberts, 1989; Adams, 1993) was a woman enrolled by her neighbours to assist in births and deaths. She washed and prepared the corpse; might also organise neighbourhood wreaths, the funeral tea and mind the house during the funeral. Some were paid for their services, others saw it as part of working-class reciprocity. Adams and Roberts both saw the decline of the layer-out in terms of the change in community life as old neighbourhoods were broken up, in the increased paid-work opportunities for women and in new possibilities for pride in the home, helped by increased prosperity.

Viewing the dead was a neighbourly mark of respect (Roberts, 1989). Whilst wakes had become uncommon in the industrial Lancashire she described, viewing the body was still customary. More people paid respects than attending funerals. It was very common for children to visit, and thus death played an enormous part in the socialisation of working-class children (ibid.: 191). Adults exercised neighbourhood pressure to view: there were often sweets or funeral cake as rewards; there were superstitions that those who touched or kissed the dead neither feared the dead nor dreamt of them. The architecture of the house meant that the front door often opened straight from the street into the front room where the coffin lay. However, there were some indications that the invasion of the grieving family's privacy was not always welcome (ibid.: 200) and householders became more selective about both visiting and receiving. As people increasingly went into hospital to die, and bodies were not then brought home, the role of neighbours at the time of a death declined.

Attendance at funerals was made more difficult for mourners and sympathisers by the replacement of parish churchyards by town or district cemeteries after 1850. Walking funerals were successively replaced by horse- and motor-driven funerals. The adoption of cremation has increased the distance that funeral attendance requires. A parallel process of steadily decreasing Church attendance (since the first decade of the twentieth century) and of a (albeit less steep) decline in religious belief has contributed to lower attendances at funerals. Secular changes have also contributed to lower attendances. The post-1945 Welfare State brought about the demise of industrial assurance, itself already threatened by the decline in the death rate of young children, for whom multiple policies were often bought. Within living memory (Roberts, 1971) the rewards of belonging to a burial or a Friendly Society often included a large turn-out at the funeral. Memberships of several clubs increased the turn-out and high attendance lent a family status. Anecdotal evidence about mining communities in South Wales spoke of levels of neighbourhood financial support as well as funeral attendance in communities characterised by a dominant and dangerous industry. The impetus for the reduction in Sunday funerals – which had bolstered funeral attendance – came from reformers within the cemetery services.

The gap between the family and the community has not yet been filled and for those who find the experience of bereavement difficult or intolerable, a range of bereavement support groups has emerged; but these are agencies or volunteers, they do not represent the instinctive response of a known local community, acting reciprocally. The family has become increasingly exposed as the major institution providing support at the time of a death. The family's role in the management of a death has been particularly affected by changes in leisure opportunities and in the role of women.

The 1950s brought fuller male employment, more disposable income and greater opportunities for mass and individual leisure. The end of military conscription in 1960 ushered in an era of conspicuous consumption and a new youth culture. Saturday paid-work was increasingly abandoned and the expanded weekends gave time for relative-visiting and house- and garden-maintenance. Television ownership was boosted by the 1953 Coronation and, from 1956, by commercial channels. The growth of the media contributed to the development of an entertainment and sporting culture. Radio and television may have proved intrusive or a solace when a home was visited by terminal illness or death. Whereas curtains were once drawn to signal and protect a household visited by death, the television and telephone enabled the outside world to insert its normalities and re-assert its values. The television made demands upon living-space: in commanding attention, it insisted on the rearrangement of furniture, room and meal-times. In older communities, the 'room for best' traditionally used at Sundays, Christmas and for coffins, was now opened up for daily use. The undertaker's chapel of rest became its substitute. Leicestershire interviewees (Jupp, 1993b) reported that they had stopped keeping the corpse at home after the installation of central heating. This might mean that between one family funeral and the next – perhaps five to twenty-five years – they had installed fitted carpets, new furniture and central heating. The home was now too pristine and the temperature too warm to keep a decomposing body cool.

The claims of the living, of hobbies and sport, of children and of home, replaced the claims of the distant dead. 'To get to the cemetery, I had to take three buses,' said a Fenland woman about her mother's grave, 'and you know what buses are like on Sundays'; when her own husband died without leaving funeral instructions, she had him cremated. There were other East Midlands interviewees for whom the attractions of cremation as a replacement for burial increased leisure time to spend with relatives. Hannon (1990) measured the 'forgetting rate', by which graves were steadily left unvisited. On the one hand, the forgetting rate could be seen as a successful outcome of the grief process. On the other, it is a casualty of weekend leisure options. When families stop visiting, neither cemetery gardeners nor Council Tax payers can be expected to take over grave maintenance (Rugg, 2006).

In traditional societies, women's roles include the burden of mourning (Bloch and Parry, 1982), whose rituals often indicated that women of child-bearing age were at risk from the pollution of death. When levels of sanitary and medical knowledge were low, beliefs and rituals interacted to protect the living from the dead. In modern Europe, industrial society and mass violent death coincided in the First World War. In the UK, the custom of mourning clothes and rituals sharply declined. By 1918, society had changed so fundamentally, with women gradually building upon the freedoms won during the War, that there was little chance that the high Victorian etiquette would be revived. 'Such etiquette', commented Taylor (1982: 270), 'depended upon the will of women to keep it going, and once that had gone, it died.'

Taylor claimed (1982) that the underlying message of ritual mourning is that a woman's sexual and emotional life (with an adult partner) has come to an end. If Taylor was correct, then it will be apparent that, in post-1945 Britain, with changes in attitude to women's work, family, marriage and divorce, mourning rituals proved increasingly anachronistic: both an obstruction in a busier and more mobile life, and inappropriate for a society beginning to take the new opportunities for new sexual and emotional freedoms, for divorce and remarriage, for new career opportunities and geographical mobility. Part of the basis for this change was new medical techniques for controlling conception and death. Although Gorer asserted that last century's taboo about sex and expressiveness about death have merely exchanged places (Gorer, 1965; but see Walter, 1998; Berridge, 2001), it is clear that, especially for women, the link between death and sexuality, between funerals and fertility, has been severed. Earlier predictions that AIDS might revive this link have proved unfounded despite HIV/AIDS becoming established in the UK.

Post-war changes in family life were illustrated in a crucial period (1958–1960) by Rosser and Harris in Swansea (Rosser and Harris, 1983). First, the extended family became more widely dispersed, both geographically, as children moved to set up their own homes, and socially, loosening the authority of the mother in a neighbourhood where her children lived close by and distancing the children who were enabled by new educational, work and marriage opportunities to move up the occupational hierarchy. Secondly, the family still retains a crucial function in providing support in a crisis, but the measure of practical help depends on the proximity of family units to each other, a proximity weakened by social and geographical mobility. *Within* families the effectiveness of the extended family largely depended upon the woman's availability to offer help; and this has been affected by the enormous changes in women's work and educational opportunities. The key relationship in the extended family is that of *wife's mother–wife–husband's mother*. The support this relationship could provide depended crucially on women being at home and not at paid work outside. The greater the level of female domesticity, the stronger the cohesion of the family and the greater support it could offer. New non-domestic opportunities for women have effected the reverse.

These changes have contributed to the decline of death rituals in contemporary society. First, they have reduced the necessity for the public demonstration of the role of widow in the family and the neighbourhood. Secondly, they have helped to set the scene for the precedence of social death before biological death. Thirdly, they have contributed to the decline of the memorialisation of the dead. When the emotional gap left by a death is less critical in both home and neighbourhood, then the social space accorded to recognition of the memory of the deceased can be lessened. Parents who occupied a vital role in the family may be honoured by a funeral no one would miss and a grave selected for accessibility. Distanced and distant parents who were once a staff but became a burden may have left so small a gap in the family that the survivors do not need a space to mark it. Those who gave the elderly little time during their life may give them even less in their death: a Sheffield funeral director told me in 1989 of the difficulty in arranging a funeral for a client: 'This businessman told me, "I can't let my mother's funeral get in the way of my diary."'

From 1884, in Britain, people have had a choice between burial and cremation for their funerals. This choice has been in part manipulated, and in part chosen. The first proponents of cremation put forward such advantages as lower funeral costs, better public health, protection of human remains from vandalism and prevention of premature burial. The last lost its salience in the earlier twentieth century (Bourke, 2005) but the first grew in prominence, accompanied by such second-generation arguments as the saving of land, its relative simplicity and the greater choice in disposing of the remains.

What were the factors behind people's choice? In 1989–1991 I compared the burial–cremation choice between small samples (totalling 58) of people in rural Lincolnshire (a village disguised as Fensham) and urban Leicester. A fuller account of the findings is given at Jupp, 1993a. The strongest links behind both burial and cremation choice were parental and marital precedent. Husbands and wives were very likely to choose the same mode of disposal. Adults were generally likely to choose the same mode of disposal as their parents. Those who chose burial gave as their other principal reasons that burial facilitated grave-visiting and remembrance and that (for Catholics and Jews) burial was their religious tradition.

Among those choosing cremation, some gave as their other principal reasons that they feared neglect of graves whilst others calculated that buried ashes could be as well visited as graves containing the full body. Indeed, the incidence of ash *burial* in family graves in Leicester was clearly chosen to permit the visiting of graves otherwise full. This led to the possibility of an intriguing calculation. Burial and cremation statistics are annually collected on the basis of *mode* of disposal, yielding an annual ratio in favour of cremation. The small Leicester sample indicated that from the perspective of *final location* of ashes, with buried bodies and interred ashes added together, human remains were more likely to be deposited under the ground (as bodies or interred ashes) than to be scattered above it. Only a more extended study could explore the prevalence and the implications of this possibility.

The village of Fensham had relatively easy access to a crematorium after the opening of Peterborough (1959) and Boston (1966). Compared with Leicester (where there had been a crematorium since 1902) Fensham could be examined as a village in the process of transition from burial traditions towards cremation. In this context, it is significant to note that those village inhabitants who were speaking about the recent cremation of their parents displayed some or all of four characteristics: they were incomers; they had had the ashes scattered; they had no restricting religious reasons to forbid cremation; and they did not anticipate succeeding generations would live near enough to tend or visit graves. Those traditional village families whose parents had been buried, when responding to questions on the occupations of their parents and grandparents, revealed that, irrespective of class, their families were static in terms of occupational mobility.

The hypothesis was tentatively suggested that change in disposal choice was linked with class mobility as determined by occupation. Local villagers possessed two forms of status: an *ascribed* status as children who have grown up in a village where their parents are known and an *achieved* status according to their success at work. The local villagers who had followed their fathers' occupation had had no need to indicate or reassert a separate status from their parents: they had inherited their parents' local standing. Whether middle or working class, their occupational and local status was identical with that of their parents and they were content to let both their parents' corpses and their status rest.

Meanwhile, precisely those villagers who had made such a success of their occupations that they had risen to a social position superior to their parents had chosen cremation for their parents' funeral. My hypothesis was that they had chosen cremation – not necessarily consciously – to signal their independence of family and local roots. The children's status having been raised by business success rather than by virtue of family inheritance or influence, the parents' role did not need to be honoured nor their link retained by the permanent interment of their bodies in the neighbourhood where they raised their children (Jupp, 1993a: 189).

Burial–cremation choice is not and has never been a purely private decision, unaffected by social context. Davies and Shaw (1995) concluded that studies to build up family funeral histories were required, so that funeral choice could be tracked and analysed over succeeding generations.

Cremation has now become the choice of over 70% of people in Britain for their funerals. Its development has been a response to and a reflection of contemporary culture, both at personal and at social levels. It relates to at least five processes in our society, of municipalisation and the growing role of the state, commercialisation, consumerisation, individualisation and secularisation (Jupp, 1997c). Once cremation became established as an alternative to burial, its major effect was to offer families a choice. On the one hand, this degree of freedom has given us the opportunity to break away from visibly communal attitudes, beliefs and practices about death and disposal and to make our own funeral decisions. On the other, our attitudes and practices at death and funerals are still affected by impersonal, social processes.

A caution needs to be entered here about constraints on choices. When *The Dead Citizens Charter* was launched as a discussion document, the head of one funeral research organisation responded that we must not take for granted people's desire to operate personal choice at the time of a funeral: her mother and her neighbours would die rather than behave in ways unacceptable to the neighbours in her street. Again, all funeral directors know that families can agonise over whether to have a secular funeral; family members do not easily risk arranging a funeral which will give offence. Again, music at funerals is a latent source of tension: on the one hand, families may want to choose music that fits the character, interests or loyalties of the person who has died, only to find the taste or expectations of other mourners have been offended (Denyer, 1997). Traditional hymns were once and necessarily communal and well-known. In a more secular society, where music is not chosen to express belief in the future life of the dead, songs are chosen to express individuality (Denison, 1999). In complementary fashion, those who sell or provide funeral services can do so in ways that match our desires for individualism. Memorial masons may wish to offer clients a wide range of memorials for graves or cremated remains. Yet churchyards, cemeteries, crematoria, gardens of rest all have their own bye-laws and limits for what is permissible: individual taste and social conformity often provide tensions, exacerbated in the heightened sense of attachments and loss that grave-visiting implies.

Whilst choice is the major product of the contemporary system of alternatives in disposal, there are five social processes which influence choice. Municipalisation is the first. In the British context, nearly all cemeteries and seven-eighths of crematoria are owned and operated by local authorities. Local authorities apply to their burial and cremation facilities the same methods of fiscal accountability that they apply to their other services. In recent years these have been reassessed, according to the Audit Commission and its successor the 'Best Value' criterion. Costs for burial outweigh those of cremation but cross-subsidy is subject to complex criteria, and whether the disposal of the dead should be subsidised as a public service is a continual issue. Local authority budgets determine the opening hours, fees and forms of memorial for cemeteries and crematoria and, for crematoria, determine the length of service times and facilities for music (West, 1996). From this perspective, crematorium authorities have more control over the style of funeral than either clergy or funeral directors, for they are the proprietors and the stage-managers.

Commercialisation is dominated by the funeral directing industry which had an annual turnover of £700 million in 2000. Their disbursements, fees paid on to burial and cremation authorities, clergy, medical certification and registration, add another third to this amount. Memorials are a third area of expenditure. In funeral directing, the post-war growth of motor transport and refrigeration increased control over the funeral arrangements at the very time when crematoria were being strategically located to serve several boroughs. The rise in cremations has thus enabled funeral directors to achieve economies of scale by undertaking several funerals in a day. This not only outbid part-time funeral directors, but stimulated commercial acquisitions whereby funeral directing chains, in a process of vertical monopoly, could provide families with access to services at every point in the funeral process.

At the same time, there are alternatives to the domination of the funeral process by the public and commercial sectors. Beveridge's proposals that there should be state support for families 'from the cradle to the grave' included support for widows and bereaved families. Post-war funeral reforms have an indirect connection in that Michael Young, who helped to draft the Labour Party's 1945 manifesto, went on to found the Consumers Association (Dench *et al.*, 1995). The Consumers Association itself has published a number of funeral surveys. The Charter theme of the 1992 Conservative Government was exploited by the National Funerals College in *The Dead Citizens Charter* (1996) and by the Institute of Burial and Cremation Administration in *The Charter for the Bereaved* (IBCA, 1996). The Consumers Association argued that 'A funeral is a distress purchase by distressed people who are not equipped for the task' (Brown, 1995: 165). This specifically characterised people arranging (and attending) funerals as consumers. That is not how bereaved people always see or saw themselves but the realisation by bereaved families of their consumer power has been heightened since the early 1990s with increasing media attention given to death and funerals.

Two characteristics of the process of secularisation are relevant here, the first being the decline in the purchase of organised religion and its institutions upon the public. Since the 1880s, the proportion of church goers within the total adult population has declined; and since the 1900s adult church attendance has declined in absolute terms. With the steep decline in Sunday School attendance since the 1930s, and changes within religious education in the schools system, very few children are now brought up with either the consciousness of a denominational label or an awareness of the Churches' life or purposes. There are therefore fewer institutional pressures upon people to know what Churches or religions teach about death or the afterlife or to take part regularly in funerary rituals.

In ways not yet fully analysed, the growth of cremation and the decline of belief in the resurrection of the body seem to have given mutual encouragement. In 1990 Davies wrote in a key passage,

> The traditional burial service focuses on the body and its resurrection future. While the modern cremation service explicitly follows that pattern, its implicit message is that the body has come to its end but the soul has gone on. The only hope that many can read into the

cremation service is the hope of a surviving soul.... What cremation allows to come to the forefront is the otherwise strongly implicit belief in a human soul which leaves the body and continues into another dimension of existence at death. (1990: 33)

Davies' words can thus be read to mean that the rise of cremation has contributed to the decline of the belief in the resurrection of the body. It is not yet clear by how much dwindling beliefs in the resurrection of the body have vacated the arena of plausible beliefs (Edwards, 1999) and thus made room for the expansion of beliefs in the immortality of the soul. Nor is it yet clear whether the cremation process, in reducing the substance of the human body and destroying its shape, has discouraged belief in its resurrection or in the need for the body's resurrection. I incline to the former position because, chronologically, articulation of declining belief in bodily resurrection preceded by 20–30 years the popularity of cremation. Yet the symbols of contemporary cremation can satisfy those who believe in either or neither.

Simultaneously, popular belief in Christian hopes of life after death has steadily declined (Hick, 1976; Davies, 1997c). Davies and Shaw's 1995 survey of 1603 people revealed that just under one third believed death was the end of human existence and just under one eighth believed in reincarnation. These findings should have dismayed those responsible for the Churches' teaching ministries. Of those professing a denominational allegiance to the Church of England, one third believed death was the end of existence and one seventh in reincarnation. Of those professing a Roman Catholic allegiance, one seventh believed death was the end and one ninth believed in reincarnation. Just over one sixth still believed they would be resurrected.

From the post-modernist perspective, it is the collapse of the Christian dominance, both in organisation and in doctrine, which is likely to have led to the free-for-all in religious practice and belief. Post-1945 immigration brought large communities of Moslems, Sikhs and Hindus into Britain for whom the law had to legislate, treating not only the major religions but also institutions of non-belief as requiring a greater equality in resources and opportunities. When all religious perspectives are considered valid, none can effectively claim uniqueness. Local authorities must arrange facilities at their cemeteries and crematoria to act as a lowest common denominator, designing space and procedures to suit all religions' requirements.

Non-belief has also been recognised, in ways that impact upon funeral ceremonies. For example, in the early 1990s the National

Secular Society led a successful campaign claiming crematoria owned by local government should not display fixed crosses or crucifixes in their chapels. As for the conduct of funerals where families have chosen a non-religious ceremony, the British Humanist Association has taken a lead in recruiting and training secular celebrants (Willson, 1989; Pearce, 2005). More recently, the organisation Civil Ceremonies has trained registrars' staff as funeral celebrants to provide ceremonies which fit families' individual needs more closely.

The rise of secular ceremonies indicates the effect of individualism upon contemporary funerals. Humanists, lacking belief in life after death, conduct funeral ceremonies which *ipso facto* are designed to celebrate a life which has completely ended. Humanist ceremonies can only reflect upon a past, not a future. With no intercessions for the dead, they take time to concentrate upon the character, values and achievements of the occupant of the coffin. Lacking traditional liturgies, they are more free to compose their own, tailored to the needs of individual families.

In the contemporary state of religious belief and practice in Britain, the role of funeral rituals has been characterised by Davies (Davies, 1995b, 1997a) as having shifted from 'prospective fulfilment of identity' to 'retrospective fulfilment of identity'. Traditional Christian funerals focused upon the body and its future existence after death: corpses were buried, or cremated, 'in sure and certain hope of the resurrection to eternal life in Jesus Christ'. For many people in Britain, the funeral rituals surrounding the death of Diana, Princess of Wales, stimulated an upsurge of imitation whereby the biographies of deceased people became of more importance in the funeral than the beliefs, either of the dead or of their community (Walter, 1999b; but contrast Denison, 2000). An increasing proportion of people in Britain admits no hope that another life awaits them after death. In this perspective, people now have to shift for themselves. Loving relationships can only be sought in this life, not the next. With no prospect of post-mortem judgement, individuals are responsible for promoting and assessing their own achievements. They must ensure that the significance of their lives is recorded, not for eternity but for posterity, in their funerals and memorials.

Morgenthau captured both the connection between life and the afterlife and the contemporary political constraints upon its realisation. In 'Death in the Nuclear Age' he wrote of the secular confidence of the man who was aware that he was 'a member in an unbroken continuing chain stretching from the past to the future' (cited in Hick, 1979: 88–90). Man may be mortal but humanity is not, and so he will be immortal in his works. Hick commented 'it is precisely this hope of immortality within the human future that is undermined by the possibility of a massive thermonuclear exchange' (Hick, 1979: 89). Whether or not our own age substitutes environmental catastrophe for nuclear tragedy, this undying fear only adds to the necessity for agnostic or atheist bereaved people to use their funerals and memorials, not only, as in cremation, to signify the end and destruction of the human body but to use the funeral ceremony to emphasise the contribution to society made by deceased people during their lives.

A unique constellation of factors has thus contributed to Britain's becoming the first modern industrial society in which the majority of its population has chosen cremation in preference to burial.

The process began at the Reformation when England became a Protestant society and, among other changes, discontinued the cult of the dead. Within just over a century, the Church of England became established as the dominant church. As long as the Church retained control over the site, rite and mode of disposal, it could control interpretations of mortality and support a plausibility structure for supernatural sanctions for morality, based upon belief in the resurrection of Jesus and in physical resurrection and post-mortem judgement for humankind.

In the nineteenth and twentieth centuries, the disposal of the dead has passed from one combination of interest groups to another: from family, neighbourhood and parish church to medical, commercial and governmental. After 1800, the national population expanded rapidly in parallel processes of industrialisation and urbanisation. In this context, the Church of England proved incapable of discharging the duties of its monopoly on the disposal of the dead, the responsibility for which passed to locally elected authorities. After 1852, no churches could compete with the new, large, better-funded local authority cemeteries.

Thus the disposal of the dead became a secular, local authority problem. Local authorities inherited from the Churches the latent problem of the custody of the dead, and of the associated growing problems which included gravestone and ground maintenance as well as the burial of the poor in an increasingly democratic society, and the scarcity of land for which other policy imperatives competed. After 1918, with the extension of the franchise and the rise of the Labour Party, town councils across the country discovered the increasing complexities of maintaining the burial tradition, issues given prominence by an influential cremation lobby and the increasing professionalisation of burial and cremation staffs. By 1939, there was a significant shift by local authorities to increase public access to cremation facilities.

The Second World War, in processes requiring much further analysis, stimulated both the general public to regard cremation more favourably and local authorities to include crematoria in their post-war reconstruction plans. In the Welfare State inaugurated by the Labour Governments of 1945–1951, increasing demands by local authorities for permissions and funding for crematoria-building were at first frustrated by the economic situation. In the increasingly prosperous 1950s there was then released an intense programme of building which led from 58 crematoria in 1950, to 148 in 1960 and 206 in 1970, the cremation rate having surpassed that for burial in 1967 (Grainger, 2005: 157–188).

The shift to cremation reveals parallel shifts in the secularisation of health and death. From George Walker's burial reforms onwards, the disposal of the dead was increasingly set in a public health reference which, when cremation proposals were denied religious sanction, also embraced cremation. The secular frame of reference in which disposal was set was extended by such issues as the increasing role of Medical Officers of Health after the 1888 Local Government Act, the campaign for birth and death registration, the Parliamentary Acts for Burial (1900) and Cremation (1902) and, after 1918, the concerns for burial ground pollution, the use of urban land and the costs of funerals both to local government and to families. Inter-war housing development contributed to the realisation by householders that keeping the dead at home was not consistent with management of a clean and healthy home. Funeral directors finally persuaded the public to entrust their dead to their new chapels-of-rest, part of the processes whereby, with new refrigeration techniques and the availability of motor transport, a greater rationalisation of their industry was stimulated. Once the body no longer needed to be watched at home, old duties could be laid aside by survivors. With the establishment of the National Health Service in 1948, the expansion of hospitals and the development of medical techniques – especially pain control – and the increasing dominance of chronic diseases as the primary causes of death meant that before 1960 the number of hospital and institutional deaths overtook the home as the normal place of death. Public health and national health thus combined to effect the distancing of death from the home and from domestic control.

For much of the nineteenth century, families' death and funeral rituals were influenced according to codes which expected funerals to function as an indication of status, of religious conviction and of family, and of local or occupational identity. But from the later nineteenth century and on through the twentieth, the social structure of families and class was changing. These changes were accelerated by two World Wars, and by a whole range of previously unavailable life-chances. In circumstances of new social and economic opportunity, families found traditional funeral rituals to be of decreasing value in terms of time, money, gender role and social consequence. There was a steady conflation of sufficient institutional interests to make cremation a prudent economic investment for Local Councils and for individual families.

At the Reformation, England had become a Protestant country in whose burial arrangements the Established Church of England had an almost unchallenged monopoly. That the UK was the first nation to industrialise meant that urban pressures on burial space were more intense than in any other country, leading to the secularisation of urban burial space in 1850. Thus, whilst general secularisation gathered apace during the period 1880–1914, the Church had lost control of its burial grounds thirty years before. Cremation was first proposed by a voluntary society led by members of the professional establishment which vigorously advocated cremation ever after; when the Church opposed cremation, cremationists organised to press a range of secular arguments for cremation which, save for the Catholic tradition, avoided religious issues. Indeed, the Church was impotent to challenge crema-tion because, first, it had already surrendered control of its burial grounds, and, secondly, cremation was found not to have been illegal; and the first crematorium was in operation so swiftly after cremation had first been proposed. The incongruity of Church opposition was further emphasised with the Cremation Act 1902 and the Cremation Regulations 1903 which were both positive towards cremation. Despite this, the cremation take-up was very low until after 1918 but attitudes to death, religion and the afterlife were all severely affected, in different ways, by the two World Wars. After 1918, local government authorities sought to discharge their responsibilities for the disposal of the dead by the promotion of cremation and investment in crematoria. The Welfare State agenda of the 1945 Labour Government stimulated funeral reforms along lines for which a reformist consensus was developing before 1939 and, in the changed post-war context of health-care, social mobility and continuing secularisation, the public steadily opted for cremation, the remaining Catholic bastion giving way in 1964.

The critical stage can be dated to the period 1939–1952 when local authorities, whilst planning for post-war reconstruction, found they could best meet their obligations for the disposal of the dead by promoting cremation. This was with the encouragement of a strong and socialist national government for whom the needs of the living far outweighed the traditional obligations paid to the dead. Within the space of thirteen years, all the major institutions which had control of, or a professional or financial stake in, the disposal of the dead, recognised and co-operated with the shift from burial to cremation: the Established Church, the medical profession, the funeral directing industry, local government and national government. For decades all these groups had been the target of cremation advocacy by a highly organised but voluntary Cremation Society which, its major task achieved, had to adapt to being only one funerals interest amongst others seeking to improve the service crematoria offered to the public.

The shift to cremation was facilitated by the decline of the religious referent in death. To speak of the disposal of the dead as a matter of economic investment is not to deny that funerals have always attracted investment according to the degree of social involvement of the deceased. It is to assert that the *economic* value of the corpse and the *emotional* value of a bereavement have become emphasised partly because of the loss of the *religious* value of death. Protestant societies denied that the survivors could do anything for body or soul that might benefit the deceased. Indeed, the corpse lost value twice: at the Reformation when survivors' influence on the dead was outlawed, and in the nineteenth century when the Church gave up its custody of the dead. The Church thereby surrendered its possession of the symbols which both offered a restored identity for the dead and prescribed moral qualifications for that restoration.

Once the Church confirmed that a 'next life' was no longer to be characterised in moral or religious terms, disposal procedures shed these characteristics too. Disposal became a matter of personal choice for the survivors: a choice exercised according to personal convenience, respect for the deceased and the self-assessed importance of family or local identity. As religious and communal involvement waned, families were freed to make arrangements to suit themselves. This coincided entirely with the duties laid upon local authorities: to dispose of the dead in such a way as to respect the wishes of the bereaved whilst exercising accountability for land resources, public health and budget priorities.

Families, with less labour power available to sustain traditional mourning and memorial tasks, were on the whole relieved to reduce the investment of the money and leisure time which an increasingly prosperous and secular society afforded them. Protestantism had argued for centuries that funerals could not serve the dead, only benefit the living. The Catholic decision in 1964 removed the last major objection to cremation. The necessity to maintain and design crematoria to suit the demands of other religious groups was consolidated by the growth of Hindu and Sikh communities in post-war Commonwealth immigration. This meant that cremation was finally free to offer itself as a practical and entirely legitimate convenience for bereaved families in a multi-cultural society.

At the outset of my research, Ivor Leverton, the London funeral director, told me, 'I could write your book for you in one word: convenience.' This book explains that disposal of the dead has become much more a matter of convenience, both personal and institutional, partly because of the loss of more ultimate categories: the Church surrendered its custody of the corpse, and modes of disposal have largely lost their theological significance. A Leicester farmer's daughter may have spoken for many individuals when she told me, 'I don't know what we have funerals for. It's just a family get-together. They haven't a religious significance.' Religion is, however, but one social institution; social institutions have always competed for control of the disposal of the dead. Contemporary debates, whether on universal issues like abortion, euthanasia and international terrorism or on more discrete issues like retained organs, funeral costs and Dr Shipman's murders all confirm that death is still too fundamental a personal, social and biological fact to be left without control and without interpretation.

Notes

Cremation legalised, 1852–1884

1. For a fuller discussion of the first cremator technology see Parsons, 2005e.
2. In the summer of 1882 cremation received an unexpected prominence because of a sporting disaster. The English national cricket team lost the series to the Australian team. *The Sporting Times* published a spoof obituary: 'In affectionate remembrance of English Cricket which died at The Oval [cricket ground] on 29th August 1882. Deeply lamented by a large circle of sorrowing friends and acquaintances. R.I.P. N.B. The body will be cremated, and the ashes taken to Australia.' For a fuller discussion, see White, 1990: 1145, 1149; Twigg, 1987.

The early years of cremation, 1884–1914

1. This relationship was changed under different circumstances in the late 1950s as a result of the purchase of the London Cremation Company by the Amalgamated Tobacco Company. The Cremation Society responded to the critical reception of the sale by organising a purchase of the majority of the shares in the London Cremation Company.

The development of cremation, 1914–1939

1. This was changed in 1938 when the Federation became independent of the Cremation Society with a new constitution and renamed The Federation of British Cremation Authorities (*Pharos*, 4:4, 1938: 8–9).
2. This proposal, by the National Council for the Disposal of the Dead, had been defeated just three weeks before in the House of Lords debate of 2 June 1938.

The advance of cremation: Wartime and reconstruction, 1939–1952

1. Mass Observation reported 'at the other, private end of the life–death cycle, it is not possible to detect, anywhere in this record for London, any sustained turning towards God or faith in – or hope for – an after-life. On the contrary, plenty of people seem almost consciously to have turned the other way, as if the whole thing was against the normal decency of death, faith and divine purpose' (Harrisson, 1990: 100).
2. The Church of England confirmed this stance in a debate on Canon Law six years later. See *The York Journal of Convocation Containing the Acts & Debates of the Convocation of York in the Sessions of 23rd and 24th May, 1951* (York: W. H. Smith & Son, 1951) pp. 6, 7, 34–37.

3. Bevan's biographer, the Rt. Hon. Michael Foot, has provided one clue to the roots of Bevan's antipathy to the traditional British way of death. Bevan was part of a pre-war Parliamentary deputation to Poland and had been astonished to discover that among the shareholders of Polish coal mines was the Prudential Assurance Company, the very firm in which so many Welsh miners were investing for their own burial insurance. From then on, Bevan was no friend of the Prudential.

4. When Bevan died in 1960, arrangements were made to scatter his ashes above Ebbw Vale, his Parliamentary constituency. On the day, there was an unexpected hitch. The ashes were stolen from the policeman's motorcycle on which they had been brought for the ceremony. There was a two-hour delay before they were recovered (Dr K. Fowler, personal communication).

The popularisation of cremation in England, 1952–2000

1. The late Geoffrey Finsberg, MP, told me in a personal communication (1988) that the Brodrick papers had passed across his desk at the Home Office but his early death prevented our arranging a further conversation, as he had offered.

Bibliography

Adams, S., 'A Gendered History of the Social Management of Death and Dying in Foleshill, Coventry during the Inter-war Years', in Clark, D. (ed.), *The Sociology of Death* (Oxford: Blackwell/The Sociological Review, 1993).

Adshead, S. D., 'Sir Christopher Wren and his Plan for London', The Royal Institute of British Architects (ed. R. Dircks), *Sir Christopher Wren A.D. 1632–1723* (London: Hodder & Stoughton, 1923), pp. 161–174.

Albery, N., Elliott, G., and Elliott, J., *The Natural Death Handbook* (London: Virgin, 1993, first edn).

Alexander, A. V., *Proceedings of the Seventh Joint Conference of Burial and Cremation Authorities*, 1938, pp. 31–2.

Allighan, G., MP., 'Burial and the State', *Report of the Conference of the Institute of Burial and Cremation Administration*, 1947, pp. 33–42.

Almond, P. C., *Heaven and Hell in Enlightenment England* (Cambridge: Cambridge University Press, 1994).

Annan, N., *Leslie Stephen: The Godless Victorian* (New York: Random House, 1984).

Anon. *The Graver Thoughts of a Country Parson* (London: Alexander Strahan & Co., 1864).

Arber, R. N., *Disposal of Cremated Remains. A European Perspective* (unpublished report to the International Cremation Federation by Roger Arber, Secretary General).

Ariès, P., *Centuries of Childhood* (London: Penguin, 1979).

Ariès, P., *The Hour of Our Death*, translated by H. Weaver (London: Allen Lane, 1981).

Ariès, P., *Images of Man and Death*, translated by J. Lloyd (Cambridge, Mass.: Harvard University Press, 1985).

Audit Commission for Local Authorities in England and Wales, 'Managing Cemeteries and Crematoria in a Competitive Environment', *Occasional Papers*, No. 8, March 1989.

Augustine, Saint, *The City of God*, translated by H. Bettenson (Harmondsworth: Penguin Books, 1984).

Augustine, Saint, *How to Help the Dead*, translated by M. Allies (London: Burns & Oates, n.d).

Badham, P., *Christian Beliefs About Life After Death* (London: SPCK, 1978).

Badham, P., with Linda Badham, *Immortality or Extinction?* (London: SPCK, 1984).

Barrow, L., *Independent Spirits: Spiritualism and English Plebeians 1850–1910*, History Workshop Series (London: Routledge & Kegan Paul, 1986).

Barry, J. A., 'The Council for the Disposition of the Dead: A Short Survey', *Journal of the Institute of Cemetery and Crematorium Superintendents*, Vol. 5, No. 1, February 1939, pp. 10–12.

Bartlett, M. J. E., 'Disposal of Chemical Waste and Its Relevance to the Funeral Service', in *Resurgam*, Vol. 34, No. 3, Autumn 1991, pp. 116–19.

Bassett, S., *Death in Towns: Urban Responses to the Dying and the Dead, 100–1600* (Leicester: Leicester University Press, 1992).

Batten, L. J., 'What is Wrong with Our Cemeteries?', *Journal of the Institute of Landscape Architects*, No. 8, October 1945, pp. 5–6.

Beaty, N. L., *The Craft of Dying: A Study in the Literary Tradition of the Ars Moriendi in England* (New Haven and London: Yale University Press, 1970).

Bennett, A., MP, 'Cremation and the Environment', *Pharos International*, Vol. 66, No. 4, 2000, pp. 8–10.

Bennett, G., *Traditions of Belief: Women, Folklore and the Supernatural Today* (London: Penguin Books, 1987).

Benson, P., 'What We would Like', *Sixth Joint Conference of Cemetery and Cremation Authorities*, Torquay, 1937, pp. 34–47.

Berger, P. L., *The Social Reality of Religion* (London: Faber, 1969).

Berridge, K., *Vigor Mortis: The End of the Death Taboo* (London: Profile Books, 2001).

Beveridge, W., *Social Insurance and Allied Services* (London: The Stationery Office Books, 1942).

Blackwood, C., 'Notes from Underground. A Retrospective on Liverpool's Gravedigger Strike', *New Society*, 3 May 1979.

Blauner, R., 'Death and Social Structure', *Psychiatry*, Vol. 29, No. 4, November 1966, pp. 378–94.

Bloch, M., *Placing the Dead: Tombs, Ancestral Villages and Kinship Organization in Madagascar* (London: Seminar Press, 1971).

Bloch, M., and Parry, J. (eds), *Death and the Regeneration of Life* (Cambridge: Cambridge University Press, 1982).

Bourke, J., *Fear. A Cultural History* (London: Virago, 2005).

Bowker, J. W., *The Sense of God: Sociological, Anthropological and Psychological Approaches to the Origin of the Sense of God* (Oxford: Oxford University Press, 1973).

Bowker, J., *The Meanings of Death* (Cambridge: Cambridge University Press, 1991).

Bradbury, M., *Representations of Death: A Social Psychological Perspective* (London: Routledge, 1999).

Briggs, K. C., 'Federation of British Cremation Authorities. Presidential Address to Conference', *Report of the Joint Conference of Burial and Cremation Authorities 1989*, 8–13.

British Medical Association, Private Practice Committee, *Medico-legal Investigation of Deaths in the Community* (London: The British Medical Association, 1963).

(Brodrick Report, The) *Report of the Committee on Death Certification and Coroners* Cmnd 4810 (London: HMSO, 1971).

Brodrick, Judge J. N. L., 'Report of the Committee on Death Certification and Coroners', *FBCA and IBCA: Report of the 31st Joint Annual Conference of Burial and Cremation Authorities*, 1972, pp. 19–26.

Brooks, C., *Mortal Remains* (Exeter: Wheaton, 1989).

Brown, C., 'Funerals – The Consumer's Perspective', *Pharos International*, Vol. 61, No. 4, 1995, pp.162–7.

Brown, P., *Père Lachaise: Elysium as Real Estate* (New York: Viking Press, 1973).

Brown, P., *The Cult of the Saints: Its Rise and Function in Latin Christianity* (University of Chicago Press, 1981).

Browne, Sir T., *Hydriotaphia: Urn Burial or A Discourse of the Sepulchral Urns Lately Found in Norfolk* [1658] (London: G. Moreton, 1894).

Burge, H. M., *The Doctrine of the Resurrection of the Body: Documents Relating to the Question of Heresy Raised against the Rev. H. D. A. Major, Ripon Hall, Oxford* (London: Mowbray, 1922).

Burns, N. T., *Christian Mortalism from Tyndale to Milton* (Cambridge, Mass.: Harvard University Press, 1972).

Bynum, C. W., *The Resurrection of the Body in Western Christianity, 200–1336* (New York: Columbia University Press, 1995).

Calder, A., *The People's War: Britain 1939–45* (London: Jonathan Cape, 1969).

Camps, F. E., 'Death Certification and Coroners', *Proceedings of the 28th Joint Conference of Burial and Cremation Authorities* 1969, pp. 47–55.

Cannadine, D., 'War and Death, Grief and Mourning in Modern Britain', in Whaley, J. (ed.), *op. cit.*, 1981, pp.187–242.

Cappers, W., *Vuurproef voor een gronddrecht: Koninklijke Vereniging voor Facultatieve Crematie 1874–1999* (Zutphen: Walburg Press, 1999).

Carr, W., *Brief Encounters: Pastoral Ministry through Baptisms, Weddings and Funerals* (London: SPCK, 1985).

Chadwick, E., *A Supplementary Report on the Results of a Special Enquiry into the Practice of Interment in Towns made at the Request of Her Majesty's Principal Secretary of State for the Home Department* [PP] Vol. XII, 1843, C.509.

Chadwick, O., *The Victorian Church*, Part 1, 3rd edn (London: Adam and Charles Black, 1971).

Chadwick, O., *The Secularization of the European Mind in the Nineteenth Century* (Cambridge: Cambridge University Press, 1975).

Chapman, G., *A Passionate Prodigality* (London: Buchan & Enright, 1985).

The Chronicle of Convocation, being a Record of the Proceedings of the Convocation of Canterbury (London: SPCK, 1942–1944).

Chulilla, J. L., 'Spain', in Davies, D. J., and Mates, L. (eds), *Encyclopedia of Cremation* (Aldershot: Ashgate, 2005).

Churches' Group on Funeral Services at Cemeteries and Crematoria, The, *Clergy and Cremation Today* (Jupp, P. C., ed.) (London: The Churches' Group on Funeral Services at Cemeteries and Crematoria/The National Funerals College, 1995).

Clark, D., *Between Pulpit and Pew: Folk Religion in a North Yorkshire Fishing Village* (Cambridge: Cambridge University Press, 1982).

Clark, D. (ed), *The Sociology of Death: Theory, Culture, Practice* (Oxford: Blackwell Publishers/The Sociological Review, 1993).

Clarke, J. M., *The Brookwood Necropolis Railway*, 3rd edn (Oxford: Oakwood Press, 1995).

Clarke, J. M., *London's Necropolis. A Guide to Brookwood Cemetery* (Stroud: Sutton, 2004).

Clarke, J. S., *Funeral Reform* (London: The Social Security League, 1944).

Clegg, F., 'Memorialisation: Available Options and their Value to the Bereaved', *Resurgam*, Vol. 31, No. 2, Summer 1988, pp. 45–8.

[Cohen Committee] *Committee on Industrial Assurance and Assurance on the Lives of Children under Ten Years of Age*, Sessional Papers 1932–1933, Vol. xiii, Cmd. 4376, 1933.

Coleman, D. C., *Courtaulds: An Economic and Social History*, Vol. 1 (Oxford: Clarendon Press, 1969).

Colvin, H., *Architecture and the After-life* (New Haven and London: Yale University Press, 1991).

Consumers' Association, *What to Do When Someone Dies*, 8th edn (London: The Consumers' Association, 2004).

Convocation of Canterbury. Joint Committee. 'Report of the Joint Committee on Questions which have Arisen in Connection with the Practice of Cremation', 1943, No. 627c. Questions concerning cremation.

Convocation of Canterbury. Lower House, 'Report of the Lower House Committee to Consider the Necessity for a form of Prayer for use at the Cremation of a Dead Body', 1942, Report No. 635.

Conway, H., *People's Parks: The Design and Development of Victorian Parks in Britain* (Cambridge, 1992).

Cope, Z., *The Versatile Victorian: Being the Life of Sir Henry Thompson, Bt. 1820–1904* (London: Harvey & Blythe, 1951).

Cox, M., *Life and Death in Spitalfields, 1700–1850* (York: Council for British Archaeology, 1996).

Cox, M. (ed.), *Grave Concerns: Death and Burial in England* (York: Council for British Archaeology, CBA Research Report 113, 1998).

Creighton, C., *A History of Epidemics in Britain* (with additional material by D. E. C. Eversley *et al.*), 2nd edn, 2 volumes (London: Cass, 1965).

Cremation Committee, *Report of the Interdepartmental Committee Appointed by the Secretary of State for the Home Department*, Cmd. 8009, 1950.

Cremation Society of England, The, *Relations Between the Cremation Society of England and Her Majesty's Government 1879–80* (London: Smith, Elder & Co., 1884).

Cremation Society of England, The, *Cremation in Great Britain* (London: The Cremation Society; 1st edn, 1909; 3rd edn, 1945).

Cremation Society of Great Britain, The, and The International Cremation Federation, *Pharos* and *Pharos International*, various issues.

Cribb, P. W., 'Some Observations on the Funeral Customs of Immigrant Communities at the Crematorium', *Resurgam*, Vol. 23, No. 1, 1980, pp. 5–7.

Cribb, P. W., 'Cremation and Pollution Factors', *Resurgam*, Vol. 31, No. 1, 1988, pp. 10–11.

Cribb, P. W., 'Fifty Years in the Cremation Movement', *Resurgam*, Vol. 32, No. 4, 1989, pp. 90–1.

Cullman, O., *Immortality of the Soul or Resurrection of the Dead?* (London: Epworth Press, 1958).

Curl, J. S., 'Introduction', in Loudon, J. C., *op. cit.*, pp. 9–22.

Curl, J. S., *A Celebration of Death*: An Introduction to Some of the Buildings, Monuments and Settings of Funerary Architecture in the Western European Tradition, 2nd edn (London: Batsford, 1993).

Curl, J. S. (ed), *Kensal Green Cemetery: The Origins and Development of the General Cemetery of All Souls, Kensal Green, London, 1824–2001* (Chichester: Phillimore, 2001).

Currie, R., Gilbert, A. and Horsley, L., *Churches and Churchgoers* (Oxford: Clarendon Press, 1977).

Dalglish, T. D., 'After the Blitz', *Journal of the National Association of Cemetery and Crematorium Superintendents*, February 1944, pp. 9–11.

Dalton, H., Untitled Address, *Proceedings of the Cremation Society Conference 1951*, pp. 3–5.

Danforth, L. M., *The Death Rituals of Rural Greece* (Princeton, NJ: Princeton University Press, 1982).

Daniell, C., *Death and Burial in Medieval England 1066–1550* (London: Routledge, 1997).

Davie, G., *Religion in Britain since 1945: Believing without Belonging* (Oxford: Blackwell, 1994).

Davies, D., *British Crematoria in Public Perspective* (Maidstone: The Cremation Society of Great Britain, 1995a).

Davies, D., 'The Theology of Cremation', in Jupp, P. C. (ed.), *Clergy and Cremation Today* (London: The Churches' Group on Funeral Services at Cemeteries and Crematoria/The National Funerals College, 1995b).

Davies, D. J., 'The Sacred Crematorium', *Mortality*, Vol. 1, No. 1, March 1996, pp. 83–94.

Davies, D., *Death, Ritual and Belief: The Rhetoric of Funerary Rites* (London: Cassell, 1997a).

Davies, D., 'Theologies of Disposal', in Jupp, P. C., and Rogers, T. (eds), *Interpreting Death: Christian Theology and Pastoral Practice* (London: Cassell, 1997b), pp. 67–84

Davies, D., 'Contemporary Belief in Life after Death', in Jupp, P. C., and Rogers, T. (eds.), *Interpreting Death: Christian Theology and Pastoral Practice* (London: Cassell, 1997c), pp. 130–142

Davies, D., 'Robert Hertz: The Social Triumph Over Death', *Mortality*, Vol. 5, No. 1, 2000, pp. 97–102.

Davies, J., 'The Martial Uses of the Mass: War Remembrance as an Elementary form of the Religious Life', in J. Davies (ed.), *Ritual and Remembrance: Responses to Death in Human Societies* (Sheffield: Sheffield Academic Press, 1994), pp.152–64.

Davies, J. D., *Cremation Today and Tomorrow* (Nottingham: Grove Books Ltd, 1990).

Davies, J. G., 'Factors Leading to the Emergence of Belief in the Resurrection of the Flesh', *Journal of Theological Studies*, Vol. 23, New Series, 1972, pp. 448–55.

Davies, W. D., *Paul and Rabbinic Judaism* (London: SPCK, 1965).

Davies, D., and Guest, M., 'Disposal of Cremated Remains', *Pharos* International, Spring 1999, pp. 26–30.

Davies, D., and Shaw, A., *Re-using Old Graves: A Report on Popular British Attitudes* (Crayford, Kent: Shaw & Sons, 1995).

Day, B., 'A Discussion Document on a Proposal to Amend the Code of Cremation Practice', *Resurgam*, Vol. 38, No. 3, 1995, pp. 147–52.

Defoe, J., 'Cremation and the Church', *The Jurist*, Vol. 31, Fall 1971.

de Deney, G. I., 'Cremation Regulations', *Proceedings of the Conference of the Cremation Society 1964*, pp. 57–62.

Denison, K., 'The Theology and Liturgy of Funerals', *Mortality*, Vol. 4, No. 1, March 1999, pp. 63–74.

Denison, K, 'The Implications of the Events Surrounding the Death and Funeral of the late Diana, Princess of Wales', *Pharos*, Vol. 66, No. 2, 2000, pp. 5–8.

Denyer, P., 'Singing the Lord's Song in a Strange Land', in Jupp, P. C., and Rogers, T. (eds), *Interpreting Death: Christian Theology and Pastoral Practice* (London: Cassell, 1997), pp. 197–202.

Department of Trade and Industry, The (DTI), *Pre-Paid Funerals: A Consultation Paper* (London: Department of Trade and Industry, July 1996).

Devlin, W., 'Cremation', *The Catholic Encyclopedia*, 1911.

Disley, E., 'Degrees of Glory: Protestant Doctrine and the Concept of Rewards Hereafter', *The Journal of Theological Studies*, Vol. 42, 1991, pp. 77–105.

Douglas, M., 'To Honour the Dead', in Dench, G., Flower, T., and Gavron, K. (eds), *Young at Eighty: The Prolific Public Life of Michael Young* (Manchester: Carcanet, 1995) pp. 209–15.

Duffy, E., 'An Apology for Grief, Fear and Anger', *Priests and People*, Vol. 5, No. 11, November 1991.

Duffy, E., *The Stripping of the Altars: Traditional Religion in England c.1400–c.1580* (New Haven and London: Yale University Press, 1992).

Duffy, E., *Saints and Sinners: A History of the Popes,* 2nd edn (New Haven: Yale University Press, 2001a)

Duffy, E., *The Voices of Morebath: Reformation and Rebellion in an English Village* (New Haven and London: Yale University Press, 2001b).

Dunk, J. and Rugg, J., *The Management of Old Cemetery Land: Now and the Future* (Crayford, Kent: Shaw & Sons, 1994).

Dunn, A., 'A Research Project into the Burial, Cremation and Disposal of Fetal Remains', unpublished thesis for the Final Diploma of the Intstitute of Burial and Cremation Administration, 1997.

Eassie, W., *Cremation of the Dead: Its History and Bearings upon Public Health* (London, 1875).

Eassie, W., 'The Systems of Cremation Now in Use upon the Continent', *Journal of the Society of Arts, 1877–78,* Vol. 26, pp. 230–239.

Ecclesiological late Cambridge Camden Society, *Funerals and Funeral Arrangements* (London: Joseph Masters, 1851).

Edwards, D. L., *After Death? Past Beliefs and Real Possibilities* (London: Cassell, 1999).

Edwards, P., 'Review of Emissions from Crematoria in the UK', *Resurgam,* Vol. 44 (2001), pp. 81–128, and *Pharos International* Vol. 67, No. 3, A1–A19, B1–B7.

Eeles, F. C., 'The Dragon of Churchyards', *Journal of the Institute of Landscape Architects,* No. 7, April 1945, pp. 11–143.

Elias, N., *The Civilizing Process: Volume 1, The History of Manners* (New York: Urizen Books, 1978).

Ellis, H. R., *The Road to Hell* (Cambridge: Cambridge University Press, 1983).

(ETRAC) Environment, Transport and Regional Affairs Committee Eighth Report, Cemeteries, Vol. I, II (London: The Stationery Office Ltd, 2001).

Emrys-Jones, A., *Disposal of the Dead* (Manchester, 1888).

Erichsen, H., *The Cremation of the Dead* (Detroit: D. O. Haynes, 1887).

Evans, R. J., *Death in Hamburg. Society and Politics in the Cholera Years 1830–1910* (London: Penguin, 1990).

Farrell, J., *Inventing the American Way of Death 1830–1920* (Philadelphia, Pa: Temple University Press, 1980).

Federation of British Cremation Authorities/Institute of Burial and Cremation Administration (Inc), *Joint Conference Reports,* various dates.

Fellows, A., *The Law of Burial and Generally of the Disposal of the Dead* (London: Haddon Best & Co. Ltd, 1940).

Field, D., Hockey, J., and Small, N., *Death, Gender and Ethnicity* (London: Routledge, 1997).

Finer, S. E., *The Life and Times of Sir Edwin Chadwick* (London: Methuen, 1952).

First and Second Reports from the Select Committee on the Death Certification Together with the Proceedings of the Committee, Minutes of Evidence, Appendix and Index, London 1893.

Firth, S., *Dying, Death and Bereavement in a British Hindu Community* (Leuvain, Belgium: Peeters, 1997).

Flanagan, K., *Seen and Unseen: Visual Culture, Sociology and Theology* (Basingstoke: Palgrave Macmillan, 2004).

Fletcher, R., *The Akenham Burial Case* (London: Wildwood House, 1974).

Forsyth, P. T., *This Life and the Next: The Effect on this Life of Faith in Another* (London: Macmillan, 1918).

Francis, D., Kellaher, L., and Neophytou, G., *The Secret Cemetery* (Oxford: Berg, 2005).

Fraser, J., address to the Social Science Congress, in J. W. Diggle, *The Lancashire Life of Bishop Fraser* (London: Sampson Low, Marston, Searle & Rivington, 1891) pp.116–9.

French, S., 'The Cemetery as Cultural Institution: The Establishment of Mount Auburn and the "Rural Cemetery" Movement', in Stannard, D. E. (ed.), *op. cit,* 1975.

Friar, B. G., 'Funeral Customs of Immigrants', *Report of the 27th Joint Conference of Burial and Cremation Authorities,* 1968, pp. 32–40.

Friar, B. G., 'The Disposal of Cremation Ashes', *Journal of the Institute of Burial and Cremation Administration,* Vol. 50, No. 2, Summer 1982, pp. 43–50.

Fry, C. M., 'The Design of British Crematoria', *Journal of the Society of Arts 1966–67,* Vol. 115, pp. 256–268.

Fulton, R. J., review of Jessica Mitford, *The American Way of Death Revisited* (London: Virago Press, 1998) in *Mortality,* Vol. 5, No. 1, 2000, pp. 103–4.

Fulton, R., and Fulton, J., 'A Psychological Aspect of Terminal Care: Anticipatory Grief', *Omega,* II, 1971, pp. 91–100.

Funeral Ombudsman Scheme, The, *Annual Reports* (London: The Funeral Ombudsman Scheme, 1994/1995–2001).

Fussell, P., *The Great War and Modern Memory* (New York and London: Oxford University Press, 1975).

Gammon, V., 'Singing and Popular Funeral Practices in the Eighteenth and Nineteenth Centuries', *Folk Music Journal,* Vol. 5, No. 4, 1988.

Garrett, H. G., 'Post-war Planning and Reform', *Journal of the National Association of Cemetery and Crematorium Superintendents,* August 1943, pp. 17–19.

Gayner, A. J., 'The Institute of Burial and Cremation Administration. Presidential Address', *Report of the Joint Conference of Burial and Cremation Authorities,* 1970, pp. 7–12.

George, V., *Social Security: Beveridge and After* (London: Routledge and Kegan Paul, 1968).

Gibson, E., and Ward, G. K., *Courage Remembered* (London: HMSO, 1989).

Gilbert, A. D., *Religion and Society in Industrial England* (London: Longman, 1976).

Gill, R., *The Myth of the Empty Church* (London: SPCK, 1993).

Gittings, C., *Death, Burial and the Individual in Early Modern England* (London: Croom Helm, 1984).

Glaser, B. G., and Strauss, A. L., *Awareness of Dying* (Chicago: Aldine, 1965).

Glossop, A., 'Joint Boards and Joint Committees for Crematoria', *Proceedings of the Cremation Conference 1947* (The Cremation Society and the Federation of British Cremation Authorities) 16 September 1947, pp. 16–22.

Le Goff, J., *The Birth of Purgatory* (London: Scolar Press, 1984).

Gordon, A., *Death is for the Living* (Edinburgh: Paul Harris, 1984).

Gore, Bishop C., An untitled address, *Proceedings of the Third Conference of Cremation Authorities, Wembley,* 1924, pp. 3–5.

Gorer, G., 'The Pornography of Death', 1955, reprinted in Gorer, G., *op. cit.,* 1965.

Gorer, G., *Death, Grief and Mourning in Contemporary Britain* (London: Cresset Press, 1965).

Gorini, P., *The First Crematory in England and the Collective Crematories,* translated by G. L. Larkins (London, 1879).

Gosden, P. H. J. H., *The Friendly Societies in England 1815–1875* (Manchester: Manchester University Press, 1961).

Grabka, G., 'Christian Viaticum: A Study of Its Cultural Background', *Traditio*, IX, 1953.

Grainger, H. J., ' "Distressingly Banal": The Architecture of Early British Crematoria', *Pharos International*, Spring 2000a, pp. 42–8.

Grainger, H. J., 'Golders Green Crematorium and the Architectural Expression of Cremation', *Mortality*, Vol. 5, No. 1, March 2000b, pp. 53–73.

Grainger, H. J., 'The Achievement of the Sir Ernest George and Alfred B. Yeates at Golders Green', in Jupp, P. C., and Grainger, H. J. (eds), *op. cit.*, 2002a, pp. 27–38.

Grainger, H. J., 'The Development of the Gordens at Golders Green Crematorium', in Jupp, P. C., and Grainger, H. J. (eds), *op. cit.*, 2002b, pp. 39–48.

Grainger, H. J., *Death Redesigned: British Crematoria: History, Architecture and Landscape* (Reading: Spire, 2005).

Grainger, H. J., *The Architecture of Sir Ernest George* (forthcoming, 2006).

Grainger, R., *The Unburied* (Worthing: Churchman, 1988).

Green, M. A., 'Dr Brighton & Dr Hyde: Deviant Doctors and Burned Bodies', *Pharos International*, Vol. 66, No. 3, 2000, pp. 8–11.

Gregory, A., *The Silence of Memory: Armistice Day, 1919–1946* (Oxford: Berg, 1994).

Guthke, K. S., *The Gender of Death: A Cultural History in Art and Literature* (Cambridge: Cambridge University Press, 1999).

HMSO, *Mortality Statistics*, various years.

Haden, H. S., *Earth to Earth. A Plea for Change of System in Our Burial of the Dead* (London, 1875).

Haden, H. S., 'Cremation as an Incentive to Crime', *Journal of the Royal Society of Arts*, Vol. 41, No. 2008, 23 November 1892, pp. 21–33.

Hallam, E., Hockey, J., and Howarth, G., *Beyond the Body: Death and Social Identity* (London: Routledge, 1999).

Hammond, J. L., and B., *Lord Shaftesbury* (London: Pelican, 1939).

Hannon, B., 'The Forgetting Rate: Evidence from a Country Cemetery', *Landscape Journal*, Spring 1990, pp. 16–21.

Harding, V., 'Burial on the Margin: Distance and Discrimination in Early Modern London', in Cox, M. (ed.), *Grave Concerns: Death and Burial in England* (York: Council for British Archaeology, CBA Research Report 113, 1998), pp. 54–64.

Harding, V., *The Dead and the Living in Paris and London, 1500–1670* (Cambridge: Cambridge University Press, 2002).

Hardy, T., 'In the Cemetery' in 'Satires of Circumstance in Fifteen Glimpses' in James Gibson (ed.), *Thomas Hardy. The Complete Poems* (London: Macmillan, 1976).

Harris, P., *What to Do When Someone Dies* (London: Consumers Association, 1st edn, 1967).

Harrisson, T., *Living Through the Blitz* (Harmondsworth: Penguin, 1990).

Hastings, A., *A History of English Christianity 1920–1985* (London: Fount, 1987).

Haynes, R., *The Society for Psychical Research 1882–1982* (London: Macdonald & Co., 1982).

Hazelgrove, J., *Spiritualism and British Society between the Wars* (Manchester: Manchester University Press, 2000)

Healey, K., 'English Churchyard Memorials', *Journal of the Society of Arts*, (Vol. 115), pp. 260–274.

Hennessey, P. J., *Families, Funerals and Finances, a Study of Funeral Expenses and How they are Paid*, Department of Health and Social Security Statistics and Research Division, Research Report No. 6 (London: HMSO, 1980).

Herring, H. T., 'Disposal of the Dead with Special Reference to Cremation', *Journal of State Medicine*, March 1924, reprinted in *Transactions of the Cremation Society, 1924*, pp. 68–74.

Hertz, R., 'A Contribution to the Study of the Collective Representation of Death', in *Death and the Right Hand*, translated by R. and C. Needham (London: Cohen & West, 1960).

Hick, J., *Death and Eternal Life* (London: Collins, 1976).

Hilton, C. L., 'The Administration of Cemeteries', *Proceedings of the Conference of the Institute of Burial and Cremation Administration*, 1947, pp. 11–21.

Hinton, J., 'The Psychology of Grief', *Report of the Thirty-first Joint Conference of Burial and Cremation Authorities 1972*, pp. 33–40.

Hockey, J. L., *Experiences of Death: An Anthropological Account* (Edinburgh: Edinburgh University Press, 1990).

Hockey, J., Katz, J., and Small, N., *Grief, Mourning and Death Ritual* (Buckingham: Open University Press, 2001).

Hodgson, H., *How to Become Dead Rich* (London: Pavilion Books, 1992).

Holder, W., *Cremation Versus Burial: An Appeal to Reason Against Prejudice* (Hull & York, 1891).

Holmes, Mrs B., *The London Burial Grounds: Notes on their History from the Earliest Times to the Present Day* (London: T. Fisher Unwin, 1896).

Hope, V., 'The Iron and Roman Ages: c.600BC to AD400', in Jupp, P. C., and Gittings, C. (eds), 1999, pp. 40–64.

Horan, P., 'Implications of the Environmental Protection Act applied to Crematoria', *Report of the Joint Conference of Burial and Cremation Authorities*, 1991, pp. 34–43.

Horder, Rt. Hon. Lord, 'Cemeteries or Playing Fields?', *Pharos*, 3:1, October 1936, pp. 16–17.

Horder, M., *The Little Genius: A Memoir of the First Lord Horder* (London: Duckworth, 1966).

Hornsby-Smith, M., *Roman Catholic Beliefs in England: Customary Catholicism and Transformations of Religious Authority* (Cambridge: Cambridge University Press, 1991).

Houlbrooke, R. (ed.), *Death, Ritual and Bereavement* (London: Routledge, 1989).

Houlbrooke, R., *Death, Religion and the Family in England, 1480–1750* (Oxford: Oxford University Press, 1998).

Houlbrooke, R., 'The Age of Decency, 1660–1760', in Jupp, P. C., and Gittings, C. (eds), *Death in England: An Illustrated History* (Manchester: Manchester University Press, 1999), pp. 174–201.

House of Commons, 'Disposal of the Dead (Regulation) Bill', morning, 30 April 1884.

Howarth, G., *The Funeral Industry in the East End of London: An Ethnographical Study*, unpublished PhD thesis, University of London, 1992.

Howarth, G., *Last Rites: The Work of the Modern Funeral Director* (Amityville, N.Y. : Baywood, 1996).

Howarth, G., 'Professionalising the Funeral Industry in England, 1700–1960', in Jupp, P. C., and Howarth, G. (eds), *The Changing Face of Death: Historical Accounts of Death and Disposal* (Basingstoke: Macmillan, 1997), pp. 120–34.

Howlett, C., 'The Cremation of Foetal Remains Procedure and Practice', *The Journal of the Institute of Burial and Cremation Administration* Vol. 65, No. 2, Summer 1997, pp. 53–6.

Huntington, R., and Metcalf, P., *Celebrations of Death: The Anthropdogy of Mortuary Ritual* (Cambridge: Cambridge University Press, 1979).

Hussein, I., 'A Proposed Solution for Extending the life of Existing Cemeteries', *Report of the Proceedings of the 52nd Joint Conference 1993* (London: Federation of British Cremation Authorities and the Institute of Burial and Cremation Administration, 1993), pp. 73–8.

Hussein, I., 'The PFI from a Public Sector Manager's perspective', *Pharos International*, Vol. 63, No. 1, Spring 1997, pp. 19–21.

Institute of Burial and Cremation Administration, The, 'A Policy Document on the Care and Disposal of Foetal Remains', *Resurgam*, Vol. 28, No. 3, Autumn 1985, pp. 70–71.

Institute of Burial and Cremation Administration, The, *Charter for the Bereaved*, 1st edn (London: The Institute of Burial and Cremation Administration, 1996) 2nd and revised edn (London: The Institute of Burial and Cremation Administration, 1998).

Irion, P. E., *Cremation* (Philadelphia, Pa.: Fortress Press, 1968).

Irwin, D., 'Sentiment and Antiquity: European Tombs, 1750–1830', in Whaley, J. (ed.), *op. cit.*, 1981, pp. 131–53.

Jalland, P., *Death in the Victorian Family* (Oxford: Oxford University Press, 1996).

Jalland, P., 'Victorian Death and Its Decline, 1850–1918', in Jupp, P. C., and Gittings, C. (eds), *Death in England: An Illustrated History* (Manchester: Manchester University Press, 1999), pp. 230–55.

James, H., *A Fitting End. Making the Most of a Funeral* (Norwich: Canterbury Press, 2004).

Jamieson, J., 'On the Origin of Cremation or the Burning of the Dead', Transactions of the Royal Society of Edinburgh, 8 (1818), pp. 83–127.

Jamieson, E. A., 'The Formation and Administration of the South-West Middlesex Crematorium', *Proceedings of the Cremation Society Conference 1954*, 6 July 1954, pp. 7–12.

Johnson, M. D., *The Dissolution of Dissent, 1850–1918* (New York and London: Garland Publishing Inc., 1987).

Jones, P. H., 'The Scope and Purpose of the Federation of British Cremation Authorities', *Pharos*, Vol. 17, No. 1, 1950, pp. 5–8.

Jones, P. H., 'The Burden of Burial: An Enquiry into the Economic Aspects of the Interment System Based on Information Supplied by Cemetery Authorities', *Pharos*, Vol. 17, No. 1, February 1951, pp. 2–4.

Jones, P. H., 'Charges for Medical Certificates', *Proceedings of the Cremation Society Conference 1953*, 27 June 1953a, pp. 29–39.

Jones, P. H., 'A National Plan for Crematoria', *Proceedings of the Cremation Society Conference 1953*, 30 June 1953b, pp. 5–16.

Jupp, P. C., 'From Dust to Ashes: The Replacement of Burial by Cremation in England 1840–1967', *The Congregational Lecture*, The Congregational Memorial Hall Trust (1978) Ltd, 1990.

Jupp, P. C., 'Cremation or burial? Contemporary Choice in City and Village', in Clark, D. (ed), *The Sociology of Death: Theory, Culture, Practice* (Oxford: Blackwell Publishers/The Sociological Review, 1993a), pp. 169–97.

Jupp, P. C., The Development of Cremation in England, 1820–1990: A Sociological Account', unpublished PhD thesis, University of London, 1993b.

Jupp, P. C., 'Enon Chapel: No Way for the Dead', in Jupp, P. C., and Howarth, G. (eds), *The Changing Face of Death: Historical Accounts of Death and Disposal* (Basingstoke: Macmillan, 1997a), pp. 90–104.

Jupp, P. C., 'The Dead Citizens Charter', *Pharos International*, Vol. 63, No. 4, Winter 1997b, pp. 18–28.

Jupp, P. C., 'The Context of Funeral Ministry Today', in Jupp, P. C., and Rogers, T. (eds), *Interpreting Death: Christian Theology and Pastoral Practice* (London: Cassell, 1997c), pp. 3–16.

Jupp, P. C., 'History of the Cremation Movement in Great Britain: The First 125 Years', *Pharos*, Spring 1999, pp. 18–25.

Jupp, P. C., 'Virtue Ethics and Death: The Final Arrangements', in Flanagan, K., and Jupp, P. C. (eds), *Virtue Ethics and Sociology: Issues of Modernity and Religion* (Basingstoke: Palgrave, 2001), pp. 217–35.

Jupp, P. C., 'The Critical Years: The Development of Cremation in England, 1918–1952', *Resurgam*, Vol. 45, No. 3, Autumn 2002, pp. 102–9.

Jupp, P. C., and Gittings, C. (eds), *Death in England: An Illustrated History* (Manchester: Manchester University Press, 1999).

Jupp, P. C., and Grainger, H. J., *Golders Green Crematorium, 1902–2002: A London Centenary in Context* (London: London Cremation Company plc, 2002).

Jupp, P. C., and Howarth, G. (eds), *The Changing Face of Death: Historical Accounts of Death and Disposal* (Basingstoke: Macmillan, 1997).

Jupp, P. C., and Rogers, T. (eds), *Interpreting Death: Christian Theology and Pastoral Practice* (London: Cassell, 1997).

Jupp, P. C., and Walter, T., 'The Healthy Society: 1918–1998', in Jupp, P. C., and Gittings, C. (eds), *Death in England: An Illustrated History* (Manchester: Manchester University Press, 1999).

Kazmier, L., 'Modernity, Britain and the Culture of Cremation', *European Journal of Palliative Care*, 2000, Vol. 7, No. 4, pp. 134–37.

Kazmier, L., 'A Symbolic Space: Rural Myth, the Great War and the Growth of Cremation', *Pharos International*, Vol. 68, No. 2, Summer 2002, pp. 2–9.

Keizer, H., 'Netherlands: Societies and Law', in Davies, D. J., and Mates, L. (eds), *Encyclopedia of Cremation* (Aldershot: Ashgate, 2005).

Kellaher, L., and Hockey, J., 'Where Have All the Ashes Gone?' *Pharos International*, Vol. 68, No. 4, Winter 2002, pp. 14–19.

Kellaher, L., Prendergast, D., and Hockey, J., 'Resistance, Renewal or Reinvention: The Removal of Ashes from Crematoria', *Pharos International*, Vol. 70, No. 4, Spring 2004, pp. 10–13.

Klass, D., Silverman, P. R., and Nickman, S. L. (eds), *Continuing Bonds: New Understandings of Grief* (London: Taylor & Francis, 1996).

Kohner, N., *A Dignified Ending. Recommendations for Good Practice in the Disposal of the Bodies and Remains of Babies Born Dead before the Legal Age of Viability* (London: The Stillbirth and Neonatal Death Society, 1992).

Kohner, N., and Henley, A., *When a Baby Dies: The Experience of late Miscarriage, Stillbirth and Neonatal Death*, revised edn (London: Routledge, 2001).

Koskinen, M., 'Burning the Body: The Debate on Cremation in Britain, 1874–1902', Tampere: Tampereen Yiliopistopaino, 2000.

Kreider, A., *English Chantries: The Road to Dissolution* (Cambridge, Mass.: Harvard University Press, 1979).

Kselman, T., 'Funeral Conflicts in Nineteenth-century France', *Comparative Studies in Society and History*, 30 (1988), 312–32.

Kselman, T. A., *Death and the Afterlife in Modern France* (Princeton, NJ: Princeton University Press, 1993).

Lampard, J. S., 'Theology in Ashes: The Failure of the Churches to Think Theologically about Cremation', *Bereavement and Belief* (London: The Churches' Group on Funeral Services at Cemeteries and Crematoria, 1993), pp. 28–36.

Lampard, J. S., *Go Forth, Christian Soul: The Biography of a Prayer* (Peterborough: Epworth, 2006).

Landers, J., *Death and the Metropolis: Studies in the Demographic History of London, 1670–1830* (Cambridge: Cambridge University Press, 1993).

Leaney, J., 'Ashes to Ashes: Cremation and the Celebration of Death in Nineteenth-Century Britain', in Houlbrooke, R. (ed.), *op. cit.*, 1989.

Light, A. E., *Bunhill Fields*, 2nd edn (London: C. J. Farncombe & Sons Ltd, 1915).

Lincoln, B., 'Revolutionary Exhumations in Spain, July 1936', *Contemporary Studies in Society and History*, Vol. 27, 1985.

Litten, J., *The English Way of Death: The Common Funeral since 1450* (London: Robert Hale, 1991).

Litten, J., 'The Funeral Trade in Hanoverian England, 1714–1760', in Jupp, P. C., and Howarth, G. (eds), *The Changing Face of Death: Historical Accounts of Death and Disposal* (Basingstoke: Macmillan, 1997) pp. 48–61.

Litten, J., 'Golders Green Crematorium and Its Early Influence in London Funerals', in Jupp, P. C., and Grainger, H. J. (eds), *Golders Green Crematorium 1902–2002: A London Centenary in Context* (London: The London Cremation Company plc, 2002), pp. 17–26.

Llewellyn, N., *Funeral Monuments in Post-Reformation England* (Cambridge: Cambridge University Press, 2000).

Lloyd, R., *The Church of England 1900–1965* (London: SCM Press, 1966).

London Planning Advisory Committee (LPAC), *Planning for Burial Space in London: Policies for Sustainable Cemeteries in the New Millennium* (London: LPAC, 1997).

Longmate, N., King Cholera (Edinburgh: Hamish Hamilton, 1966).

Longmate, N., *How We Lived Then: A History of Everyday Life during the Second World War* (London: Arrow, 1973).

Longworth, P., *The Unending Vigil: The History of the War Graves Commission* (Barnsley: Leo Cooper/Sword & Pen, revised edn, 1985).

Loudon, J. C., *On the Laying Out, Planting and Management of Cemeteries and the Improvement of Churchyards* [1843] (Redhill, Surrey: Ivelet Books, 1981).

Luby, J., 'Foetal Deaths', *Resurgam*, Vol. 35, No. 4, Winter 1992, p. 54.

Lynd, H. M., *England in the Eighteen-Eighties* (Oxford: Oxford University Press, 1945).

McDannell, C., and Lang, B., *Heaven: A History*, 2nd edn (New Haven and London: Yale Nota Bene, 2001).

McDonald, J., 'A Decade of Cremation in the Catholic Church', *Clergy Review*, 1975, pp. 381–8; a shorter version, with the same title, is published in *Proceedings of the Cremation Society Conference 1975*, pp. 15–21.

McHale, B., 'IBCA Presidential Address', *Report of the 50th Joint Conference of Burial and Cremation Authorities*, 1991, pp. 70–7.

McHale, B., 'Review of Process Guidance Notes – What the Future Holds', *Pharos International*, Vol. 67, No. 3, Autumn 2001, pp. 20–4.

Mackintosh, W. H., *Disestablishment and Liberation. The Movement for the Seperation of the Anglican Church from State Control* (London: Epworth, 1972).

McLeod, H., *Class and Religion in the Late Victorian City* (London: Croom Helm, 1974).

McManners, J., *Church and State in France 1870–1914* (London: SPCK, 1972).

McManners, J., *Death and Enlightenment: Changing Attitudes to Death Among Christians and Unbelievers in Eighteenth-Century France* (Oxford: Oxford University Press, 1981a).

McManners, J., 'Death and the French Historians', in Whaley, J. (ed.), *Mirrors of Mortality* (London: Europa, 1981b), pp. 106–30.

Major, H. D. A., *A Resurrection of Relics: A Modern Churchman's Defence in a Recent Charge of Heresy* (Oxford: Blackwell, 1922).

Makepeace, C. E., *Manchester Crematorium 1890–1990* (Manchester: Manchester Free Press, n.d. [1990]).

Manning, B. L., *The Protestant Dissenting Deputies* (Cambridge: Cambridge University Press, 1952).

Marlowe, J., *Late Victorian. The life of Sir Arnold Wilson* (London: The Cresset Press, 1967).

Marris, P., *Widows and Their Families* (London: Routledge & Kegan Paul, 1958).

Marris, P., *Loss and Change: Reports of the Institute of Communities Studies* (London: Routledge & Kegan Paul, 1968).

Marshall, P., *Beliefs and the Dead in Reformation England* (Oxford: Oxford University Press, 2002).

Martin, D. A., *A General Theory of Secularization* (Oxford: Blackwell, 1978a).

Martin, D. A., *The Dilemmas of Contemporary Religion* (Oxford: Blackwell, 1978b).

Marwick, A., *The Deluge: British Society and the First World War* (Harmondsworth: Pelican, 1967).

Meller, H., *London Cemeteries: An Illustrated Guide and Gazetteer*, 3rd edn (Aldershot: Scolar Press, 1994).

Merridale, C., *Night of Stone: Death and Memory in Russia* (London: Granta Books, 2000).

Mitchell, P., *The IBCA Exhumation Handbook* (Newark, Notts: Institute of Burial and Cremation Administration (Inc.), 1998).

Mitchison, R., *British Population Changes since 1860* (London: Macmillan, 1977).

Mitford, J., *The American Way of Death* (London: Quartet, 1980 [1963]).

Mitford, J., *The American Way of Death Revisited* (New York: Knopf, 1998).

Monopolies and Mergers Commission, *Co-operative Wholesale Society Ltd and House of Fraser plc. A Report on the Acquisition by the Co-operative and Wholesale Society Ltd. of the Scottish funerals business of the House of Fraser plc.* Cm. 229, HMSO, 1987.

Monopolies and Mergers Commission, *Service Corporation International and Plantsbrook Group Plc. A Report on the Merger Situation*, Cm. 2880, London, HMSO, May 1995.

Morley, J., *Death, Heaven and the Victorians* (London: Studio Vista, 1971).

Morrah, D., *A History of Industrial Life Assurance* (London: George Allen & Unwin, 1955).

Morris, R. J., *Cholera 1832: The Social Response to an Epidemic* (Trowbridge: Croom Helm, 1976).

Mulkay, M., and Ernst, J., 'The Changing Profile of Social Death', *European Journal of Sociology*, Vol. 32 (1991), pp. 172–96.

National Association of Cemetery and Crematorium Superintendents, *Memorandum for Planning for Post-War Reform in the Disposition of the Dead*, 1944.

National Funerals College, The, *The Dead Citizens Charter*, 1st edn (London: The National Funerals College, 1996); 2nd edn (Bristol: The National Funerals College, 1998).

Naylor, M. (as Page, M. J. A.), *Funeral Rituals in a Northern City*, unpublished PhD thesis (University of Leeds, 1989).

ap Nicholas, I., *A Welsh Heretic: Dr. William Price, Llantrisant* (Wirral: Ffynnon Press, 1940).

Nicol, R., *This Grave and Burning Question: A Centenary History of Cremation in Australia* (Adelaide: Adelaide Cemeteries Authority, 2003).

Nickelsburg, Jr., G. W. E., *Resurrection, Immortality and Eternal Life in Intertestamental Judaism*, Harvard Theological Studies XXVI (Harvard: 1972)).

Nock, A. D., 'Cremation and Burial in the Roman Empire', *Harvard Theological Review*, Vol. XXV, 1932.

Obelkevich, J., *Religion and Rural Society: South Lindsey 1825–1875* (Oxford: Clarendon Press, 1976).

O'Connor, M. C., *The Art of Dying Well: The Development of the* Ars Moriendi (New York: Columbia University Press, 1942).

Oddfellows, The, *Survey of Funeral Costs in Britain 2000*, 14th edn (Manchester: The Oddfellows, 2000).

Office of Fair Trading, *Pre-paid Funeral Plans: A Report by the Office of Fair Trading* (London: Office of Fair Trading, May, 1995).

Oliver, P., Davis, I., and Bentley, I., *Dunroamin: The Suburban Semi and Its Enemies* (London: Barrie and Jenkins, 1981).

Order of Christian Funerals (London: Geoffrey Chapman, 1990).

(Parmoor Report, The) *The Report of the Departmental Committee on the Business of Industrial Life Assurance Companies and Collecting Societies*, Sessional Papers, 1920, Vol. xviii, Cmd. 614.

Parry, J. P., *Death in Banaras* (Cambridge: Cambridge University Press, 1994).

Parsons, B., *Change and Development in the British Funeral Industry during the Twentieth Century with Special Reference to the Period 1960–1994*, unpublished PhD thesis (University of Westminster, 1997).

Parsons, B., 'Yesterday, Today and Tomorrow. The Life-cycle of the UK Funeral Industry', *Mortality*, Vol. 4, No. 2, July 1999, pp. 127–45.

Parsons, B., *The London Way of Death* (Stroud, Gloucestershire: Sutton, 2001).

Parsons, B., 'J H Kenyon: The First 125 Years' (Worthing: FSJ Communications, 2005a).

Parsons, B., 'Where did the Ashes Go? The Development of Cremation and Disposal of Ashes. Part 1: Burying the Cremated', *Journal of the Institute of Cemetery and Crematorium Management*, Vol. 73, No. 1, Spring 2005b, pp. 6–11.

Parsons, B., 'Where did the Ashes Go? The Development of Cremation and Disposal of Ashes. Part 2: Scattering and Gardens of Rest', *Journal of the Institute of Cemetery and Crematorium Management*, Vol. 73, No. 2, Summer 2005c, pp. 28–43.

Parsons, B., 'From Welbeck to Woking: William Garstin and the First Cremations', *Pharos International*, Vol. 71, No. 1, Spring 2005d, pp. 3–8.

Parsons, B., *Committed to the Cleansing Flame: The Development of Cremation in Nineteenth Century England* (Reading: Spire, 2005e).

Pearce, J., 'Where we are with Secular Funerals', in *Pharos International*, Vol. 71, No. 3, Autumn 2005, pp. 8–10.

Pharos (London: The Cremation Society of Great Britain), 1934–1985; retitled *Pharos International*, 1986–.

Pickering, W. S. F., *Anglo-Catholicism: A Study in Religious Ambiguity* (London: Routledge, 1989).

Porter, R., 'Death and the Doctors in Georgian England', in Houlbrooke, R. (ed.), *Death, Ritual and Bereavement*, pp. 77–94 (London: Routledge, 1989).

Porter, R. (ed.), 'Medical Science', *The Cambridge Illustrated History of Medicine* (Cambridge: Cambridge University Press, 1996) pp. 154–201.

Potter, H., *Hanging in Judgement: Religion and the Death-penalty in England from the Bloody Code to Absolution* (London: SCM Press, 1993).

Prevette, K. G. C., *The History of Modern Cremation in Great Britain from 1874* (London: The Cremation Society, 1974).

Prior, L., 'Actuarial Visions of Death: Life, Death and Chance in the Modern World', in Jupp, P. C., and Howarth, G. (eds), *The Changing Face of Death: Historical Accounts of Death and Disposal* (Basingstoke: Macmillan, 1997), pp. 177–93.

Prothero, S., *Purified by Fire: A History of Cremation in America* (Berkeley and Los Angeles: University of California Press, 2001).

Quasten, J., 'Vetus Superstitio et Nova Religio: The Problem of Refrigerium in the Ancient Church of North Africa', *Harvard Theological Review*, Vol. XXIII, 1940.

Queen's Bench Division, *The Queen v. Price*, Queen's Bench Division, Vol. XII, 7 February 1884, pp. 247–56.

Rald, D., 'Petition to the Council of the Church in Rome to Remove the Prohibition on Cremation', *Pharos*, 28:3, August 1962, pp. 15–19.

Reeves, J., 'The New Cremation Act', *Pharos*, Vol. 18, No. 3, August 1952, pp. 6–8,15.

Relations between the Cremation Society of England and Her Majesty's Government (London: Smith, Elder & Co., 1884).

Resurgam, The Journal of the Federation of British Cremation Authorities (1958–).

Retained Organs Commission. Annual Report, April 2001–March 2002 (London: The Retained Organs Commission, September 2002).

Richardson, R., *Death, Dissection and the Destitute* (London: Routledge & Kegan Paul, 1987).

Richardson, R., 'Why was Death so Big in Victorian Britain?', in Houlbrooke, R. (ed.), *op. cit.*, 1989, pp. 105–17.

Roberts, E., 'The Lancashire Way of Death', in Houlbrooke, R. (ed.), *op. cit.*, 1989, pp. 188–207.

Roberts, J. W., 'The Institute of Burial and Cremation Administration. Presidential Address', *Joint Conference of Burial and Cremation Authorities*, 1967, pp. 37–44.

Roberts, R., *The Classic Slum: Salford Life in the First Quarter of the Century* (Harmondsworth: Pelican, 1971).

Robertson, J. D., 'Cremation from the Cemetery Superintendent's Point of View', *Proceedings of the Tenth Conference of Cremation Authorities Ipswich*, 1931, pp. 15–23

Robinson, W., *God's Acre Beautiful or the Cemeteries of the Future* (London: The Garden Office, 1880).

Robinson, W., *Cremation and Urn Burial, or The Cemeteries of the Future* (London: 1889).

Rose, G., 'The Direction of Funeral Directing', paper given to the *First Anglo-European Funerary Congress*, organised by Memorial Advisory Bureau, Worthing, May 1991.

Rose, L., *Massacre of the Innocents: Infanticide in Britain 1800–1939* (London: Routledge & Kegan Paul, 1986).

Rosenthal, J. T., *The Purchase of Paradise: Gift Giving and the Aristocracy, 1307–1485* (London: Routledge & Kegan Paul, 1972).

Rosser, C., and Harris, C., *The Family and Social Change* (London: Routledge & Kegan Paul, 1983).

Rowell, G., *Hell and the Victorians* (Oxford: Oxford University Press, 1974).

Rowell, G., *The Liturgy of Christian Burial* (London: SPCK, 1977).

Rugg, J., *The Rise of Cemetery Companies in Britain 1820–1853*, Unpublished PhD thesis, University of Stirling, 1992.

Rugg, J., 'The Origins and Progress of Cemetery Establishment in Britain', in Jupp, P. C., and Howarth, G. (eds), *The Changing Face of Death: Historical Accounts of Death and Disposal* (Basingstoke: Macmillan, 1997), pp. 105–19.

Rugg, J., 'A New Burial Form and Its Meanings: Cemetery Establishment in the First Half of the Nineteenth Century', in Cox, M. (ed.), *Grave Concerns: Death and Burial in England* (York: Council for British Archaeology, CBA Research Report 113, 1998) pp. 44–53.

Rugg, J., 'Nonconformity and the Development of Early Cemeteries in England 1820–1850', *The Journal of the United Reformed Church History Society*, Vol. 6, No. 5, 1999, pp. 309–21.

Rugg, J., 'Managing "Civilian Deaths Due to War Operations": Yorkshire Experiences during World War II', *Twentieth Century British History*, Vol. 15, No. 2, 2004, pp. 152–73.

Rugg, J., 'Lawn Cemeteries: A Social History', forthcoming in *Urban History*, May 2006.

Russell, J., 'Cremation', *The American Ecclesiastical Review*, Vol. CLIII, July 1965.

Rutherford, H. R., *Honoring the Dead: Catholics and Cremation Today* (Collegeville, Minnesota: The Liturgical Press, 2001).

Salvesen, Lord, 'The Medico-Legal Aspect of Cremation', *Proceedings of the Sixth Annual Conference of Cremation Authorities*, 1927, pp. 79–82.

Salvesen, Lord, 'Defects of the Cremation Act, 1902', in *Pharos*, Vol. 1, No. 1, October 1934, pp. 3–6.

Seale, C., *Constructing Death: The Sociology of Dying and Bereavement* (Cambridge: Cambridge University Press, 1998)

Seale, C., and Cartwright, A., *The Year before Death* (Aldershot: Avebury, 1994).

Report from the Select Committee on the Health of Towns 17th June, 1840 [PP] 1840.

Report from the Select Committee on the Improvement of the Health of Towns with Minutes of Evidence [PP] Vol. X, 1842.

Sheppy, P. P. J., *Death, Liturgy and Ritual, Volume 1* (Aldershot: Ashgate, 2004).

Simon, Brian, *In Search of a Grandfather. Henry Simon of Manchester, 1835–1899* (Leicester: The Pendene Press, 1997).

Sloane, D. C., *The Last Great Necessity: Cemeteries in American History*, Baltimore, MD: Johns Hopkins University Press, 1991.

Smale, B., *Deathwork: A Sociological Analysis of Funeral Directing*, unpublished PhD thesis (University of Surrey, 1985).

Smale, D. A., 'A Look Back – the Original Cremation Regulations', *Resurgam*, Vol. 25, No. 3, 1992, pp. 110–16.

Smart, N., 'Death in the Judaeo-Christian Tradition', in A. Toynbee, A. K. Mant, N. Smart, J. Hinton, S. Yudkin, E. Rhode, R. Heywood and H. H. Price, *Man's Concern with Death* (London: Hodder & Stoughton, 1968), pp. 116–21.

Smith, H. L. (ed.), *War and Social Change: British Society in the Second World War* (Manchester: Manchester University Press, 1986).

Spottiswoode, J., *Undertaken with Love* (London: Robert Hale, 1991).

Stannard, D. E., *The Puritan Way of Death* (Oxford: Oxford University Press, 1977).

Stock, G., 'Quaker Burial: Doctrine and Practice', in Cox, M. (ed.), *Grave Concerns: Death and Burial in England* (York: Council for British Archaeology, CBA Research Report 113, 1998), pp. 129–43.

Stone, L., *The Family, Sex and Marriage in England 1500–1800* (Harmondsworth: Penguin, 1979).

Stoneham, Lord, untitled address, *Report of the Joint Conference of Burial and Cremation Authorities*, 1967, pp. 12–14.

Strange, J.-M., 'Tho' Lost to Sight, to Memory Dear': Pragmatism, Sentimentality and Working-class Attitudes Towards the Grave, c.1875–1914', *Mortality*, Vol. 8, No. 2, May 2003, pp. 144–59.

Strutt, A. H., 'The Report of the Interdepartmental Committee on Cremation Regulations', *Record of the Cremation Society Conference 1951*, 26 June 1951, pp. 18–23.

Strutt, Sir A. H., *Cremation Legislation* (Maidstone: The Cremation Society of Great Britain, 1976).

Sudnow, D., *Passing on: The Social Organisation of Dying* (Englewood Cliffs, NJ: Prentice Hall, 1967).

Sullivan, J. V., 'Cemeteries and the Public', *Journal of the National Association of Cemetery and Crematorium Superintendents*, May 1937, pp. 18–20.

Sutherland-Gower, R. S., *Cleanliness versus Corruption* (London: Longmans, Green & Co., 1910).

Sykes, D. T., *The Advantages of Cremation from the Cemetery Chaplain's Point of View* (London: The Cremation Society, 1931).

Taylor, L., *Mourning Dress: A Costume and Social History* (London: George Allen & Unwin, 1982).

Thomas, H., 'Changing Social Attitudes towards Cremation', *Proceedings of the Cremation Society Conference*, 1976, pp. 67–75.

Thomas, J. H., 'Life, Death and Paradise: The Theology of the Funeral', in Jupp, P. C., and Rogers, T. (eds), 1997, pp. 56–66.

Thomas, K., *Religion and the Decline of Magic: Studies in Popular Beliefs in Sixteenth- and Seventeenth-Century England* (Harmondsworth: Penguin, 1973).

Thompson, F. M. L., *The Rise of the Respectable Society 1830–1900* (London: Fontana, 1988).

Thompson, Sir H., 'The Treatment of the Body After Death', *Contemporary Review*, January 1874, pp. 553–71.

Thompson, Sir H., *Modern Cremation: Its History and Practice, with information relating to the recently improved arrangements made by the Cremation Society of England*, 1st edn, (London: 1889).

Thompson, Sir H., 'An Address on the Amendment of the Laws Relating to Certificates of Death and Coroners' Inquests', *Transactions of the Cremation Society, 1897*, pp. 30–4.

Thurston, H., *The Question of Cremation* (London: The Catholic Truth Society, 1936) reprinted from the *Westminster Cathedral Chronicle* (February 1918).

Transactions of the Cremation Society of England, Vol. 1 (1880) and Vol. 2 (1886) (London: The Cremation Society).

Tranter, N. L., *British Population in the Twentieth Century* (Basingstoke: Macmillan, 1996).

Trasler, G., ' "Mind the Gap": Funerals at the Crematorium', unpublished paper, 1998 Available from the Revd Graham Trasler, 37 Jacklyns Lane, New Arlesford, Hants SO24 9LF.

Turner, E. S., 'Cremation in Britain', *Resurgam*, Vol. 31, No. 4, Winter 1988, pp. 86–89.

Twigg, J., 'New Light on the Ashes', *The International Journal of the History of Sport*, Vol. 4, No. 2, September 1987, pp. 231–236.

Van Gennep, A., *Les rites de passage* [1909] ET *The Rites of Passage* (Chicago, IL: University of Chicago Press, 1960).

Vaughan, H. A., 'Cremation and Christianity', *Dublin Review*, Third Series, Vol. xxiii, No. 2, 1891, pp. 384–402.

Walker, D. P., *The Decline of Hell: Seventeenth-Century Discussions of Eternal Torment* (London: Routledge & Kegan Paul, 1964).

Walker, G. A., *Gatherings from Graveyards* (London, 1839).

Walker, G. A., *The Graveyards of London* (London, 1841).

Walker, G. A., *Interment and Disinterment*: The Reproduction of a Series of Letters to the *Morning Herald*, various dates, November 4th 1842 to January 12th 1843 (Longman, Brown, Green and Longmans, 1843).

Walker, G. A., *Burial Ground Incendiarism* (London, 1846).

Walker, G. A., *A Series of Lectures on the Actual Conditions of the Metropolitan Graveyards*, I-IV (Longman, Brown, Green and Longmans, 1847).

Walter, T., *Funerals and How to Improve Them* (London: Hodder & Stoughton, 1990).

Walter, T., 'Modern Death: Taboo or not Taboo?', *Sociology*, Vol. 25, No. 2, May 1991a, pp. 293–310.

Walter, T., 'The Mourning after Hillsborough', *Sociological Review*, Vol. 39, No. 3, 1991b, pp. 599–625.

Walter, T., *The Eclipse of Eternity: A Sociology of the Afterlife* (Basingstoke: Macmillan, 1996).

Walter, T., 'Classics Revisited: A Sociology of Grief', *Mortality*, Vol. 3, No. 1, 1998, pp. 83–7.

Walter, T., *On Bereavement: The Culture of Grief* (Buckingham: Open University Press, 1999a).

Walter, T. (ed.), *The Mourning for Diana* (Oxford: Berg, 1999b).

Walter, T., Pickering, M., and Littlewood, J., 'Death in the News: The Public Invigilation of Private Emotion', *Sociology*, Vol. 29, No. 4, 1995, pp. 579–96.

Ware, T., *The Orthodox Church* (London: Penguin, 1963).

Warner, W. L., *The Living and the Dead: A Study of the Symbolic Life of Americans* (New Haven: Yale University Press, 1959).

Watson, J. L., and Rawski, E. S. (eds), *Death Ritual in Late Imperial and Modern China* (Berkeley: University of California Press, 1988).

Watts, M. R., 'The Hateful Mystery', *Transactions of the United Reformed Church History Society*, Vol. 2, No. 8, October 1981.

Weatherhead, L., *After Death: A Popular Statement of the Modern Christian View of Life beyond the Grave* (London: Epworth, 1923).

Wells, T. S., 'Remarks on Cremation or Burial?', *British Medical Journal*, 18 September 1880, pp. 461–3.

West, K., 'Local Authorities: Development of Burial Grounds', unpublished paper presented to The Dead Citizens Charter conference, Westminster Central Hall, London, 31 October, 1996.

Whaley, J. (ed.), *Mirrors of Mortality: Studies in the Social History of Death* (London: Europa, 1981).

White, C. F., 'A National Plan for Crematoria', *Proceedings of the Cremation Society Conference 1954*, 6 July 1954, pp. 12–17.

White, S. R. G., 'A Burning Issue', *New Law Journal*, 10 August 1990.

White, S. R. G., 'Founder Members of the Cremation Society', *Pharos International*, Spring 1999, pp. 11–17.

White, S. R. G., 'Property in Body Parts and the Cremation Regulations', *Pharos International*, Vol. 66, No. 3, 2000, pp. 12–16.

White, S. R. G., 'Honoretta Pratt – Cremated 1769(?)', *Pharos International*, Vol. 67, No. 1, 2001a, p. 16.

White, S. R. G., 'Shipman and Others: Current Inquiries Bearing on Cremation', *Pharos International*, Vol. 67, No. 3, 2001b, pp. 15–23.

White, S. R. G., 'A Burial Ahead of Its Time? The Crookenden Burial Case and the Sanctioning of Cremation in England and Wales', *Mortality*, Vol. 7, No. 2, July 2002, pp. 171–190.

White, S. R. G., 'The Cremation Act 1902: From Private to Local to General', in *Pharos International*, Vol. 69, No. 1, Spring 2003, pp. 14–18.

Wilkins, R., *The Fireside Book of Death* (London: Robert Hale, 1990).

Wilkinson, A., *The Church of England in the First World War* (London: SPCK, 1978).

Willson, J. W., *Funerals without God: A Practical Guide to Non-religious Funerals* (London: British Humanist Association, 1989).

Wilmhurst, J. and Mrs Wilmhurst, 'What does the Public Think?', *Proceedings of the Cremation Society Conference 1975*, pp. 25–37, 94.

Wilson, B. R., *Religion in Secular Society* (Harmondsworth: Pelican, 1966).

Wilson, P., 'The Impact of the Environmental Protection Act on the Funeral Service', *Resurgam*, Vol. 34, No. 2, Summer 1991, pp. 77–8, reprinted in *Funeral Director*, Vol. 71, No. 7, July 1991, pp. 12–13.

Wilson, Sir A., and Levy, H., *Burial Reform and Funeral Costs* (Oxford: Oxford University Press, 1938).

Wilson, Sir A., and Levy, H., *Industrial Assurance* (Oxford: Oxford University Press, 1937).

Winter, J. M., 'The Demographic Consequences of the War', in Smith, H. L. (ed.), *War and Social Change: British Society in the Second World War* (Manchester: Manchester University Press, 1986), pp. 151–78.

Winter, J., *Sites of Memory, Sites of Mourning: The Great War in European Cultural History* (Cambridge: Cambridge University Press, 1995).

Wordsworth, Bishop C., *On Burning of the Body; and on Burial* (Lincoln: James Wilkinson, 1874).

Wotherspoon, G. *Cremation, Ancient and Modern: The History and Utility of the Fire Burial* (London: 1886).

Wrigley, E. A., Davies, R. S., Oeppen, J. E. and Schofield, R. S., *English Population History from Family Reconstitution 1580–1837* (Cambridge: Cambridge University Press, 1997).

Wylie, W., 'The Burning and Burial of the Dead', *Archaeologie*, Journal of the Society of Antiquaries of London, Vol. 37, 1858, pp. 455–78.

Young, E., 'Night Thoughts', edited by G. Gilfillan (Edinburgh: James Nichol, 1853).

Young, M., *The Metronomic Society* (London: Thames & Hudson, 1988).

Young, M., 'Ashes to Hashes', *The Guardian*, 8 June 1994.

Young, M. (HL, 'Municipal Crematoria: Privatisation', 30 October 1995, cols 1310–1321).

Young, M., and Cullen, L., *A Good Death: Conversations with East Londoners* (London: Routledge, 1996).

Ziegler, P., *London at War 1939–1945* (London: Sinclair-Stevenson, 1995).

Index

Printed in the United States
145139LV00003B/13/A

9 780333 692981